German
IMMIGRANT SERVANT CONTRACTS

Registered at the Port of Philadelphia,

1817–1831

Farley Grubb

Economics Department
University of Delaware

Published by Genealogical Publishing Co., Inc.
1001 N. Calvert Street, Baltimore, MD 21202
Library of Congress Catalogue Card Number 94-78264
International Standard Book Number 0-8063-1416-8
Made in the United States of America

INTRODUCTION

Book *C* of Redemptioners, transcribed below, is the key contract register covering the last major episode of European immigrant servitude in the United States. It provides an indispensable record for studying the nature of immigrant servant contracting during the last years of the institution, and for studying why European immigrant servitude disappeared (Grubb 1994a, 1994b). Because the final episode of European immigrant servitude involved German immigrants exclusively, this contract register also provides an indispensable record of German immigration to America.

While the largest peak in German immigration between 1755 and 1830 occurred during the years 1816 through 1819 (Grubb 1994b; Strassburger 1934; Wokeck 1981), the United States federal government did not start systematically collecting passenger manifests until 1820. Few surviving port records and state documents before 1820 recorded names and other information about individual passengers, and those that have survived are incomplete (Bentley and Tepper 1986; Grubb 1990a, 1990b, 1994b; Strassburger 1934). Book *C* of Redemptioners is one of the few existing documents that can be used to identify German immigrants who arrived between November 1817 and 1820, for whom no other immigration records exist. Because immigrant servant contracts were registered within 30 days of arrival, the registration date can serve as a proxy for the date of arrival (Grubb 1988, 1994b). The register can also be used to reconstruct immigrant families, since many family members entered servitude together. In addition, the register locates the initial residence of these immigrants since the township, county, and state of the immigrants' American masters are recorded (Grubb 1985b, 1994a). Thus, this contract register is a key historical document for studying a major episode of German immigration to America.

GERMAN IMMIGRANT SERVITUDE IN AMERICA

Germans comprised the largest non-British European migration to English-speaking North America during the eighteenth and early nineteenth centuries. By the Revolution, between one-third and one-half of Pennsylvania's population was composed of Germans and those of German ancestry. Like British colonists, many German colonists relied on servitude to finance the cost of their transatlantic journey. Overall, approximately half of all European emigrants to colonial British American entered servitude to pay for their passage. European immigrant servitude continued after the Revolution, with the last vestiges concentrated among German immigrants arriving at the ports of Philadelphia, Baltimore, and New Orleans. At Philadelphia, the main port of arrival, approximately 45 percent of German immigrants entered servitude during the years 1785 through 1804 (Grubb 1985a). Servitude between 1805 and 1816 appears roughly similar, although missing data makes giving exact numbers impossible. German immigrant servitude continued after the War of 1812 with roughly 42 percent of German arrivals in 1817 and 1818 entering servitude. By the early 1820s, however, immigrant servitude had permanently disappeared. The numbers of servants and the percentage of immigrants entering servitude between 1820 and 1831, when the official registration of German immigrant servants ceased, were in the single digits (Grubb 1994a, 1994b).

For those wanting to know more about both the general history of German immigration and servitude in America, I highly recommend several classic studies, including those by Diffenderffer (1899), Geiser (1901), Hansen (1940), Herrick (1926), Morris (1981), Smith (1947), and Strassburger (1934). Some examples of excellent modern studies of this topic include Grabbe (1984), Moltmann (1986), and Wokeck (1981, 1991). Finally, I have published a series of articles which focus on the quantification and economic analysis of various aspects of German immigration and servitude (Grubb 1985a, 1985b, 1986, 1987a, 1987b, 1987c, 1988, 1989, 1990a, 1990b, 1992a, 1992b, 1994a, 1994b). Instead of summarizing these sources, I will introduce

German immigrant servitude by providing the documentary history of each step of the migration and servitude process. I will give examples of contracts, government documents, and eyewitness descriptions of the process, tracing the sequence of steps the immigrant passed through from boarding the ship in Europe to having the servant contract registered in America. As much as possible, these examples will be taken from documents which are concurrent with the time period and involve the immigrants whose contracts are transcribed here.

In Europe, German immigrants signed a ship contract which gave them a choice of paying a cash price for passage and thus being "free" immigrants or paying a credit price for passage and thus being "redemptioner" immigrants. The redemptioner's ship contract specified the conditions and restrictions on "redeeming" or repaying the passage loan upon arrival in America. The ship contract also specified what provisions, destination, and behavior was to be expected both of all passengers, free and redemptioner, and the captain. While few examples of ship passenger contracts for German immigrants have survived (Grubb 1986), an excellent example of the typical contract comes from the period covered by this contract register. The names of some of the passengers on this ship appear in the register. The transportation contract is between the captain and the passengers of the Ship *Elizabeth* which arrived in Philadelphia from Amsterdam in the year 1819 (Tepper 1978, 257-8). The contract which the passengers signed reads as follows:

> We the undersigned: I, M. Adams, Captain of the Ship Elizabeth on one part, and we the passengers on the other part do obligate ourselves--
> First, We the passengers to take our passage with the above mentioned Capt. Adams to Philadelphia in North America, and to conduct ourselves as good passengers ought to do, quiet and orderly, and to be satisfied with the food mentioned at foot as per agreement with the Captain, and with regard to water and other provisions, to follow the Captain's directions as he shall find necessary through long passage or other circumstances.
> Second. We agree to take our passage on the following conditions, viz. to pay
> For those who are able to pay in Amsterdam for each person man or woman 180 fr.
> Children under four years of age are free--
> From four to twelve years to pay 90 fr.
> From twelve years and older to pay 180 fr.
> For those who are not able to pay here or only in part, the passage to be
> Children under four years of age free
> From four to twelve years 95 fr.
> From twelve years and older 190 fr. and 200 fr. as specified.
> Those who have to pay their passage in America shall be obliged to do so in ten days after their arrival. No passenger shall be allowed to leave the vessel in America without leave from the Captain and in particular those as have not paid their passage money. Should any one of the passengers die on the voyage, the family of such person shall be obliged to pay his passage, if such decease took place on more than half the distance of the voyage, but should the person die this side half the distance, the loss of the passage shall fall to the Captain.
> In return I, M. Adams obligate myself to carry these passengers to Philadelphia, to accommodate them with the necessary comfort and give them daily the here below mentioned proportion of victuals--children not to receive anything.
> Sunday--one pound Beef and half pound Rice,
> Monday--one pound Flour,
> Tuesday--one half pound Pork with pease,
> Wednesday--one pound Beef and barley,

> Thursday--like Tuesday,
> Friday--like Monday,
> Saturday--like Wednesday,
> One pound Butter, one pound Cheese, six pounds Bread,
> per week.
> One glass Gin and three quarter gallons Water per day.
> There shall also be on board a sufficiency of Vinegar to
> cleanse the vessel and for the refreshing the passengers. To all
> this we bind ourselves with our persons and property.
> Witness Van Olivier & Co.
> Amsterdam, 4 May, 1819.

After the ship docked in Philadelphia, a health officer inspected the passengers. The following is an example of the health officer's hand-written report, one which covers immigrants appearing in this register ("Book *C* of Redemptioners"):

> *Health Office, Philad*^a   *1824*
>
> *To Jacob H. Hoeckly Register of German Passengers*
> *   I do hereby report*
> *That I have received all the above named Passengers (25 in number)*
> *on board the Ship Jane Capt. John Smith, arrived (this day) at*
> *the Port of Philadelphia from Amsterdam, and that none of them*
> *are superannuated, impotent or otherwise likely to become chargeable*
> *to the Public, but all of them sound, without any defect in*
> *mind or body.*
> *   NB.*
> *   Health Officer*

Subsequently, the registrar of German passengers passed the health officer's information on to the secretary of the State of Pennsylvania, as the following hand-written letter illustrates ("Book *C* of Redemptioners"):

> *Philadelphia   1824*
>
> *Molten C. Rojeng Esq. Secretary of the Commonwealth of Pennsylvania--Harrisburg*
>
> *Sir.*
> *   Agreeably to the Act of Assembly (in such case made & provided) I hereby*
> *transmit to you the list of the names of German Passengers arrived at the Port*
> *of Philadelphia on the day of inst. from Amsterdam on board the Ship Jane*
> *Capt. John Smith-- all of whom (agreeably to the Report of the Health Officer) have*
> *been permitted & Licensed to land.*
> *   J. F. H. Register of German*
> *   Passengers*

If the health officer determined that the passengers were suitable for landing, the merchant in charge of the cargo would place advertisements in the local newspapers announcing that immigrants on board the ship were willing to enter servitude in exchange for the paying of their passage debts. The advertisements attracted buyers from the counties surrounding Philadelphia, from neighboring states, and occasionally from places as far away as Alabama, Missouri, and even Cuba. The buyers came on board the ship and negotiated with the immigrants the terms of the servant contract that would raise the required sum. Few eyewitness descriptions of this bargaining process have survived. Perhaps the most accurate and sober description is by Pastor Henry Melchior Muhlenberg, head of the German Lutheran church in Pennsylvania, who had observed the market for German redemptioner servants for many years. In 1769, he described the process as follows (Diffenderffer 1899, 192; Strassburger 1934, I, xxxvii):

> . . . announcements are printed in the newspapers, stating how many
> of the new arrivals are to be sold. Those with money are released.
> Whoever has well-to-do friends seeks a loan from them to pay the

passage, but there are only a few who succeed. The ship becomes
the market-place. The buyers make their choice among the arrivals
and bargain with them for a certain number of years and days.
They then take them to the merchant, pay their passage and their
other debts and receive from the government authorities a written
document, which makes the newcomer their property for a definite
period . . . Young and unmarried persons of both sexes are sold
first . . . Married people, widows, and the infirmed are dull sale.

The only eyewitness description of the sale of German redemptioners from the period covered
by this contract register, including servants found in this register, is by Henry Bradshaw Fearon.
This description, however, should not be taken at face value. Fearon was a well-to-do English
traveller, unfamiliar with working class conditions and institutions, and somewhat biased against
America. In his description, the errors regarding the ethnicity of the immigrants and how the
contract prices for servants were determined speak to his unfamiliarity with the institution and
process of redeeming. In addition, Fearon observed the bargaining in Philadelphia in the fall of
1817 when a flood of destitute Germans had been driven from the Rhineland by the famine and
destruction caused by the 1816 agricultural disaster known as "the year without a summer"
(Grubb 1994b, Skeen 1981; Hansen 1940, 79-106). This was a random and acute climatic crisis
unparalleled for several centuries in terms of its severe effect on the Rhineland. Thus, Fearon
observed a very atypical year with regard to the condition of German immigrants. Still, Fearon's
description is all we have and it has some merit. He wrote on Oct. 12, 1817 (Fearon 1818, 149-
52), [Note: The W. Odlin mentioned in the quotation was one of the larger purchasers and
resellers of servants recorded in the contract register transcribed here.]

A practice which has been often referred to in connection
with this country, naturally excited my attention. It is that of
individuals emigrating from Europe without money, and paying
for their passage by binding themselves to the captain, who
receives the produce of their labor for a certain number of years.
Seeing the following advertisement in the newspapers, put
in by the captain and owners of the vessel referred to, I visited
the ship, in company with a boot-maker of this city:

"THE PASSENGERS
"On board the brig Bubona, from Amsterdam, and
"who are willing to engage themselves for a limited
"time, to defray the expenses of their passage, consist
"of persons of the following occupations, besides wo-
"men and children, viz. 13 farmers, 2 bakers, 2 butch-
"ers, 8 weavers, 3 taylors, 1 gardener, 3 masons,
"1 mill-sawyer, 1 white-smith, 2 shoe-makers, 3 ca-
"binet-makers, 1 coal-burner, 1 barber, 1 carpenter,
"1 stocking-weaver, 1 cooper, 1 wheelwright, 1 brewer,
"1 locksmith. ---Apply on board of the Bubona, op-
"posite Callowhill-street, in the river Delaware, or to
"W. Odlin and Co. No. 38, South Wharves.   Oct. 2.

As we ascended the side of this hulk, a most revolting
scene of want and misery presented itself. The eye involuntarily
turned for some relief from the horrible picture of human suffering,
which this living sepulchre afforded. Mr. _____ enquired if there
were any shoemakers on board. The captain advanced: his
appearance bespoke his office; he is an American, tall, determined,
and with an eye that flashes with Algerine cruelty. He called in
the Dutch language for shoe-makers, and never can I forget the
scene which followed. The poor fellows came running up with
unspeakable delight, no doubt anticipating a relief from their

loathsome dungeon. Their clothes, if rags deserve that denomination, actually perfumed the air. Some were without shirts, others had this article of dress, but of a quality as coarse as the worst packing cloth. I enquired of several if they could speak English. They smiled, and gabbled, "No Engly, no Engly, ---one Engly talk ship." The deck was filthy. The cooking, washing, and necessary departments were close together. Such is the mercenary barbarity of the Americans who are engaged in this trade, that they crammed into one of those vessels 500 passengers, 80 of whom died on the passage. The price for women is about 70 dollars, men 80 dollars, boys 60 dollars. When they saw at our departure that we had not purchased, their countenances fell to that standard of stupid gloom which seemed to place them a link below rational beings. From my heart I execrated the *European cause* of their removal, which is thus daily compelling men to quit the land of their fathers, to become voluntary exiles in a foreign clime: ---yet Americans can think and write such sentiments as the following: "We rejoice with the patriotic Hollanders at the return of the illustrious house of Orange to their first magistracy, and do not wonder at their *enthusiastic joy* upon the occasion, when they remember that this ancient family have been always the gallants and zealous defenders of *the rights and liberties of the Dutch people.*"

An interesting occurrence is said to have taken place the other day, in connection with the German Redemptioners (as by a strange misnomer the Dutch are denominated). A gentleman of this city wanted an old couple to take care of his house; ---a man, his wife, and daughter were offered to him for sale; ---he purchased them. ---They proved to be his father, his mother, and sister!!!

After the servant contract was negotiated and the shipper (or seller in the case of a resold contract) was paid, the contract was registered by the government. After the Revolution, the Pennsylvania German Society convinced the State of Pennsylvania to keep a register of German immigrant servant contracts. These books are the only systematic records of European immigrant servants arriving in the United States after 1784. Book *A* spans 1785 through 1804 ("Book *A* of Redemptioners"); Book *B* which must have spanned 1805 through November 4, 1817, apparently is lost, and Book *C* spans from November 5, 1817, through 1831 ("Book *C* of Redemptioners"). It is this last Book which is transcribed here.

The registers contained not a complete transcription of the actual contracts, but a summarization of the key elements in the contracts. The registrar typically recorded the immigrant servant's name; the buyer's name, occupation, township, county, and state of residence; who gave the servant consent to contract if the servant was a minor; the length of servitude and the amount paid to the shipper for the contract (called the consideration); any special payments to the servant during or at the end of the contract; and any other non-standard contractual stipulation. Based on the contract example given below, it appears that the registrar simply recorded the unique information the contracting parties added to a standard format or to a pre-printed contract form.

While the parties typically used pre-printed forms which left spaces open for the parties to add their unique information, handwritten contracts consistent with these pre-printed forms were also employed and acceptable. Because few actual contracts have survived, contract registers such as the one transcribed here are the key source of information on immigrant servitude. The following example of an actual contract was appended to this contract register ("Book *C* of Redemptioners"). The hand-written information added by the contracting parties to the pre-printed form is indicated here by italics. The one piece of information atypically missing from this contract is the price, called "the consideration," paid by the master for the contract.

PHILADELPHIA, ss.

This Indenture

Witnesseth, That *Susanna Herbster of her own free will,*
and consent of her Father Laurence Herbster, for the consideration
hereinafter mentioned, to be done and performed by Christian
Schenck of the Northern Liberties, Shoemaker
as also for other good causes *she* the said *Susanna Herbster*
hath bound and put *her*self and by these Presents doth bind and put *her*self
Servant to the said *Christian Schenck*   to serve
him his Executors, Administrators and Assigns from the day of the date
hereof, for and during the full term of *Six Years*
from thence next ensuing. During all which term the said Servant *her*
said *master his*   Executors, Administrators and Assigns faithfully
shall serve, and that honestly and obediently in all things, as a good and faithful
Servant ought to do. And the said *Christian Schenck his*
Executors, Administrators and Assigns, during the said term shall find and provide for the said Servant sufficient Meat, Drink, Apparel, Washing and Lodging
And also give her Six Months Schooling. And within the first three
years of the Term of the Service of the said Susanna Herbster, to have her
confirmed at the German Lutheran Church in Philadelphia, and attend the
Lectures of the Minister, agreeable to the form of the said Church. And at the
expiration of her term to have two complete suits of clothes, one thereof to be new,
also a good Bed, Bolster Pillows & Blankets worth at least twenty five dollars.
And for the true performance hereof, both the said parties bind themselves firmly
unto each other by these Presents. In Witness whereof they have interchange-
ably set their Hands and Seals. Dated the *nineteenth*   day of
May   A. D. one thousand eight hundred and *twenty four*
      Bound before

her
Susanna X Herbster
mark

Pennsylvania State law regulated the immigration and sale of German immigrant servants. During the years covered by this contract register these laws required the registration of all German immigrant servant contracts. The registrar was to be a special officer who was familiar with both the English and German languages. Unregistered contracts were invalid, and all concerned persons were entitled to have a copy or abstract of the register. Masters were required to give German redemptioners who were minors six week's schooling for each year of service, and it was the duty of the registrar to insert this provision in the indenture. Masters were required to pay, at the end of the contract, freedom dues consisting of two complete suits or clothes, one of which to be new, or the equivalent. A bill of ladening was to be given to all passengers for all goods brought and stored in the hold of the vessel. Persons were to be put on shore with their goods for no additional charge beyond the price agreed upon in Europe. Husbands and wives who entered servitude were not to be separated except by mutual consent. Unless they agreed to separate indentures, separating them would void the indenture. Those servants bound to serve in Pennsylvania were not to be sold out of the state without their consent. The captain was to give proper food and drink and to care for the passengers on his ship during a term of 30 days after arrival during which time the passengers could negotiate with the buyers or benefactors who boarded the ship as to the conditions which would cause their passage debts to be repaid. Additional time after the 30 days was to be at the expense of the passengers. The captain was to have sick passengers removed and cared for on shore, unless they could not be moved from the ship, in which cased they were to be cared for on the ship. Passengers who died on the voyage or shortly after landing were to be reported within fifteen days of arrival, and a just account of their goods was to be rendered to the Register of Wills for the benefit of their heirs and creditors. The penalty extracted from the shipper for violating these regulations ranged from 50 to 500 dollars. For a more complete rendering of the texts and sources of these laws see Herrick (1926, 293, 305-8).

QUANTITATIVE SUMMARY OF THIS SERVANT REGISTER

Quantitative data describing the conditions of German immigrant servitude have been constructed from the contract register transcribed here. While I will briefly summarize some of these findings here, see Grubb (1989, 1992b, 1994a, 1994b) for the complete tabulations.

The first entry in the registry was on November 5, 1817, and the last entry was on December 1, 1831. The contract registry lists 1,258 entries wherein 1,933 names of separate individuals are recorded. The entries are concentrated in the years 1817, 1818, and 1819, when 370, 464, and 351 entries, respectively, were recorded. Only 73 entries were recorded between 1820 and 1831.

Within these entries a total of 1,035 new immigrant servants are recorded. In addition, these entries include the resale of 60 immigrant servants from one master to another master, the outright release of 58 immigrants servants by their masters, and the reassignment of 192 immigrant servants from the masters' purchasing agents to the master proper. In most cases, each entry records only one immigrant servant contract. The exceptions are most often for married servants and their children. Their contracts are sometimes recorded as separate entries and sometimes recorded together within one entry. In addition, a number of children of immigrant servants, while mentioned by name in the entries, were not subject to the conditions of their parents' servant contracts.

Among the 1,035 new immigrant servants were 192 married persons, 249 single adult males, 187 single adult females, and 407 dependent children (those who required consent from an adult to contract). The average contract length for single adult males was 2.7 years, and for married persons was 2.9 years. Given the significant movement in price indices during this period, the raw average of the contract prices lacks meaning. The average deflated contract debt (1795 = 100) was $100 for single adult males and $74 for married persons. For a more complete discussion of contract debts, passage fares, and contract prices and their inflation adjusted value see Grubb (1988, 1994b).

Masters came from all walks of life. Some came from well respected stations and occupations. For example, Gottlieb Kintzle was sold to James Madison of the State of Virginia (p. 9), Philipina Betz was sold to Joseph Barnes a Philadelphia attorney (p. 10), Frederick Troscher was sold to Richard Bache the postmaster (p. 16), Dorothea Werner was sold to John Geyer a Philadelphia alderman (p. 55), Barbara Schaffelin was sold to Louisa McIlhenney a gentlewomen (p. 60), Fredericca Kalender was sold to John Ross a physician (p. 61), Johan George Vogt was sold to John Biddle a major in the United States Army (p. 86), Regina Zahnin was sold to Augustus L. Baumfort a professor of mathematics (p. 89), Friderika Eitel was sold to Charles W. Bazeley the keeper of a female seminary (p. 89), and Dorothea Beck was sold to Robert B. Belville a minister of the gospel (p. 116). Most masters, however, came from a middling station in society and were the employers of those in the common trades. For example, farmers purchased 31 percent of the servants, merchants 19 percent, bakers 3 percent, innkeepers 3 percent, storekeepers 1.6 percent, victualers 1.4 percent, millers 1.3 percent, ironmasters 1.1 percent, grocers 1 percent, confectioners 0.9 percent, papermakers 0.9 percent, mariners 0.8 percent, brewers 0.7 percent, and tanners 0.7 percent. The rest of the masters were scattered among numerous trades from brassfounders and coopers to tailors and weavers.

Masters also came from all parts of the county, including the western and southern territories. For example, 11 percent came from Alabama, 2.3 percent from Missouri, 2.2 percent from Virginia, 2.1 percent from New York, 1.6 percent from North Carolina, and 0.9 percent from Illinois. One master even came from the Island of Cuba. Most masters, however, resided close to Philadelphia. For example, 37 percent came from Philadelphia county, 9 percent from Gloucester county (New Jersey), 6 percent from Lancaster county, 2.1 percent from Bucks county, 1.9 percent from Cumberland county, 1.7 from Berks county, 1.6 from Chester county, 1.6 percent from Lebanon county, and 1.6 percent from Burlington county (New Jersey). The rest of the masters were scattered mostly across the other counties of Pennsylvania, New Jersey, and Delaware.

Most masters, 74 percent, purchased only one servant, and another 16 percent purchased only two servants. A few, however, made large purchases. The seven largest were, in descending order, Benjamin B. Cooper of Gloucester county, New Jersey, who purchased 63 servants; N. Farrows of Alabama who purchased 46 servants; Francis Clopper of Alabama who purchased 30 servants; James Brown of Alabama who purchased 29 servants; Woodbridge Odlin of Gloucester county, New Jersey, who purchased 22 servants; James T. Watson of New York City who purchased 20 servants; and Jacob Bollinger of St. Louis, Missouri, who purchased 18 servants.

TRANSCRIPTION FORMAT

I transcribed this book of contract registrations completely, in order of registration, and (with minor exceptions) verbatim, including following the registrars' spelling, phrasing, punctuation, and pagination. I altered the capitalization and possessive punctuation to modern usage, spelled out all known abbreviations, and used commas in place of dashes, periods, and other rogue punctuation marks where it seemed appropriate. There are two reasons why it was important to preserve the registrars' pagination. First, registered changes in contract status, such as resales, typically refer to the original contract registration by page number. Thus, it is necessary to know the page number of the original document on which each contract appears in order to trace the activities of many of these immigrant servants. Second, the number of contracts registered per page can be used to estimate the volume of German immigrant servants arriving in Philadelphia during the years when the contract register is lost (Grubb 1994b). Thus, the pagination of the original document is a useful historical fact for expanding our knowledge into periods for which records have not survived.

While the original spelling was retained largely to preserve the purity of the original spelling of the names for genealogists, many scholars may find the spelling and phrasing to be of historical interest with regards to the evolution of language and education. In addition, most of the spelling corruption is not severe enough to cause confusion for the modern reader, such as the habit of spelling money without the "e," territory with only one "r," and mystery with an "i" in place of the first "y." The registrars do not appear to have corrupted the spelling of immigrant names to any great extent. Wholesale spelling corruption was unlikely because over 80 percent of German adult male immigrants were literate in German and bilingual translators were present when the servant contracts were written (Grubb 1987c, 1990a, 1990c, 1992a, 1994a). A couple of minor irregularities in the spelling of names do not appear to be random, however. Different registrars may have had different preferred spellings. For example, for some months the name of all people called "George" is spelled without the last "e" and in other months with the last "e." In some months the name of all people called "Elizabeth" is spelled with an "s" in place of the "z" and in other months only the "z" is used. Likewise, the addition of an "in" on the end of the last name to designate the individual as an unmarried adult female is not consistently practiced. Finally, only a couple of last names appear to be complete fabrications caused by language and translation problems. For example, on August 3, 1819, an immigrant was registered as Regina Wurtembergerin. It seems likely that whoever initially recorded the contract in Philadelphia confused the woman's principality of emigration for her last name. The same might be the case for Johan and Maria Wurtzberger who arrived October 30, 1818.

Two contracts were appended to the end of the document but were not recorded in the register. I added both to this transcription. I copied the registration style and placed these contracts in what would have been their proper location in the register. The two servants so included are Susanna Herbster (May 19, 1824) and Barbara Heinrich (Oct. 27, 1824). Finally, the term "consideration" refers to the sum paid by the master to the shipper (or to the prior master in the case of a resale or reassignment of a contract) and represents the immigrant's passage debt.

ACKNOWLEDGEMENTS

I wish to thank Anne Pfaelzer de Ortiz for providing research and editorial assistance, and the Historical Society of Pennsylvania for providing a microfilm copy of the contract registry and permission to publish a transcription of that document.

REFERENCES

Bentley, Elizabeth P. (transc.), and Michael H. Tepper (ed.) (1986), *Passenger Arrivals at the Port of Philadelphia, 1800-1819: The Philadelphia "Baggage Lists"*. Baltimore: Genealogical Publishing Co.

"Book *A* of Redemptioners, 1785-1804." Unpublished Manuscript held at the Historical Society of Pennsylvania, Philadelphia.

"Book *C* of Redemptioners, 1817-1831." Unpublished Manuscript held at the Historical Society of Pennsylvania, Philadelphia.

Diffenderffer, Frank R. (1899), "The German Immigration into Pennsylvania Through the Port of Philadelphia, and 'The Redemptioners'." *Pennsylvania German Society* **10**, 1-328.

Fearon, Henry Bradshaw (1818), *Sketches of America: A Narrative of a Journey of Five Thousand Miles Through the Eastern and Western States of America*. London: Longman, Hurst, Rees, Orme, and Brown.

Geiser, Karl F. (1901), *Redemptioners and Indentured Servants in the Colony and Commonwealth of Pennsylvania*. New Haven: Tuttle, Morehouse, and Taylor Co.

Grabbe, Hans-Jurgen (1984), "Das Ende des Redemptioner-Systems in den Vereinigten Staaten." *Amerikastudien* **29**, 277-96.

Grubb, Farley (1985a), "The Incidence of Servitude in Trans-Atlantic Migration, 1771-1804." *Explorations in Economic History* **22**, 316-39.

Grubb, Farley (1985b), "Immigrant Servant Labor: Their Occupational and Geographic Distribution in the Late Eighteenth-Century Mid-Atlantic Economy." *Social Science History* **9**, 249-75.

Grubb, Farley (1986), "Redemptioner Immigration to Pennsylvania: Evidence on Contract Choice and Profitability." *Journal of Economic History* **46**, 407-18.

Grubb, Farley (1987a), "Morbidity and Mortality on the North Atlantic Passage: Eighteenth-Century German Immigration to Pennsylvania." *Journal of Interdisciplinary History* **17**, 565-85.

Grubb, Farley (1987b), "The Market Structure of Shipping German Immigrants to Colonial America." *Pennsylvania Magazine of History and Biography* **111**, 27-48.

Grubb, Farley (1987c), "Colonial Immigrant Literacy: An Economic Analysis of Pennsylvania-German Evidence, 1727-1775." *Explorations in Economic History* **24**, 63-76.

Grubb, Farley (1988), "The Auction of Redemptioner Servants, Philadelphia, 1771-1804: An Economic Analysis." *Journal of Economic History* **48**, 583-603.

Grubb, Farley (1989), "Servant Auction Records and Immigration into the Delaware Valley, 1745-1831: The Proportion of Females Among Immigrant Servants." *Proceedings of the American Philosophical Society* **133**, 154-69.

Grubb, Farley (1990a), "German Immigration to Pennsylvania, 1709 to 1820." *Journal of Interdisciplinary History* **20**, 417-36.

Grubb, Farley (1990b), "The Reliability of U.S. Immigration Statistics: The Case of Philadelphia, 1815-1830." *International Journal of Maritime History* **2**, 29-54.

Grubb, Farley (1990c), "Growth of Literacy in Colonial America: Longitudinal Patterns,

Economic Models, and the Direction of Future Research." *Social Science History* **14**, 451-82.

Grubb, Farley (1992a), "Educational Choice in the Era Before Free Public Schooling: Evidence from German Immigrant Children in Pennsylvania, 1771-1817." *Journal of Economic History* **52**, 363-75.

Grubb, Farley (1992b), "The Long-Run Trend in the Value of European Immigrant Servants, 1654-1831: New Measurements and Interpretations." *Research in Economic History* **14**, 167-240.

Grubb, Farley (1994a), "The Disappearance of Organized Markets for European Immigrant Servants in the United States: Five Popular Explanations Reexamined." *Social Science History* **18**, 1-30.

Grubb, Farley (1994b), "The End of European Immigrant Servitude in the United States: An Economic Analysis of Market Collapse, 1772-1835." *Journal of Economic History* forthcoming.

Hansen, Marcus Lee (1940), *The Atlantic Migration 1607-1860*. Cambridge, MA: Harvard University Press.

Herrick, Cheesman A. (1926), *White Servitude in Pennsylvania*. Philadelphia: John Joseph McVey.

Moltmann, Gunter (1986), "The Migration of German Redemptioners to North America, 1720-1820." In P. C. Emmer (ed.), *Colonialism and Migration; Indentured Labour Before and After Slavery*. Boston: Martinus Nijhoff. Pp. 105-122.

Morris, Richard B. (1981), *Government and Labor in Early America*. Boston: Northeastern University Press.

Skeen, Edward C. (1981), "The Year Without a Summer: A Historical View." *Journal of the Early Republic* **1**, 51-67.

Smith, Abbot E. (1947), *Colonists in Bondage*. New York: W. W. Norton.

Strassburger, Ralph B. (1934), *Pennsylvania German Pioneers*. Norristown, PA: Pennsylvania German Society.

Tepper, Michael (ed.) (1978), *Emigrants to Pennsylvania, 1641-1819*. Baltimore: Genealogical Publishing Co.

Wokeck, Marianne S. (1981), "The Flow and Composition of German Immigration to Philadelphia, 1727-1775." *Pennsylvania Magazine of History and Biography* **105**, 249-278.

Wokeck, Marianne S. (1991), "Harnessing the Lure of the "Best Poor Man's Country": The Dynamics of German-Speaking Immigration to British North America, 1683-1783." In Ida Altman and James Horn (eds.), *"To Make America" European Emigration in the Early Modern Period*. Los Angeles: University of California Press. Pp. 204-43.

BOOK C OF REDEMPTIONERS

November 5, 1817

Catharina Klingler bound herself servant to John Gest of Philadelphia merchant to serve him four years and at the expiration of her term to have two complete suits of clothes, one thereof to be new. Consideration = $100.00.

Catharina Klinger at the same time assigned to Frederick Diller Baker of Salisbury Township Lancaster County farmer to serve him the remainder of her indenture as above recorded. Consideration = $100.00.

Hans Ulrich Kaser with his father's consent bound himself servant to Jacob Hassinger of Philadelphia merchant to serve him eight years and three months and to have six weeks schooling for every year of his servitude, and at the expiration of his term to have two complete suits of clothes, one thereof to be new. Consideration = $55.30.

Conrad Kaser with his father's consent bound himself servant to John Schwartz of Forks township Northampton county farmer to serve him seven years ten months and 16 days. And to have six weeks schooling for every year of his servitude and at the expiration of his term to have two complete suits of clothes one thereof to be new. Consideration = $66.30.

Verona Seggeser with her father's consent bound herself servant to Benjamin Fogel of Makunsky township Lehigh county farmer to serve him three years. And at the expiration of her term to have two complete suits of clothes, one thereof to be new. Consideration = $66.30.

John Seggeser with his father's consent bound himself servant to the above Benjamin Fogel to serve him five years. And to have six weeks schooling for every year of his servitude and at the expiration of his term to have two complete suits of clothes, one thereof to be new. Consideration = $66.30.

Jacob Seggeser with his father's consent bound himself servant to Joseph Trago of Stoneybrook township Chester county farmer to serve him eight years and five months. And to have six weeks schooling for every year of his servitude and at the expiration of his term to have two complete suits of clothes, one thereof to be new. Consideration = $66.30.

Anton Seiler bound himself servant to John M. Davis of Tredyffran township Chester county farmer to serve him three years. And at the expiration of his term to have two complete suits of clothes, one thereof to be new. Consideration = $76.35.

Elizabeth Seiffer bound herself servant to William Hayes of Lewisburg, Union county merchant to serve him two years and six months. And at the expiration of her term to have two complete suits of clothes, one thereof to be new, and ten dollars in cash. Consideration = $70.00.

Catherina Sterki with her father's consent bound herself servant to Richard Ashhurst of Philadelphia merchant to serve him three years. And to have six weeks schooling for every year of her servitude and at the expiration of her term to have two complete suits of clothes, one thereof to be new. Consideration = $66.30.

John Hitz with his father's consent bound himself servant to George Ricker of Manheim township Lancaster county turner to serve him nine years and one month. And to have six weeks schooling for every year of his servitude, and at the expiration of his term to have two complete suits of clothes, one thereof to be new. Consideration = $50.30.

Henry Hess bound himself servant to Daniel Crist of Buffaloe township Union county farmer to serve him two years and six months. And at the expiration of his term to have two complete suits of clothes, one thereof to be new, and forty five dollars in cash. Consideration = $50.00.

November 6, 1817

Ludwig Hoffman with Christoph Meyer's consent bound himself servant to Christian Konig of Lacock township Lancaster county farmer to serve him three years and eight months and to have six weeks schooling for every year of his servitude and at the expiration of his term to have two complete suits of clothes, one thereof to be new. Consideration = $35.00.

Maria Anna Zuber bound herself servant to James Van Uxem Junior of Morrisville, Bucks county miller to serve him three years. And at the expiration of her term to have two complete suits of clothes, one thereof to be new. Consideration = $66.30.

November 7, 1817

Dorothea Jenner bound herself servant to Jacob M. Haldeman of Allen township Cumberland county ironmaster to serve him four years. And at the expiration of her term to have two complete suits of clothes, one thereof to be new. And ten dollars in cash. Consideration = $100.00.

John Michael Dachtler with his father's consent bound himself servant to the above Jacob M. Haldeman to serve him seven years and to have six weeks schooling for every year of his servitude and at the expiration of his term to have two complete suits of clothes, one thereof to be new, and ten dollars in cash. Consideration = $62.50.

John Dachtler with his father's consent bound himself servant to the above Jacob M. Haldeman to serve him eight years. And to have six weeks schooling for every year of his servitude and at the expiration of his term to have two complete suits of clothes, one thereof to be new and ten dollars in cash. Consideration = $62.50.

Maria Barbara Dachtler with her father's consent bound herself servant to the aforesaid Jacob M. Haldeman to serve him ten years. And to have six weeks schooling for every year of her servitude and at the expiration of her term two complete suits of clothes, one thereof to be new. And ten dollars in cash. Consideration = $62.50.

John Jacob Dachtler with his father's consent bound himself servant to the above Jacob M. Haldeman to serve him nine years. And to have six weeks schooling for every year of his servitude, and at the expiration of his term to have two complete suits of clothes, one thereof to be new, and ten dollars in cash. Consideration = $62.50.

John Jacob Dachtler at the same time assigned to John Haldeman of Columbia, Lancaster county merchant to serve him the remainder of his indenture as above recorded. Consideration = $90.00.

Carolina Huber assigned by Jonathan Fell Junior to Frederick Hoeckley of the Northern Liberties to serve him the remainder of her indenture as recorded in Book B page 102. Consideration = $90.00.

Elizabeth Kaser with her father's consent bound herself servant to John Gruver of Springfield township Bucks county miller, to serve him seven years and five months. And to have six weeks schooling for every year of her servitude and at the expiration of her term to have two complete suits of clothes, one thereof to be new, and a cow, and a spinningwheel and four dollars in cash. Consideration = $32.30.

John Burger with his father's consent bound himself servant to Michael Ulrich of Sweetara township Dauphin county farmer, to serve him four years. And have one quarter schooling during his servitude and at the expiration of his term to have two complete suits of clothes, one thereof to be new. Consideration = $80.30.

Peter Rauch bound himself servant to Francis Miquet of Philadelphia hairdresser, to serve him three years. And at the expiration of his term to have two complete suits of clothes, one thereof to be new. Consideration = $76.35.

November 8, 1817

Magdalena Grohe with her father's consent bound herself servant to Philip Justice of the Northern Liberties carpenter, to serve him five years and seven months and to have six weeks schooling for every year of her servitude, and at the expiration of her term to have two complete suits of clothes, one thereof to be new. Consideration = $30.00.

Barbara Kaser with her father's consent to go to the State of New Jersey bound herself servant to Joseph Hancock of Mansfield township Burlington county New Jersey farmer to serve him three years. And to have one quarter schooling during her servitude, and at the expiration of her term to have two complete suits of clothes, one thereof to be new. Consideration = $50.30.

4

John George Beck with his father's consent bound himself servant to Peter Reinhard of Lancaster, Pennsylvania sadler to serve him eight years and eleven months, and to have six weeks schooling for every year of his servitude, and at the expiration of his term to have two complete suits of clothes, one thereof to be new. Consideration = $70.00.

John George Beck at the same time assigned to George Kleist of Lancaster, Pennsylvania brewer, to serve him the remainder of his indenture as above recorded. Consideration = $70.00.

Samuel Freidiger bound himself servant to John Irwin of Shippensburg, Pennsylvania merchant to serve him four years and at the expiration of his term to have two complete suits of clothes, one thereof to be new. And ten dollars in cash. Consideration = $74.30.

Catharina Kober bound herself servant to John Lardner of Oxford township Philadelphia county gentleman to serve him four years. And at the expiration of her term to have two complete suits of clothes, one thereof to be new. Consideration = $114.80.

November 10, 1817

Moritz Muller bound himself servant to Jacob Sigrist of Lebanon township Lebanon county farmer, to serve him three years and six months. And at the expiration of his term to have two complete suits of clothes, one thereof to be new and twenty dollars in cash. Consideration = $66.30.

Catharina Gerockin bound herself servant to William Ward of New Millford, Susquahannah county merchant to serve him four years. And at the expiration of her term to have two complete suits of clothes, one thereof to be new. Consideration = $40.00.

Fredericca Gerockin bound herself servant to the above William Ward to serve him four years. And at the expiration of her term to have two complete suits of clothes, one thereof to be new. Consideration = $100.00.

John Michael Beck with his father's consent to go to the Misoury territory bound himself servant to Francis Nicolas Dethier of the Misoury territory merchant to serve him six years and ten months. And to have six weeks schooling for every year of his servitude and at the expiration of his term to have two complete suits of clothes, one thereof to be new. Consideration = $100.00.

Jacob Frederick Gerock with his mother's consent to go to the Misoury territory bound himself servant to the above Francis Nicolas Dethier to serve him eight years three months and 23 days. And to have six weeks schooling for every year of his servitude and at the expiration of his term to have two complete suits of clothes, one thereof to be new. Consideration = $75.00.

Rosina Klinck with her father's consent to go to the Misoury bound herself servant to Emanuel De Hadiamont of the Misoury territory merchant to serve him four years. And to have six weeks schooling during her servitude, and at the expiration of her term to have two complete suits of clothes, one thereof to be new. Consideration = $120.00.

William Frederick Kreh with E. Rising's consent to go to Misoury bound himself servant to the aforesaid Emanuel De Hodiamont to serve him three years and seven months. And at the expiration of his term to have two complete suits of clothes, one thereof to be new. Consideration = $100.00.

Landolin Stregel with his wife's consent bound himself servant to Parkes Boyd of Philadelphia pewterer, to serve him three years. And to have fifteen dollars per year in lieu of apparel, and no freedom suit. Considerations = $15.00.

Anna Maria Stregel with her husband's consent bound herself servant to the above Parkes Boyd to serve him three years, and to have fifteen dollars per year in lieu of apparel, and no freedom suit. Consideration = $15.00.

John Jacob Mollenkopff with his mother's consent bound himself servant to the above Parkes Boyd to serve him nine years and six months. And to have six weeks schooling for every year of his servitude and at the expiration of his term to have two complete suits of clothes, one thereof to be new, or twenty six 67/100 dollars in cash at the option of the master. Consideration = $35.00.

November 11, 1817

John Michael Motz with his wife's consent bound himself servant to Samuel J. Robbins of Philadelphia merchant to serve him six years. And at the expiration of his term to have two complete suits of clothes, one thereof to be new. And if the consideration is refunded with all expenses within ninety days then this indenture to be null and void. Consideration = $25.00.

John Michael Motz at the same time assigned to Michael P. Casselly of Greensburg, Westmoreland county merchant to serve him the remainder of his indenture as above recorded. Consideration = $25.00.

Christina Johanna Motz with her husband's consent bound herself servant to the above Samuel J. Robbins to serve him six years. And at the expiration of her term to have two complete suits of clothes, one thereof to be new, her indenture to be null and void on the above conditions. Considerations = $25.00.

Christina Johanna Motz at the same time assigned to the above Michael P. Casselly to serve him the remainder of her indenture as above recorded. Consideration = $25.00.

Jacob Motz with his father's consent bound himself servant to the above Samuel J. Robbins to serve him eleven years. And to have six weeks schooling for every year of his servitude and at the expiration of his term to have two complete suits of clothes, one thereof to be new, his indenture to be null and void on the above conditions. Consideration = $25.00.

Jacob Motz at the same time assigned to the above Michael P. Casselly to serve him the remainder of the indenture as above recorded. Consideration = $25.00.

John Motz with his father's consent bound himself servant to the aforesaid Samuel J. Robbins to serve him twelve years and nine months. And to have six weeks schooling for every year of his servitude, and at the expiration of his term to have two complete suits of clothes, one thereof to be new, his indenture to be null and void on the aforesaid conditions. Consideration = $25.00.

John Motz at the same time assigned to the aforesaid Michael P. Casselly to serve him the remainder of his indenture as above recorded. Consideration = $25.00.

Barbara Motz with her father's consent bound herself servant to the above Samuel J. Robbins to serve him ten years and ten months. And to have six weeks schooling for every year of her servitude and at the expiration of her term to have two complete suits of clothes, one thereof to be new, her indenture to be null and void on the aforesaid conditions. Consideration = $25.00.

Barbara Motz at the same time assigned the the above Michael P. Casselly to serve him the remainder of her indenture as above recorded. Consideration = $25.00.

John Jacob Volz with E. Rising's consent to go to the Misoury bound himself servant to E. F. F. Joseph De Resimont to serve him three years. And to have six weeks schooling for every year of his servitude and at the expiration of his term to have two complete suits of clothes, one thereof to be new. And to receive customary salary for nine months of the above term. Consideration = $80.00.

William Godlob Schweitzer with his consent to go to the Misoury bound himself servant to the above E. F. F. Joseph De Resimont to serve him three years. And at the expiration of his term to have two complete suits of clothes, one thereof to be new and to receive customary salary for eighteen months of the above term. Consideration = $40.00.

Eva Margaretta Rasig bound herself servant to Henry Hartzel Junior to serve him three years and six months at at the expiration of her term to have two complete suits of clothes, one thereof to be new. And fifteen dollars in cash the master lives at Rockhill township Bucks county farmer. Consideration = $76.80.

November 12, 1817

John Fogt with his consent to go to New Jersey bound himself servant to Ephraim Lloyd of Salem New Jersey farmer to serve him three years. And at the expiration of his term to have two complete suits of clothes, one thereof to be new. And forty four dollars in cash. Consideration = $34.15.

Catharina Wuterich with her consent to go to New Jersey bound herself servant to the above Ephraim Lloyd to serve him three years and at the expiration of her term to have two complete suits of clothes, one thereof to be new, and forty four dollars in cash. Consideration = $34.15.

Christian Stahl bound himself servant to Peter Knapp of Ohly, Berks county farmer to serve him three years & six months and at the expiration of his term to have two complete suits of clothes, one thereof to be new. Consideration = $75.00.

Christian Stahl at the same time assigned to John Knapp of the above place, to serve him the remainder of his indenture as above recorded. Consideration = $75.00.

November 13, 1817

Ludwig Frederick Krayl with E. Rising's consent bound himself servant to John Stauffer of Lampeter township Lancaster county farmer to serve him three years and two months. And to have six weeks schooling for every year of his servitude and at the expiration of his term to have two complete suits of clothes, one thereof to be new. Consideration = $76.80.

John Christoph Bauer with his wife's consent bound himself servant to Daniel Reigart of Lancaster, Pennsylvania merchant to serve him three years. And at the expiration of his term to have two complete suits of clothes, one thereof to be new. Consideration = $30.00.

Barbara Bauer with her husband's consent bound herself servant to the above Daniel Reigart to serve him three years and at the expiration of her term to have two complete suits of clothes, one thereof to be new. Consideration = $30.00.

Margretta Bauer with her father's consent bound herself servant to the above Daniel Reigart, to serve him thirteen years and to have six weeks schooling for every year of her servitude and at the expiration of her term to have two complete suits of clothes, one thereof to be new. Consideration = $20.00.

Jacob Kohler with his father's consent to go to Virginia bound himself servant to George Richards of Philadelphia merchant to serve him six years and nine months. And to have six weeks schooling for every year of his servitude. And at the expiration of his term to have two complete suits of clothes, one thereof to be new. Consideration = $60.00.

Jacob Kohler at the same time assigned to Richard Furt of Petersburg, Virginia merchant to serve him the remainder of his indenture as above recorded. Consideration = $60.00.

John Schaffner with his consent to go to Virginia bound himself servant to the above George Richards to serve him two years & six months. And at the expiration of his term to have two complete suits of clothes, one thereof to be new. (This indenture is this day 14th Nov. cancelled by consent of the parties.) Consideration = $100.00.

John Schaffner at the same time assigned to the above Richard Furt to serve him the remainder of his indenture as above recorded. Consideration = $100.00.

John David Klingler with his father's consent bound himself servant to Jacob Seibert of Heidelberg township Lebanon county farmer to serve him nine years and one month. And to have six weeks schooling for every year of his servitude. And at the expiration of his term to have two complete suits of clothes, one thereof to be new. Consideration = $70.00.

Ludwig Buehrer with his father's consent bound himself servant to Nathaniel Gilman of Philadelphia merchant to serve him twelve years and three months. And to have six weeks schooling for every year of his servitude, and at the expiration of his term to have two complete suits of clothes, one thereof to be new. Consideration = $76.40.

George Michael Kembach bound himself servant to John Schwar of Cocalico township Lancaster county farmer to serve him three years and three months. And at the expiration of his term to have two complete suits of clothes, one thereof to be new. Consideration = $95.80.

George Michael Kembach at the same time assigned to Henry Eberle of Elizabeth township Lancaster county miller to serve him the remainder of his indenture as above recorded. Consideration = $95.80.

Carolina Graff bound herself servant to William Taylor Junior of Philadelphia merchant to serve him three years and six months. And at the expiration of her term to have two complete suits of clothes, one thereof to be new, and twenty dollars in cash. And in case her husband should refund the above consideration with all expenses then this indenture to be null and void. Consideration = $40.00.

John George Heimedinger bound himself servant to John Stieg of Philadelphia baker to serve him fourteen months. And to receive one dollar per week wages in lieu of apparel and no freedom suit. And also to have six weeks schooling during his servitude. Consideration = $36.40.

Ludwig Frederick Krayl assigned by John Stauffer to George Yohe of Philadelphia innkeeper to serve him the remainder of his indentured as recorded page 7. Consideration = $90.00.

November 14, 1817

Valentine Hassinger assigned by Jacob Hassinger to Christopher Wagner of Braunswick township Sckuylkill county farmer to serve him the remainder of his indenture as recorded in Book B, page 327. Consideration = $76.00.

Melcher Hitz with his father's consent bound himself servant to Henry Geiger of Hempfield township Westmoreland county farmer to serve him eight years one month & 20 days. And to have six weeks schooling for every year of his servitude, and at the expiration of his term to have two complete suits of clothes, one thereof to be new. Consideration = $50.00.

Melcher Hitz at the same time assigned to Simon Singer of Greensburg, Westmoreland county innkeeper to serve him the remainder of his indenture as above recorded. Consideration = $50.00.

Martin Bletscher with his consent to go to New Jersey bound himself servant to Wesley Budd of Morris river township Cumberland county New Jersey iron master, to serve him three years. And at the expiration of his term to have two complete suits of clothes, one thereof to be new. And seventy two dollars in cash. Consideration = $18.00.

Jacob Hampff with his wife's consent bound himself servant to David Rickebach of Trederffran township Chester county farmer to serve him three years. And at the expiration of his term to have two complete suits of clothes, one thereof to be new and twenty dollars in cash. The child to be fed and clothed gratis and to be free with the parent. Consideration = $40.00.

Rosina Hampff with her husband's consent bound herself servant to the above David Rickebach to serve him three years and at the expiration of her term to have two complete suits of clothes, one thereof to be new. The child to be fed and clothed gratis and to be free with the parent. Consideration = $40.00.

November 15, 1817

Sabina Schalin bound herself servant to Walter Midlin of Southwark Philadelphia county mariner to serve him four years and at the expiration of her term to have two complete suits of clothes, one thereof to be new. Consideration = $76.35.

John George Kromer bound himself servant to Henry Lewis of Radnor township Delaware county farmer to serve him two years. And at the expiration of his term to have two complete suits of clothes, one thereof to be new. Consideration = $64.20.

Christian Gohl with his consent to go to New Jersey bound himself servant to Charles Ellis of Mansfield township Burlington county farmer to serve him two years. And at the expiration of his term to have two complete suits of clothes, one thereof to be new, and twenty dollars in cash. Consideration = $44.20.

Ignats Boeam with his consent to go to Virginia bound himself servant to George Richards of Philadelphia merchant to serve him two years and six months. And at the expiration of his term to have two complete suits of clothes, one thereof to be new. Consideration = $77.00.

Ignats Boeam at the same time assigned to Richard Furt of Petersburg, Virginia merchant to serve him the remainder of his indenture as above recorded. Consideration = $77.00.

Conrad Pulvermuller with E. Green's consent to go to Virginia bound himself servant to George Richards of Philadelphia merchant to serve him three years. And to have twelve weeks schooling during his servitude and at the expiration of his term to have two complete suits of clothes, one thereof to be new. Consideration = $76.67.

Conrad Pulvermuller at the same time assigned to James Samuel of Ville Bourough, Virginia merchant to serve him the remainder of his indenture as above recorded. Consideration = $76.67.

Gottlieb Kintzle with the same consent bound himself servant to the above George Richards to serve him three years. And at the expiration of his term to have two complete suits of clothes, one thereof to be new. Consideration = $76.67.

Gottlieb Kintzle at the same time assigned to James Madison of the State of Virginia merchant to serve him the remainder of his indenture as above recorded. Consideration = $76.67.

John Kegh with his consent to go to Mississippi bound himself servant to Jean Claude Benoit Boutiere of Aigleville, Mississippi territory to serve him four years. And at the expiration of his term to have two complete suits of clothes, one thereof to be new. And one dollar per month in cash as it comes due. Consideration = $76.00.

Felix Hurtzler with the same consent bound himself servant to the above Jean Claude B. Boutiere to serve him four years. And at the expiration of his term to have two complete suits of clothes, one thereof to be new, and one dollar per month in cash as it comes due. Consideration = $50.00.

John Jacob Buser with the same consent bound himself servant to Charles de Brosse of the above place and territory to serve him four years. And at the expiration of his term to have two complete suits of clothes, one thereof to be new, and one dollar in cash as it comes due per month. Consideration = $50.00.

Jacob Leuthweiller with his wife's consent bound himself servant to Jacob Steman of Manheim township Lancaster county miller, to serve him three years and six months. And at the expiration of his term to have two complete suits of clothes, one thereof to be new. Consideration = $76.00.

Maria Leuthweiller with her husband's consent bound herself servant to the above Jacob Steman to serve him three years and six months. And at the expiration of her term to have two complete suits of clothes, one thereof to be new. Consideration = $76.00.

November 17, 1817

George Klingler bound himself servant to Martin Light of Bardhall township Lebanon county farmer to serve him three years and six months. And at the expiration of his term to have two complete suits of clothes, one thereof to be new. And twenty dollars in cash if he serves faithfully. Consideration = $100.00.

Philipina Betz bound herself servant to Joseph Barnes esquire of Philadelphia attorney to serve him three years. And at the expiration of her term to have two complete suits of clothes, one thereof to be new. Consideration = $97.50.

Susanna Magdelena Betz with her mother's consent bound herself servant to the above Joseph Barnes esquire to serve him four years and four months. And to have six weeks schooling for every year of her servitude and at the expiration of her term to have two complete suits of clothes, one thereof to be new. Consideration = $97.50.

November 18, 1817

Frederick Hetz with E. Rising's consent bound himself servant to Samuel Longstreth of Philadelphia merchant to serve him four years. And to have six weeks schooling for every year of his servitude, and at the expiration of his term to have two complete suits of clothes, one thereof to new. Consideration = $76.30.

Frederick Hetz at the same time assigned to John Creigh of Landesburgh, Cumberland county M.D. to serve him the remainder of his indenture as above recorded. Consideration = $76.30.

Samuel Burckhart with consent of his wife bound himself servant to Michael Lapp of Leacock township Lancaster county farmer to serve him three years. And at the expiration of his term to have two complete suits of clothes, one thereof to be new. The child to be fed and clothed gratis and to be free with the parent. Consideration = $47.00.

Barbara Burckhart with consent of her husband bound herself servant to the above Michael Lapp to serve him three years. And at the expiration of her term to have two complete suits of clothes, one thereof to be new. The child to be fed and clothed gratis and to be free with the parent. Consideration = $47.00.

Josiah Kuhn with his father's consent bound himself servant to the above Michael Lapp to serve him eleven years. And to have six weeks schooling for every year of his servitude and at the expiration of his term to have two complete suits of clothes, one thereof to be new. Consideration = $40.00.

John Mathias Kober with his father's consent bound himself servant to Mathias Smyser Junior of Yorktown, Pennsylvania farmer to serve him three years and eleven months, and to have six weeks schooling for every year of his servitude and at the expiration of his term to have two complete suits of clothes, one thereof to be new. Consideration = $116.40.

Adam Kuhn bound himself servant to Gideon Cox of Philadelphia merchant to serve him six years. And at the expiration of his term to have two complete suits of clothes, one thereof to be new. And thirty dollars in cash. Consideration = $70.00.

Adam Kuhn at the same time assigned to Robert Babcock of Bucks county, Pennsylvania farmer to serve him the the remainder of his indenture as above recorded. Consideration = $70.00.

Benedict Kuhn with his father's consent bound himself servant to the above Gideon Cox to serve him sixteen years & six months. And to have six weeks schooling for every year of his servitude. And at the expiration of his term to have two complete suits of clothes, one thereof to be new. Consideration = $37.00.

Benedict Kuhn at the same time assigned to the above Robert Babcock to serve him the remainder of his indenture as above recorded. Consideration = $37.00.

Andreas Staengel bound himself servant to the above Gideon Cox to serve him five years. And at the expiration of his term to have two complete suits of clothes, one thereof to be new, and forty dollars in cash. Consideration = $76.35.

Andreas Staengel at the same time assigned to the above Robert Babcock to serve him the remainder of his indenture as above recorded. Consideration = $76.35.

Catharina Kurn with her father's consent bound herself servant to Adam Hocker of Derry township Dauphin county farmer to serve him three years, and to have six weeks schooling for every year's servitude, and at the expiration of her term to have two complete suits of clothes, one thereof to be new. Consideration = $100.00.

November 19, 1817

Dominicus Muller with his wife's consent to go to New Jersey bound himself servant to Joseph Lodge of Billingsford, Gloucester county New Jersey farmer to serve him three years. And at the expiration of his term to have two complete suits of clothes, one thereof to be new. The child to be fed and clothed gratis and to be free with the parent. Consideration = $45.70.

Maria Muller with her husband's consent as foresaid bound herself servant to the above Joseph Lodge to serve him three years. And at the expiration of her term to have two complete suits of clothes, one thereof to be new. The child to be fed and clothed gratis and to be free with the parent. Consideration = $45.70.

November 20, 1817

Elizabeth Barbara Kuern with her father's consent bound herself servant to Abraham Stoltzfuss of Leacock township Lancaster county farmer to serve him seven years and six months. And to have six weeks schooling for every year of her servitude and at the expiration of her term to have two complete suits of clothes, one thereof to be new. Consideration = $60.00.

John Klinck with his father's consent bound himself servant to Christian Hess of Salsburry township Lancaster county miller to serve him eleven years and seven months. And at the expiration of his term to have two complete suits of clothes, one thereof to be new. And also six weeks schooling for every year of his servitude. Consideration = $47.50.

John Klinck at the same time assigned to Joseph Horst of Leacock township Lancaster county farmer to serve him the remainder of his indenture as above recorded. Consideration = $47.50.

Gottlieb Klinck with his father's consent bound himself servant to the above Christian Hess to serve him fourteen years five months & 16 days. And to have six weeks schooling for every year of his servitude. And at the expiration of his term to have two complete suits of clothes, one thereof to be new. Consideration = $47.50.

Gottlieb Klinck at the same time assigned to Christian Roop of Salsburry township Lancaster farmer to serve him the remainder of his indenture as above recorded. Consideration = $47.50.

Anna Maria Fritz with her father's consent bound herself servant to Frederick Fisher of the Northern Liberties grocer to serve him four years and three months. And to have six weeks schooling for every year of her servitude. And at the expiration of her term to have two complete suits of clothes, one thereof to be new. Consideration = $78.40.

John Schaffner with his wife's consent bound himself servant to Michael T. Simpson of Fairview township York county Pennsylvania farmer to serve him four years. And at the expiration of his term to have two complete suits of clothes, one thereof to be new. And one hundred dollars in cash. Consideration = $81.85.

Catharina Schaffner with her husband's consent bound herself servant to the above Michael T. Simpson to serve him four years. And at the expiration of her term to have two complete suits of clothes, one thereof to be new. Consideration = $81.85.

November 21, 1817

Jacob Raab bound himself servant to Jacob Kraut of Bedminster township Bucks county farmer to serve him three years. And at the expiration of his term to have two complete suits of clothes, one thereof to be new. Consideration = $78.50.

Zacharias Bletscher with consent of his wife to go to New Jersey bound himself servant to Wesley Budd of Morris river township Cumberland county New Jersey ironmaster to serve him three years & six months. And at the expiration of his term to have two complete suits of clothes, one thereof to be new. And forty dollars in cash. The child Barbara to be fed and clothed gratis and to be free with the parent. Consideration = $25.00.

Elizabeth Bletscher Junior with consent of her father as above, bound herself servant to the above Wesley Budd to serve him thirteen years. And to have six weeks schooling for every year of her servitude and at the expiration of her term to have two complete suits of clothes, one thereof to be new. And a good cow. Consideration = $20.00.

November 22, 1817

Mathias Ley bound himself servant to Henry Karmone of Anville township Lebanon county farmer to serve him three years. And at the expiration of his term to have two complete suits of clothes, one thereof to be new. Consideration = $76.35.

November 24, 1817

Margaretta Hantle with her father's consent bound herself servant to Jacob V. Hunter of Rockland township Berks county ironmaster to serve him four years and eight months. And to have six weeks schooling for every year of her servitude, and at the expiration of her term to have two complete suits of clothes, one thereof to be new. Consideration = $80.40.

Catharina Seefried bound herself servant to Henry Most of Penn township Philadelphia county farmer to serve him two years eleven months and 14 days. And at the expiration of her term to have two complete suits of clothes, one thereof to be new. Consideration = $76.30.

Mathias Fruh with his wife's consent to go to the Mobille bound himself servant to Woodbridge Odlin of Philadelphia merchant to serve him three years. And at the expiration of his term to have two complete suits of clothes, one thereof to be new. The child Dorthea Junior to be fed and clothed gratis and to be free with the parent. Consideration = $76.35.

Dorothea Fruh with her husband's consent as aforesaid bound herself servant to the above Woodbridge Odlin to serve him three years. And at the expiration of her term to have two complete suits of clothes, one thereof to be new. The child Dorothea Junior to be fed and clothed gratis and to be free with the parent. Consideration = $76.35.

Johanna Rudolph with the aforesaid consent bound herself servant to the above Woodbridge Odlin to serve him three years. And at the expiration of her term to have two complete suits of clothes, one thereof to be new. The child Johanna Junior to be fed and clothed gratis and to be free with the mother. Consideration = $76.35.

Gottlob Rudolph with his mother's consent as aforesaid bound himself servant to the above Woodbridge Odlin to serve him nine years and six months. And to have six weeks schooling for every year of his servitude, and at the expiration of his term to have two complete suits of clothes, one thereof to be new. Consideration = $38.35.

Jacob Schaffer with his wife's consent as aforesaid bound himself servant to the above Woodbridge Odlin to serve him three years. And at the expiration of his term to have two complete suits of clothes, one thereof to be new. The children Adam and Solomea to be fed and clothed gratis and to be free with the parent. Consideration = $76.35.

Solomea Schaffer with her husband's consent as aforesaid bound herself servant to the above Woodbridge Odlin to serve him three years. And at the expiration of her term to have two complete suits of clothes, one thereof to be new. The children Adam and Solomea to be fed and clothed gratis and to be free with the parent. Consideration = $76.35.

Philip Weber with his mother's consent as aforsaid bound himself servant to the above Woodbridge Odlin to serve him nine years and six months. And to have six weeks schooling for every year of his servitude and at the expiration of his term to have two complete suits of clothes, one thereof to be new. Consideration = $38.35.

Daniel Reiniger with his wife's consent as aforesaid bound himself servant to the said Woodbridge Odlin to serve him three years. And at the expiration of his term to have two complete suits of clothes, one thereof to be new. The children Christian and Daniel to be fed and clothed gratis and to be free with the parent. Consideration = $76.35.

Barbara Reiniger with her husband's consent as aforesaid bound herself servant to the above Woodbridge Odlin to serve him three years. And at the expiration of her term to have two complete suits of clothes, one thereof to be new. The children Christian and Daniel to be fed and clothed gratis and to be free with the parent. Consideration = $76.35.

Barbara Reiniger Junior with her father's consent as aforesaid bound herself servant to the above Woodbridge Odlin to serve him nine years. And to have six weeks schooling for every year of her servitude, and at the expiration of her term to have two complete suits of clothes, one thereof to be new. Consideration = $38.35.

Andreas Klepser with his wife's consent bound himself servant to William Ker Junior of Porter township Huntingdon county farmer to serve him three years. And at the expiration of his term to have two complete suits of clothes, one thereof to be new. The two children to be fed and clothed gratis and to be free with the parent. Consideration = $30.00.

Johanna Elizabeth Klepser with her husband's consent bound herself to the above William Ker Junior to serve him three years. And at the expiration of her term to have two complete suits of clothes, one thereof to be new. The two children to be fed and clothed gratis and to be free with the parent. Consideration = $30.00.

Andreas Klepser Junior with his father's consent bound himself servant to the above William Ker Junior to serve him eight years and nine months. And to have six weeks schooling for every year of his servitude and at the expiration of his term to have two complete suits of clothes, one thereof to be new. Consideration = $25.00.

Jacob Klepser with his father's consent bound himself servant to the above William Ker Junior to serve him nine years and six months. And to have six weeks schooling for every year of his servitude and at the expiration of his term to have two complete suits of clothes, one thereof to be new. Consideration = $25.00.

Jeremias Klepser with his father's consent bound himself servant to the above William Ker Junior to serve him fourteen years and six months. And to have six weeks schooling for every year of his servitude. And at the expiration of his term to have two complete suits of clothes, one thereof to be new. Consideration = $25.00.

Michael Schaffer with his wife's consent bound himself servant to Nathan Woods of Dickenson township Cumberland county farmer to serve him three years and six months. And at the expiration of his term to have two complete suits of clothes, one thereof to be new. And fifty dollars in cash if he conducts himself well. The child to be fed and clothed gratis and to be free with the parent. Consideration = $30.00.

Christiana Schaffer with her husband's consent bound herself servant to the above Nathan Woods to serve him three years and six months. And at the expiration of her term to have two complete suits of clothes, one thereof to be new. The child to be fed and clothed gratis and to be free with the parent. Consideration = $30.00.

November 25, 1817

Joseph Anthonia Thal assigned by Frederick Foering to Tyonius Thall the father of the said servant, to serve him the remainder of his indenture as recorded in Book B, page 255. Consideration = $50.00.

Louisa Troscher with E. Rising's consent bound herself servant to Charles W. Beasley of Philadelphia teacher, to serve him three years. And to have six weeks schooling for every year of her servitude and at the expiration of her term to have two complete suits of clothes, one thereof to be new. Consideration = $85.00.

John Ludwig Troscher with E. Rising's consent bound himself servant to the above Charles W. Beasley to serve him eight years and nine months. And to have six weeks schooling for every year of his servitude and at the expiration of his term to have two complete suits of clothes, one thereof to be new. Consideration = $85.00.

November 26, 1817

Wernhard Mesmer bound himself servant to George Heberling of upper Nazareth township Northampton county farmer to serve him three years, and at the expiration of his term to have two complete suits of clothes, one thereof to be new, and twenty four dollars 60 cents in cash. Consideration = $54.60.

Eva Breitenstein assigned by William Sutton to Elizabeth Fillar of Philadelphia to serve her the remainder of her indenture as recorded in Book B, page 142. Consideration = $10.00

Frederick Troscher with E. Rising's consent bound himself servant to Richard Bache esquire of the City of Philadelphia, postmaster, to serve him six years and five months. And to have six weeks schooling for every year of his servitude. And at the expiration of his term to have two complete suits of clothes, one thereof to be new. Consideration = $85.00.

Gottlieb Handle with his wife's consent bound himself servant to Woodbridge Odlin of Philadelphia merchant to serve him three years. And at the expiration of his term to have two complete suits of clothes, one thereof to be new. The two children John and Maria to be fed and clothed gratis and to be free with the parent. Consideration = $76.30.

Johanna Handle with her husband's consent bound herself servant to the above Woodbridge Odlin, to serve him three years. And at the expiration of her term to have two complete suits of clothes, one thereof to be new. The two children John and Maria to be fed and clothed gratis and to be free with the parent. Consideration = $76.30.

Johanna Handle Junior with her father's consent bound herself servant to the above Woodbridge Odlin, to serve him five years and six months. And to have six weeks schooling for every year of her servitude and at the expiration of her term to have two complete suits of clothes, one thereof to be new. Consideration = $38.30.

Baltus Handle with his father's consent bound himself servant to the above Woodbridge Odlin, to serve him thirteen years, and to have six weeks schooling for every year of his servitude and at the expiration of his term to have two complete suits of clothes, one thereof to be new. Consideration = $38.30.

Conrad Reizner bound himself servant to the above Woodbridge Odlin to serve him three years. And at the expiration of his term to have two complete suits of clothes, one thereof to be new. Consideration = $76.30.

Diederich Rasig with his wife's consent bound himself servant to the above Woodbridge Odlin to serve him three years. And at the expiration of his term to have two complete suits of clothes, one thereof to be new. Consideration = $76.30.

Eva Rasig with her husband's consent bound herself servant to the above Woodbridge Odlin to serve him three years, and at the expiration of her term to have two complete suits of clothes, one thereof to be new. Consideration = $76.30.

Jacob Rasig with his father's consent bound himself servant to the above Woodbridge Odlin, to serve him eight years. And to have six weeks schooling for every year of his servitude. And at the expiration of his term to have two complete suits of clothes, one thereof to be new. Consideration = $38.30.

Magdalena Rasig with her father's consent bound herself servant to the above Woodbridge Odlin, to serve him eight years and three months, and to have six weeks schooling for every year of her servitude and at the expiration of her term to have two complete suits of clothes, one thereof to be new. Consideration = $38.30.

John Daniel Eisenbraun bound himself servant to the above Woodbridge Odlin to serve him three years. And at the expiration of his term to have two complete suits of clothes, one thereof to be new. And if the above servant can refund the consideration at any time during his servitude then this indenture to be null and void. Consideration = $76.30.

Philip Kober with his wife's consent bound himself servant to the aforesaid Woodbridge Odlin, to serve him three years. And at the expiration of his term to have two complete suits of clothes, one thereof to be new. And forty dollars in cash. The child Juliana to be fed and clothed gratis and to be free with the parent. Consideration = $38.30.

Catharina Kober with her husband's consent bound herself servant to the above Woodbridge Odlin to serve him three years. And at the expiration of her term to have two complete suits of clothes, one thereof to be new, and forty dollars in cash. The child Juliana to be fed and clothed gratis and to be free with the parent. Consideration = $38.30.

Christoph Kober with his father's consent bound himself servant to the above Woodbridge Odlin, to serve him eleven years. And to have six weeks of schooling for every year of his servitude, and at the expiration of his term to have two complete suits of clothes, one thereof to be new. Consideration = $38.30.

Christina Kober with her father's consent bound herself servant to the above Woodbridge Odlin to serve him eleven years. And to have six weeks of schooling for every year of her servitude. And at the expiration of her term to have two complete suits of clothes, one thereof to be new. Consideration = $38.30.

November 27, 1817

Joseph Buhrer with his wife's consent bound himself servant to the above Woodbridge Odlin to serve him three years. And at the expiration of his term to have two complete suits of clothes, one thereof to be new. The two children Ignatius and Francis to be fed and clothed gratis and to be free with the parent. Consideration = $76.30.

Joseph Buhrer at the same time assigned to George Mower of Southampton township Cumberland county farmer to serve him the remainder of his indenture as above recorded. Consideration = $76.30.

Othilia Buhrer with her husband's consent bound herself servant to the above Woodbridge Odlin, to serve him three years. And at the expiration of her term to have two complete suits of clothes, one thereof to be new. The two children Ignatius and Francis to be fed and clothed gratis and to be free with the parent. Consideration = $76.30.

Othilia Buhrer at the same time assigned to the above George Mower to serve him the remainder of her indenture as above recorded. Consideration = $76.30.

Maria Franzisca Buhrer with her father's consent bound herself servant to the above Woodbridge Odlin to serve him eleven years and to have six weeks schooling for every year of her servitude and at the expiration of her term to have two complete suits of clothes, one thereof to be new. Consideration = $38.30.

Maria Franzisca Buhrer at the same time assigned to the above George Mower to serve him the remainder of her indenture as above recorded. Consideration = $38.30.

Jacob Fritz with his wife's consent bound himself servant to the above Woodbrige Odlin, to serve him three years. And at the expiration of his term to have two complete suits of clothes, one thereof to be new. And nineteen dollars in cash. And if the consideration is refunded within six months then this indenture to be null and void. Consideration = $57.30.

Anna Maria Fritz with her husband's consent bound herself servant to the above Woodbridge Odlin, to serve him three years. And at the expiration of her term to have two complete suits of clothes, one thereof to be new. And nineteen dollars in cash. And if the above consideration is refunded within six months then this indenture to be null and void. Consideration = $57.30.

George Fritz with his father's consent bound himself servant to the above Woodbridge Odlin, to serve him eight years. And to have six weeks schooling for every years of his servitude, and at the expiration of his term to have two complete suits of clothes, one thereof to be new, and if the consideration is refunded within six months then this indenture to be null and void. Consideration = $38.30.

John Fritz with his father's consent bound himself servant to the above Woodbridge Odlin to serve him nine years. And to have six weeks schooling for every years of his servitude, and at the expiration of his term to have two complete suits of clothes, one thereof to be new. And if the consideration is refunded within six months then this indenture to be null and void. Consideration = $38.30.

Daniel Fritz with his father's consent bound himself servant to the above Woodbridge Odlin to serve him thirteen years, and to have six weeks schooling for every years of his servitude, and at the expiration of his term to have two complete suits of clothes, one thereof to be new, and if the consideration is refunded within six months then this indenture to be null and void. Consideration = $38.30.

Dorothea Kingeter bound herself servant to the above Woodbridge Odlin, to serve him three years. And at the expiration of her term to have two complete suits of clothes, one thereof to be new, her infant to be fed and clothed gratis and be free with with the mother. Consideration = $76.30.

John Kingeter with his mother's consent bound himself servant to the above Woodbridge Odlin, to serve him seven years. And to have six weeks schooling for every year of his servitude, and at the expiration of his term to have two complete suits of clothes, one thereof to be new. Consideration = $38.30.

Frederick Kingeter with his mother's consent bound himself servant to the above Woodbridge Odlin, to serve him twelve years. And to have six weeks schooling for every year of his servitude, and at the expiration of his term to have two complete suits of clothes, one thereof to be new. Consideration = $38.30.

Henry Kochenburger with his wife's consent bound himself servant to the aforesaid Woodbridge Odlin to serve him three years and at the expiration of his term to have two complete suits of clothes, one thereof to be new, and fifty six dollars in cash with interest from this day. The children Martin & Catharina to be fed and clothed gratis and to be free with the parent. Consideration = $20.00.

Catharina Kochenburger with her husband's consent bound himself servant to the above Woodbridge Odlin to serve him three years and at the expiration of her term to have two complete suits of clothes, one thereof to be new, and fifty six dollars in cash with interest from this day. The children Martin & Catharina to be fed and clothed gratis and to be free with the parent. Consideration = $20.00.

Eva Kochenburger with her father's consent bound herself servant to the above Woodbridge Odlin, to serve him ten years and six months, and to have six weeks schooling for every year of her servitude, and at the expiration of her term to have two complete suits of clothes, one thereof to be new. Consideration = $38.30.

Elizabeth Kochenburger with her father's consent bound herself servant to the above Woodbridge Odlin, to serve him thirteen years. And to have six weeks schooling for every year of her servitude, and at the expiration of her term to have two complete suits of clothes, one thereof to be new. Consideration = $38.30.

Franz Ludwig Kuhne with his wife's consent bound himself servant to the above Woodbridge Odlin, to serve him three years, and at the expiration of his term to have two complete suits of clothes, one thereof to be new. The three children to be fed and clothed gratis and to be free with the parent. Consideration = $76.30.

Teresia Kuhne with her husband's consent bound herself servant to the above Woodbridge Odlin, to serve him three years, and at the expiration of her term to have two complete suits of clothes, one thereof to be new. The three children to be fed and clothed gratis and to be free with the parent. Consideration = $76.30.

John George Hahn with his wife's consent bound himself servant to the above Woodbridge Odlin, to serve him three years. And at the expiration of his term to have two complete suits of clothes, one thereof to be new. The three children to be fed and clothed gratis and to be free with the parent. Consideration = $76.30.

Barbara Hahn with her husband's consent bound herself servant to the aforesaid Woodbridge Odlin, to serve him three years, and at the expiration of her term to have two complete suits of clothes, one thereof to be new. The three children to be fed and clothed gratis and to be free with the parent. Consideration = $76.30.

Michael Pfeiffer with his wife's consent bound himself servant to the above Woodbridge Odlin, to serve him three years, and at the expiration of his term to have two complete suits of clothes, one thereof to be new. The infant to be fed and clothed gratis and to be free with the parent. Consideration = $76.30.

Catharina Pfeiffer with her husband's consent bound herself servant to the above Woodbridge Odlin, to serve him three years. And at the expiration of his term to have two complete suits of clothes, one thereof to be new. The infant to be fed and clothed gratis and to be free with the parent. Consideration = $76.30.

George Arnold with his wife's consent bound himself servant to the above Woodbridge Odlin, to serve him three years. And at the expiration of his term to have two complete suits of clothes, one thereof to be new. And twenty dollars in cash. Consideration = $56.30.

Barbara Arnold with her husband's consent bound herself servant to the above Woodbridge Odlin, to serve him three years, and at the expiration of her term to have two complete suits of clothes, one thereof to be new. Consideration = $76.30.

Jacob Arnold with his father's consent bound himself servant to the above Woodbridge Odlin, to serve him nine years and ten months. And to have six weeks schooling for every year of his servitude and at the expiration of his term to have two complete suits of clothes, one thereof to be new. Consideration = $38.30.

Frederick Arnold with his father's consent bound himself servant to the above Woodbridge Odlin, to serve him eight years, and to have six weeks schooling for every year of his servitude and at the expiration of his term to have two complete suits of clothes, one thereof to be new. Consideration = $38.30.

Frederick Arnold at the same time assigned to John Schaffer of Colebrookdale township Berks county farmer to serve him the remainder of his indenture as above recorded. Consideration = $80.00.

Michael Pfeiffer Junior with his father's consent bound himself servant to the above Woodbridge Odlin, to serve him ten years, and to have six weeks schooling for every year of his servitude, and at the expiration of his term to have two complete suits of clothes, one thereof to be new. Consideration = $38.30.

Ludwig Schmidt bound himself servant to Philip Steininger of Whitehall township Lehigh county farmer, to serve him three years. And at the expiration of his term to have two complete suits of clothes, one thereof to be new. Consideration = $76.35.

Ludwig Arnold with consent to go to New Jersey bound himself servant to William Johnson of Lowerpennsneck Salem county New Jersey farmer to serve him three years. And at the expiration of his term to have two complete suits of clothes, one thereof to be new. And fifty dollars in cash. Consideration = $38.00.

November 28, 1817

John Jacob Denger bound himself servant to Clayton Earl of Philadelphia merchant to serve him two years and at the expiration of his term to have two complete suits of clothes, one thereof to be new. Consideration = $40.00.

Caspar Fuchs and Margaretta his wife bound themselves servants with their consent to go to the State of Delaware to the above Clayton Earl to serve him four years. And at the expiration of their term to have each two complete suits of clothes, one thereof to be new. And twenty dollars in cash and if they conduct themself well they shall have twenty dollars more. The children to be fed and clothed gratis and to be free with the parents. Consideration = $100.00.

Caspar Fuchs and his wife Margaretta at the same time assigned to Philip Raybold of New Castle county State of Delaware, to serve him the remainder of their indenture as above recorded. Consideration = $100.00.

John George Beck and Anna Maria his wife with their consent to go to the State of Delaware bound themselves servant to the above Clayton Earl to serve him four years, and at the expiration of their term to have each two complete suits of clothes, one thereof to be new. And twenty dollars in cash and if they conduct themself well they shall have twenty dollars more. Consideration = $100.00.

John George Beck and Anna Maria his wife at the same time assigned to the above Philip Raybold to serve him the remainder of their indenture as above recorded. Consideration = $100.00.

Frederick Frey with his father's consent to go to New Jersey bound himself servant to Edward Harris of Moorestown Burlington county New Jersey farmer to serve him twelve years & eight months and to have six weeks schooling for every year of his servitude and at the expiration of his term to have two complete suits of clothes, one thereof to be new. Consideration = $46.20.

Henry Hochstrasser bound himself servant to Abraham Dettweiler of Francony township Montgomery county farmer to serve him three years at at the expiration of his term to have two complete suits of clothes, one thereof to be new, or thirty dollars in cash at the servant's option. Consideration = $76.00.

John Egger bound himself servant to Joseph Taylor of Goshen township Chester county farmer, to serve him two years and at the expiration of his term to have two complete suits of clothes, one thereof to be new, or forty dollars in cash at the option of the servant. Consideration = $50.00.

Christian Klingler with his wife's consent bound himself servant to Henry Gessenheimer of Pottsgrove Pennsylvania minister to serve him three years. And at the expiration of his term to have two complete suits of clothes, one thereof to be new, and twenty dollars in cash. The two children to be fed & clothed gratis and to be free with the parent. Consideration = $15.00.

Judith Klingler with her husband's consent bound herself servant to the above Henry Gessenheimer, to serve him three years. And at the expiration of her term to have two complete suits of clothes, one thereof to be new. The two children to be fed & clothed gratis and to be free with the parent. Consideration = $15.00.

Christina Klingler with her father's consent bound herself servant to the above Henry Gessenheimer to serve him seven years, and to have six weeks schooling for every year of her servitude and at the expiration of her term to have two complete suits of clothes, one thereof to be new. Consideration = $15.00.

John Klingler with his father's consent bound himself servant to the above Henry Gessenheimer to serve him eleven years, and to have six weeks schooling for every year of her servitude and at the expiration of her term to have two complete suits of clothes, one thereof to be new. Consideration = $15.00.

Conrad Schettler with his wife's consent bound himself servant to the above Henry Gessenheimer to serve him three years. And at the expiration of his term to have two complete suits of clothes, one thereof to be new, and twenty dollars in cash. Consideration = $75.00.

Juliana Schettler with her husband's consent bound herself servant to the above Henry Gessenheimer to serve him three years, and at the expiration of her term to have two complete suits of clothes, one thereof to be new. Consideration = $75.00.

Jacob Hauser with George Devries' consent to go to the Missoury territory bound himself servant to Jacob Bollinger of the Missoury territory St. Louis to serve him four years, and to have eighteen weeks schooling during his servitude, and at the expiration of his term to have two complete suits of clothes, one thereof to be new & twenty dollars in cash. Consideration = $76.35.

Jacob Lutz with the same consent as aforesaid bound himself servant to the before mentioned Jacob Bollinger to serve him four years and to have six weeks schooling for every year of his servitude, and at the expiration of his term to have two complete suits of clothes, one thereof to be new. Consideration = $76.35.

John Schultz with his own consent as aforesaid bound himself servant to the above Jacob Bollinger to serve him three years and six months. And at the expiration of his term to have two complete suits of clothes, one thereof to be new. Consideration = $76.35.

John Amandus Sauder with George Devries' consent as aforesaid bound himself servant to the above Jacob Bollinger, to serve him four years and to have nine weeks schooling during his servitude and at the expiration of his term to have two complete suits of clothing, one thereof to be new. Consideration = $76.35.

Nicholas Stumpf with his own consent as aforesaid bound himself servant to the above Jacob Bollinger to serve him three years and six months and at the expiration of his term to have two complete suits of clothes, one thereof to be new. Consideration = $76.35.

Philip Kreiner with his own consent as aforesaid bound himself servant to the above Jacob Bollinger to serve him three years and six months. And at the expiration of his term to have two complete suits of clothes, one thereof to be new. Consideration = $76.35.

Michael Goetsche with his own consent as aforesaid bound himself servant to the above Jacob Bollinger to serve him three years and six months. And at the expiration of his term to have two complete suits of clothes, one thereof to be new. Consideration = $76.35.

George Muhle with George Devries' consent as aforesaid bound himself servant to the above Jacob Bollinger to serve him four years, and to have fifteen weeks schooling during his servitude and at the expiration of his term to have two complete suits of clothing, one thereof to be new. Consideration = $76.35.

Mathias Frey with his own consent as aforesaid bound himself servant to the before mentioned Jacob Bollinger to serve him three years and six months and at the expiration of his term to have two complete suits of clothes, one thereof to be new. Consideration = $76.35.

Gottfried Rau with George Devries' consent as aforesaid bound himself servant to the above Jacob Bollinger, to serve him five years, and to have six weeks schooling for every year of his servitude, and at the expiration of his term to have two complete suits of clothing, one thereof to be new. Consideration = $76.35.

Christopher Trautwein with his own consent as aforesaid bound himself servant to the above Jacob Bollinger to serve him four years, and at the expiration of his term to have two complete suits of clothes, one thereof to be new. Consideration = $76.35.

Jacob Koepfler with his own consent as aforesaid bound himself servant to the above Jacob Bollinger to serve him three years and six months. And at the expiration of his term to have two complete suits of clothes, one thereof to be new, and twenty dollars in cash. Consideration = $76.35.

David Schaefner with his own consent as aforesaid bound himself servant to the above Jacob Bollinger to serve him three years and six months and at the expiration of his term to have two complete suits of clothes, one thereof to be new. Consideration = $76.35.

Joseph Gender with George Devries' consent as aforesaid bound himself servant to the above Jacob Bollinger to serve him seven years and six months and to have six weeks schooling for every year of his servitude, and at the expiration of his term to have two complete suits of clothing, one thereof to be new. Consideration = $76.35.

Frederick Bisschopf of his own consent as aforesaid bound himself servant to the above Jacob Bollinger to serve him three years and six months. And at the expiration of his term to have two complete suits of clothes, one thereof to be new. Consideration = $76.35.

Ferdinand Gullarowitch with his own consent as aforesaid bound himself servant to the before mentioned Jacob Bollinger to serve him three years and six months and at the expiration of his term to have two complete suits of clothes, one thereof to be new. Consideration = $76.35.

John Engelhardt with George Devries' consent as aforesaid bound himself servant to the above Jacob Bollinger, to serve him three years and six months and to have six weeks schooling during his servitude. And at the expiration of his term to have two complete suits of clothing, one thereof to be new. Consideration = $76.35.

Jacob Schmidt with his own consent as aforesaid bound himself servant to the above Jacob Bollinger to serve him three years and six months. And at the expiration of his term to have two complete suits of clothes, one thereof to be new. Consideration = $76.35.

November 29, 1817

Hartman Wilde with the consent of his wife bound himself servant to Woodbridge Odlin of Philadelphia merchant, to serve him three years. And at the expiration of his term to have two complete suits of clothes, one thereof to be new and forty one dollars and fifty cents in cash. Consideration = $34.95.

Hartman Wilde assigned, transferred, and released of all claims of service by Woodbridge Odlin for consideration refunded by the above servant the first day of December. Consideration = $34.95.

Elizabeth Wilde with the consent of her husband bound herself servant to Woodbridge Odlin to serve him three years. And at the expiration of his term to have two complete suits of clothes, one thereof to be new and forty one dollars and fifty cents in cash. Consideration = $34.95.

Elizabeth Wilde assigned, transferred and released of all claims of service by Woodbridge Odlin, for consideration refunded by the above servant the first day of December. Consideration = $34.95.

John Jacob Hartman Senior with his wife's consent bound himself servant to Woodbridge Odlin of Philadelphia merchant to serve him three years. And at the expiration of his term to have two complete suits of clothes, one thereof to be new and thirty dollars 20 cents in cash. Consideration = $31.30.

Elizabeth Hartman with her husband's consent bound herself servant to the above Woodbridge Odlin to serve him three years. And at the expiration of her term to have two complete suits of clothes, one thereof to be new. And thirty dollars 20 cents in cash. Consideration = $31.30.

John Jacob Hartman Junior with his father's consent bound himself servant to the above Woodbridge Odlin to serve him fourteen years, and to have six weeks schooling for every year of his servitude and at the expiration of his term to have two complete suits of clothes, one thereof to be new. Consideration = $38.30.

Albrecht Eichelberger with his wife's consent bound himself servant to the above Woodbridge Odlin to serve him three years. And at the expiration of his term to have two complete suits of clothes, one thereof to be new. And thirty dollars 80 cents in cash. The child to be fed and clothed gratis and to be free with the parent. Consideration = $60.75.

Margaretta Eichelberger with her husband's consent bound herself servant to the above Woodbridge Odlin to serve him three years. And at the expiration of her term to have two complete suits of clothes, one thereof to be new. The child to be fed and clothed gratis and to be free with the parent. Consideration = $60.75.

John Ulrich Kohler bound himself servant to the above Woodbridge Odlin to serve him three years. And at the expiration of his term to have two complete suits of clothes, one thereof to be new. And thirty eight dollars in cash. Consideration = $76.30.

Henry Kohler with his father's consent bound himself servant to the above Woodbridge Odlin, to serve him nine years and to have six weeks schooling for every year of his servitude. And at the expiration of his term to have two complete suits of clothes, one thereof to be new. And if the consideration is refunded at any time during his servitude then this indenture to be null and void. Consideration = $38.30.

Lontze Hutz bound himself servant to the above Woodbridge Odlin, to serve him three years. And at the expiration of his term to have two complete suits of clothes, one thereof to be new. And twenty eight dollars in cash. The child Catharina to be fed and clothed gratis and to be free with the parent. Consideration = $48.30.

Philip Hutz with his father's consent bound himself servant to the aforesaid Woodbridge Odlin, to serve him twelve years. And to have six weeks schooling for every year of his servitude and at the expiration of his term to have two complete suits of clothes, one thereof to be new. Consideration = $38.30.

Theresa Laube bound herself servant to the above Woodbridge Odlin to serve him three years. And at the expiration of her term to have two complete suits of clothes, one thereof to be new. The child to be fed and clothed gratis and to be free with the mother. Consideration = $76.30.

Joseph Laube with his mother's consent bound himself servant to the above Woodbridge Odlin, to serve him ten years and to have six weeks schooling for every year of his servitude and at the expiration of his term to have two complete suits of clothes, one thereof to be new. Consideration = $38.30.

Andreas Nagele with his wife's consent bound himself servant to the above Woodbridge Odlin, to serve him three years. And at the expiration of his term to have two complete suits of clothes, one thereof to be new, and sixty five dollars in cash and if the consideration is refunded at anytime during his servitude then this indenture to be null & void. Consideration = $10.80.

Walburga Nagele with her husband's consent bound herself servant to the above Woodbridge Odlin, to serve him three years. And at the expiration of her term to have two complete suits of clothes, one thereof to be new, and sixty five dollars in cash, and if the consideration is refunded at anytime during his servitude then this indenture to be null & void. Consideration = $10.80.

Abraham Obrist bound himself servant to the above Woodbridge Odlin, to serve him three years. And at the expiration of his term to have two complete suits of clothes, one thereof to be new. Consideration = $75.30.

Anna Obrist with her father's consent bound herself servant to the above Woodbridge Odlin, to serve him eleven years and six months and to have six weeks schooling for every year of her servitude and at the expiration of her term to have two complete suits of clothes, one thereof to be new. Consideration = $38.30.

Henry Rinderknecht with his wife's consent bound himself servant to the above Woodbridge Odlin, to serve him three years. And at the expiration of his term to have two complete suits of clothes, one thereof to be new, and twenty three dollars in cash. The children to be fed and clothed gratis and to be free with the parent. Consideration = $53.30.

Elizabeth Rinderknecht with her husband's consent bound herself servant to the above Woodbridge Odlin, to serve him three years, and at the expiration of her term to have two complete suits of clothes, one thereof to be new. And twenty three dollars in cash. The children to be fed and clothed gratis and to be free with the parent. Consideration = $53.30.

Fredericca Kurz with Captain Beard's consent bound herself servant to Marinus W. Pike of Philadelphia gilder, to serve him three years and six months, and to have six weeks schooling for every year of her servitude, and at the expiration of her term to have two complete suits of clothes, one thereof to be new. And two dollars in cash. Consideration = $76.35.

December 1, 1817

Jacobina Rost assigned by Joseph Langer to Jacob Schmidgall of Immerton township Berks county farmer, to serve him the remainder of her indenture as recorded in Book B, page 278. Consideration = $95.37.

Jacobina Rost at the same time assigned by Jacob Schimdgall to Adam Everly of Philadelphia perfumer to serve him the remainder of her indenture as recorded in Book B, page 278. Consideration = $95.37.

December 2, 1817

George Arnold assigned by Woodbridge Odlin to George Craighead of Carlisle, Cumberland county farmer, to serve him the remainder of his indenture as recorded page 21. Consideration = $56.30.

Barbara Arnold assigned by Woodbridge Odlin to the above George Craighead to serve him the remainder of her indentured as recorded page 21. Consideration = $76.30.

Jacob Arnold assigned by Woodbridge Odlin to the above George Criaghead to serve him the remainder of his indenture as recorded page 21. Consideration = $38.30.

Albrecht Eichelberger assigned by Woodbridge Odlin to John G. Bull of Tredyffrin township Chester county farmer to serve him the remainder of his indenture as recorded page 27. Consideration = $60.75.

Margaretta Eichelberger assigned by Woodbridge Odlin to the above John G. Bull to serve him the remainder of her indenture as recorded page 27. Consideration = $60.75.

Michael Pfeiffer Junior assigned by Woodbridge Odlin to Jacob Andrew of Derry township Dauphin county, hatter, to serve him the remainder of his indenture as recorded page 21. Consideration = $76.30.

December 3, 1817

Mathias Fruh assigned by Woodbridge Odlin to John Weidman of Cocalico township Lancaster county farmer to serve him the remainder of his indenture as recorded page 14. Consideration = $76.35.

Dorothea Fruh assigned by Woodbridge Odlin to the above John Weidman to serve him the remainder of her indenture as recorded page 14. Consideration = $76.35.

Joest Spat assigned by Joseph Lehman agent for Clement Rass to Mrs. Ewing of Philadelphia widow to serve her the remainder of his indenture as recorded in Book B, page 218. Consideration = $50.00.

John Jacob Hartman Senior assigned by Woodbridge Odlin to Daniel Peter of Oley township Berks county farmer, to serve him the remainder of his indenture as recorded page 27. Consideration = $31.30.

Elizabeth Hartman assigned Woodbridge Odlin to the above Daniel Peter to serve him the remainder of her indenture as recorded page 27. Consideration = $31.30.

John Jacob Hartman Junior assigned by Woodbridge Odlin to the above Daniel Peter, to serve him the remainder of his indenture as recorded page 27. Consideration = $38.30.

Henry Kochenburger assigned by Woodbridge Odlin to Leonard Kapp of Heidelberg township Lebanon county farmer, to serve him the remainder of his indenture as recorded page 20. Consideration = $20.00.

Catharina Kochenburger assigned by Woodbridge Odlin to the above Leonard Kapp, to serve him the remainder of her indenture as recorded page 20. Consideration = $20.00.

Eva Kochenburger assigned by Woodbridge Odlin to the above Leonard Kapp, to serve him the remainder of her indenture as recorded page 20. Consideration = $38.30.

Elizabeth Kochenburger assigned by Woodbridge Odlin to the above Leonard Kapp, to serve him the remainder of her indenture as recorded page 20. Consideration = $38.30.

Conrad Reiszner assigned by Woodbridge Odlin to John Strohm of Lebanon township Lebanon county farmer, to serve him the remainder of his indenture as recorded page 17. Consideration = $76.30.

Johanna Lakasin released and discharged by Will Herman from all further claims of her services of her indenture as recorded in Book B, page 260. The consideration being refunded. Consideration = $32.50.

Johanna Lakasin bound herself servant to Lewis Lowry of Penn township Philadelphia county victuler, to serve him fifteen months. And at the expiration of her term to have no freedom suit. Consideration = $32.50.

December 4, 1817

George Rittberger with his wife's consent bound himself servant to Charles Bell of Philadelphia merchant to serve him three years. And at the expiration of his term to have two complete suits of clothes, one thereof to be new. And twenty five dollars in cash, and also fifty cents pocket money per month. The infant to be fed and clothed gratis and to be free with the parent. Consideration = $30.00.

Christiana Rittberger with her husband's consent bound herself servant to the aforesaid Charles Bell, to serve him three years. And at the expiration of her term to have two complete suits of clothes, one thereof to be new, and twenty five dollars in cash, and also fifty cents pocket money per month. The infant to be fed and clothed gratis and to be free with the parent. Consideration = $30.00.

Gottlieb Rittberger with his father's consent bound himself servant to the above Charles Bell to serve him thirteen years and three months, and to have six weeks schooling for every year of his servitude. And at the expiration of his term to have two complete suits of clothes, one thereof to be new. Consideration = $20.00.

December 5, 1817

John Kingeter assigned by Woodbridge Odlin to Jacob Benner of Moreland township Philadelphia county to serve him the remainder of his indenture as recorded page 19. Consideration = $76.30.

December 6, 1817

John Adam Bernhard assigned by John Pierce to Frederick Stall of Penn township Philadelphia county ropemaker to serve him the remainder of his indenture as recorded in Book B, page 241. Consideration = $60.00.

December 8, 1817

John Krieger with his consent to go to New Jersey bound himself servant to Samuel L. Howell of Gloucester county New Jersey farmer to serve him one year. And at the expiration of his term to have two complete suits of clothes, one thereof to be new, and twenty four dollars in cash. Consideration = $25.00.

Norbert Vogt with his step father's consent as above bound himself servant to the aforesaid Samuel L. Howell, to serve him two years, and to have six weeks schooling during his servitude, and at the expiration of his term to have two complete suits of clothes, one thereof to be new. Consideration = $55.00.

Anton Vogt with the same consent as above bound himself servant to the aforesaid Samuel L. Howell to serve him two years & six months and to have one quarter schooling during his servitude and at the expiration of his term to have two complete suits of clothes, one thereof to be new. Consideration = $55.00.

Maria Agatha Vogt with the same consent as above bound herself servant to the aforesaid Samuel L. Howell to serve him three years and two months. And to have six weeks schooling for every year of her servitude, and at the expiration of her term to have two complete suits of clothes, one thereof to be new. Consideration = $55.00.

John George Vogt with the same consent as above bound himself servant to the aforesaid Samuel L. Howell to serve him nine years and four months, and to have six weeks schooling for every year of his servitude and at the expiration of his term to have two complete suits of clothes, one thereof to be new. Consideration = $55.00.

Norbert Haas with John Krieger's consent as above bound himself servant to the aforesaid Samuel L. Howell to serve him two years and six months, and to have six weeks schooling for every year of his servitude, and at the expiration of his term to have two complete suits of clothes, one thereof to be new. Consideration = $55.00.

December 9, 1817

Christian Grauser with Gottlieb Grundelock's consent bound himself servant to Andreas Harman of Philadelphia baker to serve him one year and eleven months. And to have one quarter schooling during his servitude, and at the expiration of his term to have two complete suits of clothes, one thereof to be new, and thirty dollars in cash. Valuable consideration.

Jacob Schaffer assigned by Woodbridge Odlin to George Blank of upper Sackon township Lehigh county farmer, to serve him the remainder of his indenture as recorded page 14. Consideration = $76.35.

Solomea Schaffer assigned by Woodbridge Odlin to George Blank as above, to serve him the remainder of her indenture as recorded page 14. Consideration = $76.35.

Philip Weber assigned by Woodbridge Odlin to George Blank as above, to serve him the remainder of his indenture as recorded page 14. Consideration = $38.35.

John Glohr assigned by Christian Erb to David Erb of Warwick township Lancaster county farmer to serve him the remainder of his indenture as recorded in Book B, page 151. Consideration = $107.34.

December 10, 1817

Diederich Rasig assigned by Woodbridge Odlin to George Wenner Junior of Whitehall township Lehigh county farmer, to serve him the remainder of his indenture as recorded page 17. Consideration = $76.30.

Eva Rasig assigned by Woodbridge Odlin to the above George Wenner Junior to serve him the remainder of her indenture as recorded page 17. Consideration = $76.30.

Jacob Rasig assigned by Woodbridge Odlin to the above George Wenner Junior to serve him the remainder of his indenture as recorded page 17. Consideration = $38.30.

Magdalena Rasig assigned by Woodbridge Odlin to the above George Wenner Junior to serve him the remainder of her indenture as recorded page 17. Consideration = $38.30.

December 11, 1817

Dorothea Kingeter assigned by Woodbridge Odlin to George Benner of Moreland township Philadelphia county farmer to serve him the remainder of her indenture as recorded page 19. Consideration = $38.30.

Frederick Kingeter assigned by Woodbridge Odlin to Jacob Benner of Northern Liberties carter, to serve him the remainder of his indenture as recorded page 19. Consideration = $38.30.

Franz Basseler bound himself servant to John Ehlers of Philadelphia to serve him three years. And at the expiration of his term to have two complete suits of clothes, one thereof to be new. The child to be fed and clothed gratis and to be free with the father. Consideration = $98.50.

Franz Basseler at the same time assigned to Mr. Ziegler of Harmony, Pennsylvania to serve him the remainder of his indenture as recorded page 32. Consideration = $98.50.

Jacob Bury with his wife's consent bound himself servant to the aforesaid John Ehlers to serve him three years, and at the expiration of his term to have two complete suits of clothes, one thereof to be new. The child to be fed and clothed gratis and to be free with the parent. Consideration = $93.70.

Jacob Bury at the same time assigned to Mr. Ziegler as aforesaid to serve him the remainder of his indenture as above recorded. Consideration = $93.70.

Barbara Bury with her husband's consent bound herself servant to the above John Ehlers, to serve him three years and at the expiration of her term to have two complete suits of clothes, one thereof to be new. The child to be fed & clothed gratis and to be free with the parent. Consideration = $93.70.

Barbara Bury at the same time assigned to the above Mr. Ziegler to serve him the remainder of her indenture as above recorded. Consideration = $93.70.

December 12, 1817

Elizabeth Catharina Stum assigned by Margaretta Coleman to Andrew Stum the father of the servant, to serve him the remainder of her indenture as recorded in Book B, page 186. Consideration = $15.00.

December 13, 1817

Elizabeth Messerschmidt bound herself servant to Woodbridge Odlin of Philadelphia merchant to serve him two years. And at the expiration of her term to have two complete suits of clothes, one thereof to be new. And if the consideration is refunded at any time during her servitude then this indenture to be null and void. Consideration = $48.60.

Fredericka Ludy with her father's consent to go to New Jersey bound herself servant to Samuel L. Howell of Gloucestertown Gloucester county New Jersey farmer, to serve him three years. And to have six weeks schooling for every year of her servitude. And at the expiration of her term to have two complete suits of clothes, one thereof to be new. Consideration = $90.00.

Fredericka Ludy at the same time assigned to Joshua L. Howell of Deptford township Gloucester county N. Jersey, to serve him the remainder of her indenture as above recorded. Consideration = $90.00.

John Jacob Ludy with his father's consent as aforesaid bound himself servant to the above Samuel L. Howell to serve him six years and four months. And to have six weeks schooling for every year of his servitude, and at the expiration of her term to have two complete suits of clothes, one thereof to be new. Consideration = $90.00.

John Jacob Ludy at the same time assigned to the above Joshua L. Howell to serve him the remainder of his indenture as above recorded. Consideration = $90.00.

Maria Ludy with her father's consent bound herself servant to Joseph Lownes of Philadelphia silversmith to serve him ten years and six months. And to have six weeks schooling for every year of her servitude, and at the expiration of her term to have two complete suits of clothes, one thereof to be new. Consideration = $90.00.

Maria Elizabeth Ludy with her consent to go to New Jersey bound herself servant to Thomas Newbold of Springfield township Burlington county New Jersey farmer, to serve him three years. And at the expiration of her term to have two complete suits of clothes, one thereof to be new. Consideration = $80.00.

John Jacob Mollenkopff with consent of John Jacob Rehm bound himself servant to John Myers of Formanuch township Mifflin county farmer, to serve him three years. And to have six weeks schooling for every year of her servitude, and at the expiration of her term to have two complete suits of clothes, one thereof to be new. Consideration = $90.00.

John Jacob Mollenkopff at the same time assigned to Robert Wilson of the above township to serve him the remainder of his indenture as above recorded. Consideration = $90.00.

December 15, 1817

Anton Adam with his wife's consent bound himself servant to Michael Newbold of Philadelphia grazier to serve him three years. And at the expiration of his term to have two complete suits of clothes, one thereof to be new. And forty dollars in cash. The child Rosa to be fed and clothed gratis and to be free with the parent. Consideration = $40.00.

Serafin Adam with her husband's consent bound herself servant to the above Michael Newbold to serve him three years. And at the expiration of her term to have two complete suits of clothes, one thereof to be new. And forty dollars in cash. The child Rosa to be fed and clothed gratis and to be free with the parent. Consideration = $40.00.

Daniel Adams with his father's consent bound himself servant to the above Michael Newbold to serve him twelve years and three months. And to have six weeks schooling for every year of his servitude, and at the expiration of his term to have two complete suits of clothes, one thereof to be new. Consideration = $30.00.

December 17, 1817

Anna Schlegel assigned by Henry Freed to David Allebough of Skipech township Montgomery county farmer to serve him the remainder of her indenture as recorded in Book B, page 343. Consideration = $26.00.

Philip Hutz assigned by Woodbridge Odlin to Henry Resh esquire of Lancaster county, to serve him the remainder of his indenture as recorded page 28. Consideration = $38.30.

Henry Rinderknecht assigned by Woodbridge Odlin to John Charles of Lancaster county farmer, to serve him the remainder of his indenture as recorded page 28. Consideration = $53.30.

Elizabeth Rinderknecht assigned by Woodbridge Odlin to the above John Charles to serve him the remainder of her indenture as recorded page 29. Consideration = $53.30.

Michael Pfeiffer assigned by Woodbridge Odlin to Jacob Charles of Lancaster county farmer to serve him the remainder of his indenture as recorded page 21. Consideration = $76.30.

Catharina Pfeiffer assigned by Woodbridge Odlin to the above Jacob Charles to serve him the remainder of her indenture as recorded page 21. Consideration = $76.30.

John Gottlieb Reichert with his consent to go to New Jersey bound himself servant to Jacob Grevison of Gloucester State of New Jersey farmer, to serve him three years. And at the expiration of his term to have two complete suits of clothes, one thereof to be new. And five dollars in cash if he conducts himself well. Consideration = $90.00.

December 18, 1817

Catharina Duwe with her father's consent bound herself servant to George Breidenhart of Philadelphia upholsterer, to serve him four years & ten months. And to have six weeks schooling for every year of her servitude and at the expiration of her term to have two complete suits of clothes, one thereof to be new. Consideration = $45.00.

December 19, 1817

Henry Ludwig Duwe with his father's consent to go to New Jersey bound himself servant to Joseph Groff of Woolwich township Gloucester county New Jersey farmer to serve him thirteen years and two months. And to have six weeks schooling for every year of his servitude and at the expiration of his term to have two complete suits of clothes, one thereof to be new. Consideration = $45.00.

December 22, 1817

Ferena Deppeler bound herself servant to James Potter of Potter's township Centre county merchant to serve him three years and at the expiration of her term to have two complete suits of clothes, one thereof to be new. Consideration = $80.30.

Aloise Gamp with E. Rising's consent bound himself servant to William Musser of Philadelphia merchant, to serve him three years. And to have six weeks schooling for every year of his servitude. And at the expiration of his term to have two complete suits of clothes, one thereof to be new. Consideration = $76.00.

John Gamp with E. Rising's consent bound himself servant to William Musser of Philadelphia merchant, to serve him seven years eleven months & 15 days. And to have six weeks schooling for every year of his servitude, and at the expiration of his term to have two complete suits of clothes, one thereof to be new. Consideration = $36.60.

John Gamp at the same time assigned to George Musser of Lancaster gentleman to serve him the remainder of his indenture as above recorded. Consideration = $36.60.

Barbara Deppeler with her father's consent bound herself servant to Henry Schreiner of Philadelphia merchant to serve him three years eleven months & 12 days. And to have six weeks schooling for every year of her servitude, and at the expiration of her term to have two complete suits of clothes, one thereof to be new. Consideration = $76.30.

Ursula Deppeler with her father's consent bound herself servant to Richard Gray of Philadelphia mariner to serve him seven years and seven months. And to have six weeks schooling for every year of her servitude, and at the expiration of her term to have two complete suits of clothes, one thereof to be new. Consideration = $45.30.

Catharina Fritzinger bound herself servant to George Toppal of Southwark innkeeper to serve him three years and six months. And at the expiration of her term to have two complete suits of clothes, one thereof to be new. Consideration = $80.30.

Frederick Weiss with his father's consent bound himself servant to George Steiner of Philadelphia baker, to serve him three years and six months, and to have six weeks schooling for every years of his servitude, and at the expiration of his term to have two complete suits of clothes, one thereof to be new. Consideration = $75.00.

December 23, 1817

Sibila Catharina Bader bound herself servant to Andrew Hodge of Philadelphia merchant to serve him three years. And at the expiration of her term to have two complete suits of clothes, one thereof to be new, and twelve dollars in cash if she conducts herself to the satisfaction of her master. Consideration = $90.00.

Sibila Catharina Bader at the same time assigned to Robert H. Rose of Susquehanna county Pennsylvania gentleman to serve him the remainder of her indenture as above recorded. Consideration = $90.00.

December 24, 1817

Carl Rayhle with his wife's consent bound himself servant to David Haimbach of Upper Milford township Lehigh county ironmaster, to serve him eighteen months, and at the expiration of his term to have two complete suits of clothes, one thereof to be new. Consideration = $46.30.

Catharina Rayhle with her husband's consent bound herself servant to the aforesaid David Haimbach to serve him eighteen months. And at the expiration of her term to have two complete suits of clothes, one thereof to be new. Consideration = $46.30.

John Christian Zimmerman with E. Rising's consent bound himself servant to Christian Kreider of Lebanon township Lebanon county farmer to serve him four years, and to have one quarter schooling during his servitude and at the expiration of his term to have two complete suits of clothes, one thereof to be new. And forty dollars in cash. Consideration = $80.00.

December 25, 1817

Leonzy Gerspach with consent of John Melbeck bound himself servant to Philip Wolf of Allen township Northampton county farmer, to serve him three years, and to have one quarter schooling during his servitude, and at the expiration of his term to have two complete suits of clothes, one thereof to be new, and six dollars in cash. Consideration = $70.70.

December 26, 1817

Margaretta Nollin bound herself servant to Robert Babcock of Bucks county farmer to serve him six years. And at the expiration of her term to have two complete suits of clothes, one thereof to be new. Consideration = $76.30.

Nicholas Noll bound himself servant to the above Robert Babcock to serve him five years. And at the expiration of his term to have two complete suits of clothes, one thereof to be new. And twenty dollars in cash. Consideration = $76.30.

George Noll with his father's consent bound himself servant to the above Robert Babcock to serve him five years three months & 27 days. And to have six weeks schooling for every year of his servitude and at the expiration of his term to have two complete suits of clothes, one thereof to be new. Consideration = $76.30.

Mariana Hutz with Samuel Newbold's consent bound herself servant to Nathan Trotter of Philadelphia merchant to serve him five years and ten months. And to have six weeks schooling for every year of her servitude, and at the expiration of her term to have two complete suits of clothes, one thereof to be new and thirty eight dollars in cash. Consideration = $38.30.

Maria Schib bound herself servant to John Naglee of the Northern Liberties lumber merchant to serve him three years, and at the expiration of her term to have two complete suits of clothes, one thereof to be new. Consideration = $76.00.

December 27, 1817

Lorenz Winter bound himself servant to Jesse Gyger of Lardnor township Delaware county farmer to serve him two years, and at the expiration of his term to have two complete suits of clothes, one thereof to be new. Consideration = $60.70.

Michael Fritzinger with his father's consent bound himself servant to William Murdock of Philadelphia merchant to serve him five years and eight months. And to have six weeks schooling for every year of his servitude, and at the expiration of his term to have two complete suits of clothes, one thereof to be new. Consideration = $76.00.

Michael Fritzinger at the same time assigned to Joseph M. Downing of Dowingstown Chester county, to serve him the remainder of his indenture as above recorded. Consideration = $76.00.

Margarette Elizabeth Fritzinger with her father's consent bound herself servant to the above William Murdock to serve him five years and eight months, and to have six weeks schooling for every year of her servitude, and at the expiration of her term to have two complete suits of clothes, one thereof to be new. Consideration = $60.00.

Margarette Elizabeth Fritzinger at the same time assigned to the above Joseph M. Downing to serve him the remainder of her indenture as above recorded. Consideration = $60.00.

December 29, 1817

Anna Maria Deppeler with her father's consent bound herself servant to Francis L. Cooch of Philadelphia merchant to serve him six years and six months. And to have six weeks schooling for every year of her servitude and at the expiration of her term to have two complete suits of clothes, one thereof to be new. Consideration = $50.00.

Aloise Gamp assigned by William Musser to Michael Hurst of Donegal township Lancaster county farmer to serve him the remainder of his indenture as recorded page 35. Consideration = $76.00.

Christian Ludy Senior with consent of his wife to go to New Jersey bound himself servant to Thomas Clayton of Philadelphia hatter to serve him three years. And at the expiration of his term to have two complete suits of clothes, one thereof to be new. And twenty dollars in cash. The two children to be fed and clothed gratis and to be free with the parent. Consideration = $20.00.

Christian Ludy Senior at the same time assigned to Joshua L. Howell of Gloucester county New Jersey farmer, to serve him the remainder of his indenture as above recorded. Consideration = $20.00.

Margaretta Ludy with her husband's consent as above bound herself to the above Thomas Clayton to serve him three years and at the expiration of her term to have two complete suits of clothes, one thereof to be new. And twenty dollars in cash. The two children to be fed and clothed gratis and to be free with the parent. Consideration = $20.00.

Margaretta Ludy at the same time assigned to the above Joshua L. Howell to serve him the remainder of her indenture as above recorded. Consideration = $20.00.

Christian Ludy Junior with his father's consent as aforesaid bound himself to the aforesaid Thomas Clayton to serve him three years, and to have one quarter schooling during his servitude, and at the expiration of his term to have two complete suits of clothes, one thereof to be new, and twenty dollars in cash. Consideration = $90.00.

Christian Ludy Junior at the same time assigned to the aforesaid Joshua L. Howell to serve him the remainder of his indenture as above recorded. Consideration = $90.00.

December 30, 1817

Francisca Wunderlin with her father's consent to go to New York bound herself servant to John H. Contoit Junior of the City of New York confectioner to serve him seven years and ten months. And to have six weeks schooling for every year of her servitude and at the expiration of her term to have two complete suits of clothes, one thereof to be new. Consideration = $76.30.

John Mutter bound himself servant to Abraham Meyer of Uppersalfort township Montgomery county farmer to serve him three years. And at the expiration of his term to have two complete suits of clothes, one thereof to be new, and ten dollars in cash. Consideration = $76.30.

Jacob Adam Huber bound himself servant to George Deery of Vincent township Chester county farmer to serve him three years, and at the expiration of his term to have two complete suits of clothes, one thereof to be new. And ten dollars in cash. Consideration = $76.30.

Jacob Adam Huber at the same time assigned to Peter Deery of Vincent township Chester county farmer to serve him the remainder of his indenture as above recorded. Consideration = $76.30.

December 31, 1817

John Morad with his sister's consent bound himself servant to James Wood of Philadelphia merchant to serve him eight years and twenty days. And to have six weeks schooling for every year of his servitude and at the expiration of his term to have two complete suits of clothes, one thereof to be new and thirty eight dollars in cash with interest from this date. Consideration = $76.30.

Catharina Kramer bound herself servant to Peter Aughinbauch of Chambersburg, Pennsylvania merchant to serve him three years. And at the expiration of her term to have two complete suits of clothes, one thereof to be new. And thirteen dollars 20 cents in cash. Consideration = $63.10.

Lucas Mesch bound himself servant to Thomas Lindsay of Chambersburg, Pennsylvania innkeeper to serve him three years and at the expiration of his term to have two complete suits of clothes, one thereof to be new, and twelve dollars in cash. Consideration = $66.70.

Lucas Mesch at the same time assigned to John Lindsay esquire of Chambersburg, Pennsylvania to serve him the remainder of his indenture as recorded above. Consideration = $66.70.

John Palmer bound himself servant to Abraham Stouffer of Lower Providence township Montgomery county farmer to serve him three years. And at the expiration of his term to have two complete suits of clothes, one thereof to be new, and eighteen dollars in cash. Consideration = $86.30.

Jacob Stoll assigned by Henry D. Oberholtz to Daniel Schlichter of Upper Hanover township Montgomery county farmer to serve him the remainder of his indenture as recorded in Book B, page 263. Consideration = $63.00.

Jacob Kachel assigned by Henry D. Oberholtz to Issac Bechtel of Colebrookdale township Berks county farmer to serve him the remainder of his indenture as recorded in Book B, page 262. Consideration = $55.75.

Baltasar Beiler assigned by Henry D. Oberholtz to John M. Bechtel of Hareford township Berks county farmer to serve him the remainder of his indenture as recorded in Book B, page 282. Consideration = $82.75.

George Zeile assigned by Henry D. Oberholtz to Henry Bauman of Hareford township Berks county farmer to serve him the remainder of his indenture as recorded in Book B, page 282. Consideration = $46.00.

John Stoltz assigned by Henry D. Oberholtz to Leonard Miller of Douglass township Montgomery county to serve him the remainder of his indenture as recorded in Book B, page 282. Consideration = $31.00.

Peter Thron assigned by Henry D. Oberholtz to John A. Bechtel of Hareford township Berks county farmer to serve him the remainder of his indenture as recorded in Book B, page 287. Consideration = $41.25.

Martin Zimmerman bound himself servant to Thomas Lindsay of Chambersburg Pennsylvania innkeeper to serve him three years. And at the expiration of his term to have two complete suits of clothes, one thereof to be new. And twenty dollars in cash. Consideration = $76.30.

Samuel Kayser with his mother's consent bound himself servant to the above Thomas Lindsay to serve him nine years eleven months & 7 days. And to have six weeks schooling for every year of his servitude, and at the expiration of his term to have two complete suits of clothes, one thereof to be new. Consideration = $65.00.

Samuel Kayser at the same time assigned to Andrew Lindsay of McConneltown, Bedford county innkeeper, to serve him the remainder of his indenture as above recorded. Consideration = $65.00.

Catharina Zimmerman bound herself servant to Peter Aughinbaugh of Chambersburg Pennsylvania merchant to serve him three years and six months, and at the expiration of her term to have two complete suits of clothes, one thereof to be new. And ten dollars in cash. Consideration = $76.30.

Catharina Zimmerman at the same time assigned to John Stump of Green township Franklin county miller, to serve him the remainder of her indenture as above recorded. Consideration = $76.30.

January 1, 1818

John Andrew Schneider bound himself servant to John Geisinger of Hanover township Northampton county farmer to serve him three years. And at the expiration of his term to have two complete suits of clothes, one thereof to be new. And fifteen dollars in cash. Consideration = $76.30.

John Stocker with E. Rising's consent bound himself servant to Joseph Daniel of Hanover township Northampton county farmer, to serve him three years, and to have one quarter schooling during his servitude, and at the expiration of his term to have two complete suits of clothes, one thereof to be new and five dollars in cash. Consideration = $71.90.

Magdalena Schultz bound herself servant to Thomas Lindsay of Chambersburg Pennsylvania innkeeper to serve him three years and six months. And at the expiration of her term to have two complete suits of clothes, one thereof to be new. And ten dollars in cash. Consideration = $76.30.

Magdalena Schultz at the same time assigned to Andrew Lindsay of McConneltown, Bedford county innkeeper, to serve him the remainder of her indenture as above recorded. Consideration = $76.30.

Christian Noll bound himself servant to John Miller of Gomoro township Berks county tanner, to serve him three years and at the expiration of his term to have two complete suits of clothes, one thereof to be new, and ten dollars in cash. Consideration = $76.30.

Christian Noll at the same time assigned to Daniel Ruth of Gomoro township Berks county farmer to serve him the remainder of his indenture as above recorded. Consideration = $76.30.

Diena Du Pong with her father's consent bound herself servant to Anthony Teisseire of Philadelphia merchant to serve him five years. And to have six weeks schooling for every year of her servitude and at the expiration of her term to have two complete suits of clothes, one thereof to be new. Consideration = $76.30.

Landelin Stregel assigned by Parkes Boyd to Christian G. Schmidt of Philadelphia baker to serve him the remainder of his indenture as recorded page 5. Consideration = $20.00.

Anna Maria Stregel assigned by Parkes Boyd to the above Christian G. Schmidt, to serve him the remainder of her indenture as recorded page 5. Consideration = $20.00.

January 2, 1818

Martin Zimmerman assigned by Thomas Lindsay to Andrew Lindsay of McConneltown, Bedford county innkeeper, to serve him the remainder of his indenture as recorded page 40. Consideration = $76.30.

Jost Volmiker with his wife's consent to go to Virginia bound himself servant to John Ehlers of Philadelphia merchant to serve him three years and six months. And at the expiration of his term to have two complete suits of clothes, one thereof to be new. The child to be fed & clothed gratis and to be free with the parent. Consideration = $85.00.

Jost Volmiker at the same time assigned to Louis Beeler of Alexandria, Virginia, to serve him the remainder of his indenture as recorded page 41. Consideration = $85.00.

Catharina Volmiker with her husband's consent to go to Virginia bound herself servant to John Ehlers of Philadelphia merchant to serve him three years and six months. And at the expiration of her term to have two complete suits of clothes, one thereof to be new. The child to be fed & clothed gratis and to be free with the parent. Consideration = $85.00.

Catharina Volmiker at the same time assigned to the above Louis Beeler to serve him the remainder of her indenture as above recorded. Consideration = $85.00.

January 3, 1818

Christian Frederick Oestereicher bound himself servant to John Boal of Greenwood township Cumberland county farmer to serve him three years and at the expiration of his term to have two complete suits of clothes, one thereof to be new. Consideration = $90.00.

Conrad Geiger with Paul Keim's consent bound himself servant to Charles Mercier of Philadelphia confectioner to serve him five years and eleven months. And to have six weeks schooling for every year of his servitude, and at the expiration of his term to have two complete suits of clothes, one thereof to be new and twenty dollars in cash. Consideration = $38.30.

Benedict Kayser with his mother's consent bound himself servant to the above Charles Mercier to serve him eight years and five months. And to have six weeks schooling for every year of his servitude, and at the expiration of his term to have two complete suits of clothes, one thereof to be new and ten dollars in cash. Consideration = $50.30.

January 5, 1818

Catharina Abel bound herself servant to Isaac Oberholtz of Norrinton township Montgomery county farmer to serve him four years, and at the expiration of her term to have two complete suits of clothes, one thereof to be new. Consideration = $76.30.

Mary Ann Jack with her mother's consent bound herself servant to William L. Potts of Philadelphia iron merchant to serve him six years and eleven months. And to have six weeks schooling for every year of her servitude, and at the expiration of her term to have two complete suits of clothes, one thereof to be new. Consideration = $38.30.

Henry Riggebacher assigned by John Walker to David Hess of Northampton county farmer and gun barrel maker to serve him the remainder of his indenture as recorded in Book B, page 179, with consent of Thomas Coats Junior agent for David Hess. Consideration = $45.00.

January 6, 1818

Fredericka Catharina Hardorfer bound herself servant to John L. Glaser of Philadelphia merchant to serve him four years. And at the expiration of her term to have two complete suits of clothes, one thereof to be new, and forty dollars in cash. Consideration = $85.00.

Joseph Denz with his mother's consent bound himself servant to David Urffer of Upper Hanover township Montgomery county farmer to serve him thirteen years. And to have six weeks schooling for every year of his servitude and at the expiration of his term to have two complete suits of clothes, one thereof to be new. Consideration = $38.30.

Salome Nollin with her grandfather's consent to go to Newark State of New Jersey and from there to the State of Ohio, bound herself servant to Backus Wilbur of Newark New Jersey minister to serve him nine years one month & 3 days. And to have six weeks schooling for every year of her servitude, and at the expiration of her term to have two complete suits of clothes, one thereof to be new. Consideration = $38.30.

January 7, 1818

Mariana Morad with her sister's consent bound herself servant to Ralph Eddows Junior of Lower Dublin township Philadelphia county farmer to serve him eight years and six months and to have six weeks schooling for every year of her servitude and at the expiration of her term to have two complete suits of clothes, one thereof to be new. Consideration = $38.30.

Joseph Morad with his sister's consent bound himself to the above Ralph Eddows Junior to serve him nine years and six months. And to have six weeks schooling for every year of his servitude, and at the expiration of his term to have two complete suits of clothes, one thereof to be new. Consideration = $38.30.

January 8, 1818

Maria Begert bound herself servant to John L. Glaser of Philadelphia merchant to serve him three years, and at the expiration of her term to have two complete suits of clothes, one thereof to be new, and forty dollars in cash. Consideration = $20.00.

January 9, 1818

George Gerhardt bound himself servant to James Bryan of Springfield township Bucks county farmer to serve him three years, and at the expiration of his term to have two complete suits of clothes, one thereof to be new, and twenty dollars in cash. Consideration = $76.30.

January 10, 1818

Joseph Mehchior Baumgartner with E. Rising's consent bound himself servant to Nathan De Benneville of Harrisburg Pennsylvania merchant to serve him seven years & four months and to have six weeks schooling for every year of his servitude and at the expiration of his term to have two complete suits of clothes, one thereof to be new. Consideration = $57.00.

Maria Dorothea Alter bound herself servant to Fred D. Baker of Sallsbury township Lancaster county farmer, to serve him three years & six months. And at the expiration of her term to have two complete suits of clothes, one thereof to be new. Consideration = $76.35.

Maria Dorothea Alter at the same time assigned to Margareth Baker of the above township, to serve her the remainder of her indenture as above recorded. Consideration = $76.35.

January 12, 1818

John Ruff bound himself servant to Daniel Shelly of Allen township Cumberland county farmer to serve him three years. And at the expiration of his term to have two complete suits of clothes, one thereof to be new. And fifteen dollars in cash. Consideration = $76.30.

Jacob Debold bound himself servant to the above Daniel Shelly to serve him three years. And at the expiration of his term to have two complete suits of clothes, one thereof to be new and ten dollars in cash. Consideration = $76.30.

Anthon Baumgartner bound himself servant to the above Daniel Shelly to serve him three years. And at the expiration of his term to have two complete suits of clothes, one thereof to be new. Consideration = $76.30.

Anthon Baumgartner at the same time assigned to Daniel Mohler of Allen township Cumberland county farmer to serve him the remainder of his indenture as above recorded. Consideration = $76.30.

Philip Kober assigned by Woodbridge Odlin to Peter Bechtle of Cresum, Philadelphia county papermaker to serve him the remainder of his indenture as recorded page 18. Consideration = $38.30.

Catharina Kober assigned by Woodbridge Odlin to the above Peter Bechtle to serve him the remainder of her indenture as recorded page 18. Consideration = $38.30.

Christoph Kober assigned by Woodbridge Odlin to the above Peter Bechtle to serve him the remainder of his indenture as recorded page 18. Consideration = $38.30.

Christina Kober assigned by Woodbridge Odlin to the above Peter Bechtle to serve him the remainder of her indenture as recorded page 18. Consideration = $38.30.

January 13, 1818

Rudolph Deppeler with his father's consent bound himself servant to George Wilt of Greenwood township Lancaster county farmer to serve him five years and nine months. And to have six weeks schooling for every year of his servitude, and at the expiration of his term to have two complete suits of clothes, one thereof to be new and ten dollars in cash. Consideration = $76.30.

Jacob Deppeler with his father's consent bound himself servant to the above George Wilt to serve him fourteen years and six months. And to have six weeks schooling for every year of his servitude, and at the expiration of his term to have two complete suits of clothes, one thereof to be new, and ten dollars in cash. Consideration = $38.30.

Clemenz Urban with his father's consent bound himself servant to John Grabial Junior of Terry township Union county farmer to serve him seven years & two months. And to have six weeks schooling for every year of his servitude, and at the expiration of his term to have two complete suits of clothes, one thereof to be new, and ten dollars in cash. Consideration = $38.30.

Jacob Volmicker bound himself servant to Gottlieb Saner of Mannor township Lancaster county farmer to serve him four years & six months. And at the expiration of his term to have two complete suits of clothes, one thereof to be new, and twenty dollars in cash. Consideration = $80.00.

Elizabeth Volmicker bound herself servant to the above Gottlieb Saner to serve him four years & six months, and at the expiration of her term to have two complete suits of clothes, one thereof to be new, and twenty dollars in cash. Consideration = $80.00.

January 14, 1818

Francis Joseph Urban bound himself servant to Jesse Bowman of Bryercreek township Columbia county farmer, to serve him four years. And at the expiration of his term to have two complete suits of clothes, one thereof to be new, and forty dollars in cash. Consideration = $76.30.

Francis Joseph Urban Junior with his father's consent bound himself servant to the above Jesse Bowman to serve him ten years and two months and to have six weeks schooling for every years of his servitude, and at the expiration of his term to have two complete suits of clothes, one thereof to be new. Consideration = $38.30.

Francis Joseph Urban Junior at the same time assigned to John Bowman of the above place, to serve him the remainder of his indenture as above recorded. Consideration = $38.30.

Henry Gotz bound himself servant to Daniel Young of Hanover township Northampton county farmer, to serve him three years. And at the expiration of his term to have two complete suits of clothes, one thereof to be new. And ten dollars in cash. Consideration = $90.00.

John Staiber bound himself servant to George Young of Hanover township Lehigh county farmer, to serve him four years. And at the expiration of his term to have two complete suits of clothes, one thereof to be new. And twenty dollars in cash. Consideration = $100.00.

Lambert Herzog with his wife's consent to go to New Jersey bound himself servant to William McKnight of Burdentown State of New Jersey farmer, to serve him five years, and at the expiration of his term to have two complete suits of clothes, one thereof to be new. Consideration = $71.90.

Rosina Herzog with her husband's consent as above bound herself to the above William McKnight to serve him five years. And at the expiration of his term to have two complete suits of clothes, one thereof to be new. Consideration = $71.90.

January 15, 1818

Jacob Friedrick Amholtz bound himself servant to Leonard Stup of Heidelberg township Berks county farmer to serve him three years. And at the expiration of his term to have two complete suits of clothes, one thereof to be new, and eighteen dollars in cash. Consideration = $59.00.

Lonzi Hutz with E. Rising's consent bound himself servant to Samuel Hershberger of Cocalicoe township Lancaster county farmer to serve him three years. And to have one quarter schooling during his servitude, and at the expiration of his term to have two complete suits of clothes, one thereof to be new. Consideration = $76.30.

Lonzi Hutz at the same time assigned to John Hershberger of Hanover township Adams county farmer to serve him the remainder of his indenture as above recorded. Consideration = $76.30.

January 16, 1818

John Rudolph Hunziker it is agreed to remitt him one year and ten months of his term of servitude as recorded in Book B, 244, provided if he conducts himself well, dated this day and signed by the master Henry O. Heyll.

January 17, 1818

George Meyer with his wife's consent to go to Virginia bound himself servant to Silas H. Smith of Staunton, Virginia merchant to serve him three years. And at the expiration of his term to have two complete suits of clothes, one thereof to be new, and fourteen dollars in cash. The child to be fed and clothed gratis and to be free with the parent. Consideration = $62.00.

Christina Meyer with her husband's consent as aforesaid bound herself servant to the above Silas H. Smith, to serve him three years. And at the expiration of her term to have two complete suits of clothes, one thereof to be new, and fourteen dollars in cash. The child to be fed and clothed gratis and to be free with the parent. Consideration = $62.00.

George Hausman with his wife's consent as aforesaid bound himself servant to the above Silas H. Smith, to serve him three years. And at the expiration of his term to have two complete suits of clothes, one thereof to be new, and nine dollars in cash. Consideration = $67.00.

Maria Magdalena Hausman with her husband's consent as aforesaid bound herself to the above Silas H. Smith, to serve him three years, and at the expiration of her term to have two complete suits of clothes, one thereof to be new, and nine dollars in cash. Consideration = $67.00.

John Dieringer with his consent as aforesaid bound himself servant to the above Silas H. Smith to serve him three years. And at the expiration of his term to have two complete suits of clothes, one thereof to be new, and ten dollars in cash. Consideration = $22.00.

John Dieringer Junior with his father's consent as aforesaid bound himself servant to the above Silas H. Smith to serve him fourteen years. And to have six weeks schooling for every year of his servitude, and at the expiration of his term to have two complete suits of clothes, one thereof to be new. And ten dollars in cash. Consideration = $20.00.

George Fritzinger bound himself servant to John Gile of New Britton township Bucks county farmer, to serve him three years, and at the expiration of his term to have two complete suits of clothes, one thereof to be new, and twenty nine dollars in cash. Consideration = $47.30.

Jacob Frederick Moore bound himself servant to John Planck of the Northern Liberties cooper to serve him two years eleven months & 21 days. And at the expiration of his term to have two complete suits of clothes, one thereof to be new or thirty dollars in cash at the option of the servant, and 12.5 cents every week, payable as it comes due. Consideration = $76.30.

Christian Debolt with E. Rising's consent bound himself servant to the above John Planck to serve him three years and one month. And to have six weeks schooling for every year of his servitude, and at the expiration of his term to have two complete suits of clothes, one thereof to be new. Consideration = $76.35.

January 19, 1818

Paul Keim with his wife's consent bound himself servant to Philip Brechbill of Lebanon township Lebanon county farmer, to serve him two years and six months. And at the expiration of his term to have two complete suits of clothes, one thereof to be new, and ten dollars in cash. Consideration = $56.30.

Catharina Keim with her husband's consent bound himself servant to the above Philip Brechbill to serve him two years and six months. And at the expiration of her term to have two complete suits of clothes, one thereof to be new, and ten dollars in cash. Consideration = $56.30.

January 20, 1818

John Deppeler with his wife's consent bound himself servant to John Groh of Donegal township Lancaster county farmer to serve him two years and six months. And at the expiration of his term to have two complete suits of clothes, one thereof to be new. Consideration = $57.30.

Anna Maria Deppeler with her husband's consent bound herself servant to the above John Groh to serve him two years and six months. And at the expiration of her term to have two complete suits of clothes, one thereof to be new. Consideration = $57.30.

Joseph Meyer bound himself servant to Thees Hollmann of Philadelphia clerk to serve him three years and at the expiration of his term to have two complete suits of clothes, one thereof to be new. Consideration = $76.35.

George Kientzle bound himself servant to the above Thees Hollmann to serve him three years, and at the expiration of his term to have two complete suits of clothes, one thereof to be new. Consideration = $76.35.

Susana Catharina Noll with her mother's consent bound herself servant to John Auig of Philadelphia clerk to serve him thirteen years, and to have six weeks schooling for every year of her servitude, and at the expiration of her term to have two complete suits of clothes, one thereof to be new, and ten dollars in cash. Consideration = $10.00.

Fanchette Morad bound herself servant to George Richner of Moyamensing township Philadelphia county farmer to serve him three years, and at the expiration of her term to have two complete suits of clothes, one thereof to be new and five dollars in cash. Consideration = $76.30.

January 21, 1818

Maria Meyer bound herself servant to Christian Mast of Carnervon township Lancaster county farmer to serve him three years & six months. And at the expiration of her term to have two complete suits of clothes, one thereof to be new. Consideration = $76.35.

January 22, 1818

Simon Kagi bound himself servant to John Musser of Whitedeer township Union county farmer to serve him four years. And at the expiration of his term to have two complete suits of clothes, one thereof to be new. And forty dollars in cash. Consideration = $76.30.

John Kagi with his father's consent bound himself servant to the above John Musser to serve him thirteen years, and to have six weeks schooling for every year of his servitude and at the expiration of his term to have two complete suits of clothes, one thereof to be new. Consideration = $38.30.

John Albert bound himself servant to Michael Kohr of Bethel township Lebanon county miller, to serve him three years. And at the expiration of his term to have two complete suits of clothes, one thereof to be new. And twenty eight dollars in cash. Consideration = $48.30.

Theresia Wunderlin with her father's consent bound herself servant to the above Michael Kohr to serve him three years and six months. And to have twelve weeks schooling during her servitude. And at the expiration of her term to have two complete suits of clothes, one thereof to be new. Consideration = $85.30.

Theresia Wunderlin at the same time assigned to Valentin Schauffler to serve him the remainder of her indenture as above recorded, his resident at Jonestown Lebanon county. Consideration = $85.30.

Anna Maria Noll bound herself servant to Michael Shiller of Leacock township Lancaster county farmer to serve him two years. And at the expiration of her term to have two complete suits of clothes, one thereof to be new. Consideration = $80.30.

January 24, 1818

Jacob Frederick Moore assign by John Planck to Michael Schenck of Terry township Dauphin county miller to serve him the remainder of his indenture as recorded page 47. Consideration = $76.30.

Hans Ulrich Kaser assigned by Jacob Hassinger to James Wallace of West Hanover township Dauphin county farmer to serve him the remainder of his indenture as recorded page 1. Consideration = $55.30.

January 29, 1818

Joseph Studer with his wife's consent bound himself servant to John Mootzar of Formanough township Mifflin county farmer to serve him five years. And at the expiration of his term to have two complete suits of clothes, one thereof to be new. Consideration = $76.45.

Joseph Studer at the same time assigned to Daniel Mootzar of Tobian township Cumberland county farmer to serve him the remainder of his indenture as above recorded. Consideration = $76.45.

Anna Maria Studer with her husband's consent bound herself to the above John Mootzar to serve him five years. And at the expiration of her term to have two complete suits of clothes, one thereof to be new. Consideration = $76.45.

Anna Maria Studer at the same time assign to the aforesaid Daniel Mootzar to serve him the remainder of her indenture as above recorded. Consideration = $76.45.

Jacob Studer with his father's consent bound himself servant to the above John Mootzar to serve him eleven years & nineteen days. And to have six weeks schooling for every year of his servitude, and at the expiration of his term to have two complete suits of clothes, one thereof to be new. Consideration = $38.30.

January 30, 1818

Christina Catharina Seitz bound herself servant to Thomas C. Luders of Northern Liberties brewer to serve him four years. And at the expiration of her term to have two complete suits of clothes, one thereof to be new. The child to be fed and clothed gratis and to be free with the parent. Consideration = $60.00.

Christina Catharina Seitz at the same time assigned to George Young of Betlahem township Northampton county farmer to serve him the remainder of her indenture as above recorded. Consideration = $60.00.

Marietta Morad with E. Rising's consent bound herself servant to Thomas C. Luders of the Northern Liberties brewer, to serve him three years & ten months. And to have six weeks schooling for every year of her servitude, and at the expiration of her term to have two complete suits of clothes, one thereof to be new. Consideration = $38.30.

Marietta Morad at the same time assigned to John Samuel Haman of Nazareth township Northampton county innkeeper, to serve him the remainder of her indenture as above recorded. Consideration = $38.30.

Maria Ursula Jack with her consent to go to Kentucky bound herself servant to Benjamin Smith of Shelbyville State of Kentucky merchant to serve him one year. And at the expiration of her term to have two complete suits of clothes, one thereof to be new. Consideration = $12.00.

John Jack with his mother's consent as above bound himself servant to the aforesaid Benjamin Smith to serve him eleven years. And to have six weeks schooling for every year of his servitude, and at the expiration of his term to have two complete suits of clothes, one thereof to be new. Consideration = $38.00.

February 4, 1818

Jacob Lemle with George Devries' consent bound himself servant to Jacob Swertswelder of Salsburry township Lancaster county miller to serve him eight years. And to have six weeks schooling for every year of his servitude. And at the expiration of his term to have two complete suits of clothes, one thereof to be new. Consideration = $76.35.

Maria Juliana Alter with George Devries' consent bound herself servant to the above Jacob Swertswelder, to serve him three years and six months. And to have six weeks schooling for every year of her servitude. And at the expiration of her term to have two complete suits of clothes, one thereof to be new. Consideration = $76.35.

February 7, 1818

Barbara Hofer with Philip Justice's consent bound herself servant to Alexander McKinley of the Northern Liberties bricklayer to serve him four years and nine months. And to have six weeks schooling for every year of her servitude, and at the expiration of her term to have two complete suits of clothes, one thereof to be new. Consideration = $40.00.

John George Tantzer with his wife's consent bound himself servant to John L. Glaser of Philadelphia merchant to serve him three years, and at the expiration of his term to have two complete suits of clothes, one thereof to be new, and one hundred dollars in cash. Consideration = $35.00.

Elizabeth Tantzer with her husband's consent bound herself servant to the above John L. Glaser to serve him three years. And at the expiration of her term to have two complete suits of clothes, one thereof to be new. Consideration = $35.00.

Theresa Tantzer with her father's consent bound herself servant to the aforesaid John L. Glaser to serve him three years and have six weeks schooling for one year of her servitude, and at the expiration of her term to have two complete suits of clothes, one thereof to be new. Consideration = $35.00.

Barbara Tantzer with her father's consent bound herself servant to the above John L. Glaser to serve him seven years and three months. And to have six weeks schooling for every year of her servitude, and at the expiration of her term to have two complete suits of clothes, one thereof to be new. Consideration = $29.00.

Joseph Schultz bound himself servant to the above John L. Glaser to serve him three years, and at the expiration of his term to have two complete suits of clothes, one thereof to be new. Consideration = $80.00.

Barbara Schultz with her father's consent bound herself servant to the above John L. Glaser to serve him nine years and ten months. And to have six weeks schooling for every year of her servitude and at the expiration of her term to have two complete suits of clothes, one thereof to be new. Consideration = $40.00.

February 10, 1818

Carolina Graff assigned by William Taylor Junior to James Tatham of Clarmont Seminary Philadelphia county teacher to serve him the remainder of her indenture as recorded page 8. Consideration = $40.00.

February 12, 1818

Salome Maur bound herself servant to Woodbridge Odlin of Philadelphia merchant to serve him three years. And at the expiration of her term to have two complete suits of clothes, one thereof to be new. Consideration = $76.30.

February 19, 1818

Magdalena Wursthorn with Henry Fricke's consent bound herself to Isaac Norris of Philadelphia hatter to serve him eight years four months & 9 days. And to have six weeks schooling for every year of her servitude, and at the expiration of her term to have two complete suits of clothes, one thereof to be new. And also promise to give her eighteen dollars & 80 cents in cash and one piece of coarse linnen, five sheets being in a chest belonging to her parents deceased. Consideration = $36.30.

February 27, 1818

Christian Klingler released and discharged by his master Henry Gessenheiner from all further services whatsoever of his indenture as recorded page 23. Consideration = $15.00.

Judith Klingler released and discharged by her master Henry Gessenheiner from all further services whatsoever of her indenture as recorded page 23. Consideration = $15.00.

Christina Klingler assigned by Henry Gessenheiner to her father Christian Klingler to serve him the remainder of her indenture as recorded page 23. Consideration = $15.00.

John Klingler assigned by Henry Gessenheiner to his father Christian Klingler to serve him the remainder of his indenture as recorded page 23. Consideration = $15.00.

February 28, 1818

Frederick Sailer with his mother's consent bound himself servant to Joseph Henry of the Northern Liberties gun maker to serve him six years seven months & 10 days. And to have six weeks schooling for every year of his servitude and at the expiration of his term to have two complete suits of clothes, one thereof to be new. Consideration = $38.35.

March 7, 1818

Barbara Kayser bound herself servant to Charles F. Keilig of Philadelphia furrier, to serve him three years. And at the expiration of her term to have two complete suits of clothes, one thereof to be new. And twenty dollars in cash. Consideration = $47.30.

Barbara Kayser at the same time assigned to Thomas Lindsay of Chambersburg, Pennsylvania innkeeper to serve him the remainder of her indenture as above recorded. Consideration = $47.30.

John Kopp assigned by G. W. Mentz to Gottlieb Kopp the father of the servant to serve him the remainder of his indenture as recorded in Book B, page 256. Consideration = $25.00.

March 9, 1818

John George Ellwanger released and discharged at his particular request by Jacob Beck from all further services of his indenture as recorded in Book B, page 206. Consideration = $81.00.

March 14, 1818

Joseph Meyer assigned by Theese Hollmann to David Shoemaker of Springfield township Montgomery county to serve him the remainder of his indenture as recorded page 48. Consideration = $76.35.

March 16, 1818

Salome Maur assigned by Woodbridge Odlin to Jacob Sommer of Moreland township Philadelphia county esquire to serve him the remainder of her indenture as recorded page 51. Consideration = $76.30.

Johanna Handle Junior assigned by Woodbridge Odlin to Francis Cavellero Sarmiento esquire of Philadelphia to serve him the remainder of her indenture as recorded page 17. Consideration = $70.00.

March 17, 1818

Gottlieb Handle released and discharged at his particular request by Woodbridge Odlin from all further service of his indenture as recorded page 17. Consideration = $20.00.

Johanna Handle released and discharged at her particular request by Woodbridge Odlin from all further services of her indenture as recorded page 17. Consideration = $20.00.

March 25, 1818

David Bauer released and discharged by Luther Frank at his particular desire from all further services of his indenture as recorded in Book B, page 204. Consideration = $94.00.

Johanna Rudolph assigned by Woodbridge Odlin to Alexander Scott of Nottingham township Washington county Pennsylvania to serve him the remainder of her indenture as recorded page 14. Consideration = $76.35.

Gottlob Rudolph assigned by Woodbridge Odlin to the above Alexander Scott to serve him the remainder of his indenture as recorded page 14. Consideration = $38.35.

April 1, 1818

Maria Anna Walsser assigned by George Yohe to her father Doris Walsser to serve him the remainder of her indenture as recorded in Book B, page 208. Consideration = $100.00.

April 7, 1818

Philip Jacob Vogt Junior assigned by William M. Lane to Chester Chattin of Philadelphia carpenter to serve him the remainder of his indenture as recorded in Book B, page 100. Consideration = $30.00.

April 10, 1818

John Michael Staiger bound himself with consent of John Brunner to Jacob Emhardt of Germantown Philadelphia county taylor for two years & six months to have six weeks schooling for every year of his servitude & when free to have two suits of clothes one of which be new. Consideration = $80.00.

April 14, 1818

Samuel Bollinger assigned by John Angue to his father Samuel Bollinger to serve him the remainder of his indenture as recorded in Book B, page 279. Consideration = $77.00.

April 15, 1818

Anna Maria Dower bound herself to John R. C. Smith of Philadelphia merchant for three years to have when free two complete suits clothes, one thereof to be new. Her infant child to be fed & clothed gratis & to be free with the mother. Consideration = $80.00.

April 18, 1818

Gotlib Buhl assigned by James Abercromby Junior to Samuel W. Wetheral of Philadelphia drugist to serve him the remainder of his indenture as recorded in Book B, page 104. Consideration = $130.00.

May 9, 1818

Lambert Herzog assigned by William McKnight to John Smith esquire of Philadelphia to serve him two years & eight months from this date. Indenture recorded page 45. Consideration = $75.00.

Rosanna Herzog assigned by William McKnight to John Smith esquire of Philadelphia to serve him two years & eight months from this date. Indenture recorded page 45. Consideration = $75.00.

June 22, 1818

John Conrad Houssel assigned by James Williams to Frederick Scholer of Philadelphia baker to serve him the remainder of his indenture as recorded Book B, page 256. Consideration = $50.00.

July 11, 1818

Michael Hoerper bound himself to E. W. Hoskin of Philadelphia merchant to serve him five years and when free to have two suits clothes, one thereof to be new. Consideration = $200.00

July 18, 1818

Philip Hoffman with consent of his father bound him servant to John M. Scherzinger of Philadelphia oil & eoulerman to serve him five years & seven months. And to have six weeks schooling for every year of his servitude and at the expiration of his term to have thirty dollars in lieu of freedoms. Consideration = $80.00.

Maria Dorethea Leibfried assigned by William Snare to herself for the consideration of thirty dollars paid by John D. Eisenhun.

July 20, 1818

The indenture between John Peter Ravann & his master Joseph Borie is this day cancelled & the said servant given free in consideration of fifteen dollars paid the said master by servant. [Signed] John Peter Ravann   Joseph Borie

July 22, 1818

Nicholas Hoffman with his father bound himself to Frederick Gaul of Philadelphia brewer for three years to have six weeks schooling and at the end of his servitude two complete suits of clothes one thereof to be new or thirty dollars in cash at the option of the servant. Consideration = $85.00.

July 24, 1818

Catharina Hoffman with her father's consent bound to William Geiss of Philadelphia merchant for seven years to have six weeks schooling every year of her servitude and at the expiration of her term to have two complete suits of clothes one thereof to be new. Consideration = $70.00.

Dorethea Werner with the consent of John Ruppert bound herself to John Geyer of Philadelphia alderman for three years to have at the expiration of her term two complete suits clothes one of which to be new. Consideration = $72.00.

August 1, 1818

Jacob Sagesser with consent of his father is bound to John Langstroth of Philadelphia papermaker for five years three months & 28 days, to be taught the art trade & mystery of paper making, to have six weeks schooling for every year of his servitude & when free to have two complete suits of clothes one thereof to be new. Valuable consideration.

John Sagesser with consent of his father is bound to above John Langstroth for six years seven months & 24 days, to be taught the art trade & mystery of paper making, to have six weeks schooling for every year of his servitude & when free to have two complete suits of clothes one thereof to be new. Valuable consideration.

August 6, 1818

Elizabeth Gising assigned by William Hurlick to serve herself the remainder of her indenture as recorded in Book B, page 102. Consideration = $25.00

August 14, 1818

John Nicholas Statz in consideration of full compensation made his master Jacob Emhart is by him released from all further servitude of his indenture recorded in Book B, page 161.

John Gotlieb Wolf in consideration of full compensation made his master Jacob Emhart is by him released from all further servitude of his indenture recorded as above.

John George Gehle in consideration of full compensation made his master Jacob Emhart is by him released from all further servitude of his indenture recorded Book B, page 108.

August 25, 1818

Sophia Kuhn with consent of her father bound to John Burge of Philadelphia confectioner, to serve five years, to have six weeks schooling and at the expiration of his term two complete suits clothes one thereof to be new. Consideration = $80.00.

August 28, 1818

Nicholas Beck with consent of his step father to go to New Jersey bound himself to Thomas Jones Junior of Philadelphia merchant for nine years, to have six weeks schooling for every year of his servitude & at the expiration of his term to have two complete suits of clothes, one to be new. Consideration = $81.00.

Nicholas Beck at the same time assigned to Thomas Jones of Salem New Jersey farmer to serve the remainder of his indenture as above recorded. Consideration = $81.00.

Maria Rosina Schmidt bound herself to Melchior Larer of Philadelphia brewer for three years to have two complete suits of clothes, one to be new. Consideration = $81.50.

Maria Magdalena Sieger bound herself to Thomas Graham merchant of Philadelphia for two years, to have when free two suits clothes one of which to be new. Consideration = $41.50.

George Weimer with consent of his father is bound to Frederick Foering esquire of the Northern Liberties for eight years nine months & two days, to have six weeks schooling for every year of his servitude & at the expiration of his term two complete suits of clothes one thereof to be new. Consideration = $81.00.

Anna Maria Kuhn with her father's consent is bound to Conrad Mandel of Philadelphia baker for three years, to have at the expiration of her term two suits of clothes, one thereof to be new. Consideration = $70.00.

Ludwig Kuhn with his father's consent is bound to Jacob Ernst baker of Philadelphia for seven years, to have forty two weeks schooling during his term & at the expiration of which two suits clothes, one to be new. Consideration = $70.00.

Rosina Catharina Motz bound herself to Ebenezer McCutchen merchant Philadelphia for three years, to have at the end of her term two suits clothes, one to be new. Consideration = $81.50.

Susanna Gries bound herself to John K. Graham grocer, Philadelphia for three years, at the expiration of her term to have two suits of clothes & nine dollars cash. Consideration = $70.00.

August 29, 1818

Daniel Weimer with consent of his father to go to Ohio State is bound to Henry Weaver merchant Philadelphia for seven years & two months to have forty two weeks schooling & at the expiration of his term two suits of clothes one to be new. Consideration = $81.50.

August 31, 1818

Catharina Stahl with consent of her father is bound to William Montgomery Junior merchant of Philadelphia for three years & six months, to have twelve weeks schooling, and at the end of her term two suits clothes, one to be new. And in case of the death of her mother she to be given up to her father, he paying a reasonable compensation for the remainder of her term. Consideration = $80.00.

Catharina Dorathea Lust bound to Frederick Dreer cabinet maker Philadelphia for three years to have at the end of her term two suits clothes, one to be new. Consideration = $81.50.

John Jacob Mayer with consent of Christian G. Schmidt bound to Samuel Shoemaker esquire attorney at law Philadelphia for two years & six months to have ten weeks schooling & at the end of his term two suits clothes, one to be new. Consideration = $65.00.

Martin Digel with consent of John Brunner is bound to Thomas Hope exchange broker Philadelphia for one year & nine months, to have twelve weeks schooling & at the of his term two suits clothes, one to be new. Consideration = $40.00.

Andrew Gehring with his consent to go to New Jersey bound himself to Jacob Greverson, farmer, Waterford township Gloucester county for three years, to have at the end of his term two suits clothes, one to be new, & five dollars cash if he conducts himself well. Consideration = $81.50.

Christian Braun bound himself to Benjamin Woolston carter of the Northern Liberties to have at the end of his term two suits clothes, one to be new, bound for three years. Consideration = $81.50.

Gottlieb Frederick Rehfus bound to John M. Taylor merchant Philadelphia for three years to have at the end of his term two suits clothes, one to be new. Consideration = $81.50.

Gottlieb Frederick Rehfus at the same time assigned to Edward Fox esquire Philadelphia to serve him the remainder of his indenture as above recorded. Note. This assignment not being accepted by Edward Fox, the servant was bound as per next page. Consideration = $81.50.

John Ernst Kuhnle with consent of Peter Christian is bound to Michael Sager for one year & six months, to have nine weeks schooling, & at the end of his term two suits clothes, one to be new. Consideration = $37.50.

September 1, 1818

John Gerber bound to Christian Zug, farmer, East Whiteland township Chester county for two years & six months, to have at the end of his term two suits clothes, one to be new. Consideration = $81.50.

September 2, 1818

John Schaeffer & his wife Anna Maria bound to James P. Morris, farmer, Bristol township, Bucks county, for three years to have each two suits clothes, at the end of their term, one of which to be new, their child to be fed & clothed during their term & to be free with the parents. Consideration = $163.00.

Jacob Eberhard bound to Jonathan Maule blacksmith Philadelphia for two years to have at the end of his term two suits clothes, one to be new. Consideration = $57.50.

Frederick Almendinger bound to Denny Rodgers merchant Shippensburg Cumberland county for two years & six months, to have two suits of clothes one to be new & thirty dollars in cash at the end of his term. Consideration = $38.00.

Frederick Almendinger at the same time assigned to James Lim farmer Franklin county to serve him the remainder of his indenture as above recorded. Consideration = $38.00.

Jacob Kubler with his consent to go to Ohio is bound to E. Hinman distiller Cincinnate for three years, to have at the end of his term two suits clothes, one to be new. Consideration = $81.50.

John L. Gunther with his consent to go to Ohio is bound to E. Hinman distiller Cincinnate for three years, to have at the end of his term two suits of clothes, one to be new. Consideration = $81.50.

Jacob Lum bound to Peter Hertzog & Company sugar refiners, Northern Liberties for two years & six months, to have at the end of his term two suits clothes, one thereof to be new. Consideration = $81.50.

John Dulmer bound to the above Peter Hertzog & Company for two years & six months to have at the end of his term two complete suits clothes one thereof to be new, and twenty three dollars fifty cents cash, if not paid him by Jacob Lum. Consideration = $58.00.

September 3, 1818

Gottlieb Frederick Rehfus with his consent to go to Georgia is bound to Benjamin Picquet merchant Augusta, for three years, to have at the end of his term two suits clothes, one thereof to be new. Consideration = $81.50.

John Albrecht Dishinger with his consent to go to Georgia, is bound to the above Benjamin Picquet for three years, to have two suits clothes, one thereof to be new. Consideration = $81.50.

John Andrew Gaissert with his consent to go to Georgia is bound to the above Benjamin Picquet for three years to have two suits clothes, one thereof to be new. Consideration = $81.50.

September 4, 1818

Jacob Frederick Goetz bound to George Houck, farmer Coealtico township Lancaster county, for three years, to have at the end of his term two suits clothes, one thereof to be new, & eight dollars cash. Consideration = $81.50.

Christian Heidlauf bound to Charles Fahnestock, innkeeper, East Whiteland township Chester county, for two years & six months, to have at the end of his term sixty six dollars fifty cents cash. Consideration = $65.00.

Jacob Frederick Bauman bound to Antoni Rotshiller, locksmith Northern Liberties for three years, to have at the end of his term two suits clothes one thereof to be new. Consideration = $81.50.

September 5, 1818

John Jacob Scheffel with his uncle's consent is bound to Nicholas Scholtheis baker Philadelphia for three years, to find his own clothing & in lieu thereof to be paid by his master six dollars per month during his servitude as the same shall come due. Consideration = $81.50.

September 7, 1818

Julianna Maderin bound to John Wilson, innkeeper, Philadelphia for three years, to have at the end of her term two suits clothes, one thereof to be new. Consideration = $81.50.

John Renninger bound to John Harman, millwright, Plymouth township Montgomery county for three years, to have at the end of his term two suits clothes, one thereof to be new. Consideration = $81.50.

John Reinwald bound to the above John Harman for three years, to have at the end of his term two suits clothes & fourteen dollars fifty cents cash. Consideration = $67.00.

Jacob Froelich & Elizabeth his wife is bound to William Lardner, Lower Dublin township Philadelphia county farmer for one year & six months, to have at the end of their term each two suits clothes. Their child to be fed & clothed during their servitude & to be free with the parents. Consideration = $63.00.

September 8, 1818

Catharina Wetterin bound to Frederick Schwikkard wafer maker Northern Liberties for one year & six months, to have at the end of her term two suits of clothes one thereof to be new. Consideration = $30.00.

September 9, 1818

Catharina Elizabeth Weymer with consent of her father is bound to John Steel auctionear Philadelphia for nine years two months & twenty days, to have fifty five weeks schooling, & at the end of her term two complete suits of clothes one thereof to be new. Consideration = $60.00.

Catharina Elizabeth Weymer at the same time assigned to Doctor Agnew of Harrisburg to serve him the remainder of her indenture as above recorded. Consideration = $60.00.

Elizabeth Rosanna Werthele with consent of her father is bound to David Woelpper, victuler, Penn township for three years, to have at the end of her term two complete suits of clothes, one thereof to be new, and during her servitude twelve weeks schooling. Consideration = $81.50

Anna Maria Brunin is bound to John Fries gentleman Philadelphia for three years, to have at the end of her term two complete suits of clothes, one thereof to be new. Consideration = $81.50.

John Michael Treisendanz with consent of Abraham Stein is bound to James Fassitt, merchant, Philadelphia for four years, to have twenty four weeks schooling, & at end of his term two complete suits of clothes, one thereof to be new, & if he conducts himself to the satisfaction of his master to have six months of his time relinquished. Consideration = $81.50.

Dorothea Widmeyer with her father's consent is bound to Daniel H. Miller merchant Philadelphia for three years & six months, to have eight weeks schooling & at the end of her term two complete suits of clothes one to be new. Consideration = $81.50.

September 11, 1818

Maria Kirkhoven is bound to Richard Streeper confectioner Philadelphia for three years, to have at the end of her term two complete suits of clothes, one thereof to be new. Consideration = $81.50.

Christian Widmeyer with consent of .... is bound to Mathew Egart Bethlahem Northampton county for six years & six months & 19 days to have thirty nine weeks schooling & at the end of his term two complete suits of clothes, one thereof to be new. Consideration = $81.50.

Dorothea Maria Wolf with her father's consent is bound to John Hollmann clerk Philadelphia for four years, to have twenty four weeks schooling & at the end of her term two complete suits of clothes, one thereof to be new. Consideration = $81.50.

Dorothea Maria Wolf at the same time assigned to Louisa McIlhenney gentlewomen Penn township to serve her the remainder of her indenture as above recorded. Consideration = $81.50.

Maria Magdalena Weimer with her father's consent is bound to John Steel, auctioneer, Philadelphia for seven years & three months, to have forty four weeks schooling & at the end of her term two complete suits of clothes one thereof to be new. Consideration = $81.50.

September 12, 1818

Elizabeth Wiedmanin to Joseph Rapin gentleman, Northern Liberties, for five years to have at the end of her term two complete suits of clothes, one thereof to be new. Consideration = $81.50.

John Grupp with consent of his mother Elizabeth Wiedmanin to the above Joseph Rapin for fifteen years & six months to have six weeks schooling for every year of his servitude & at the end of his term two complete suits of clothes one to be new. Consideration = $40.75.

Barbara Schaffelin to John Hollmann clerk Philadelphia for three years, to have at the end of her term two complete suits of clothes, one thereof to be new. Consideration = $81.50.

Barbara Schaffelin at the same time assigned to Louisa McIlhenney, gentlewoman, Penn township to serve her the remainder of her indenture as above recorded. Consideration = $81.50.

Jacob Petz with consent of .... to Henry Meyers, farmer Concord township Deleware county for four years, to have twenty four weeks schooling & at the end of his term two complete suits of clothes, one thereof to be new. And if he conducts himself well twenty dollars. Consideration = $81.50.

Fredericca Kalender to John Ross physician, New Garden township Chester county for three years, to have two complete suits of clothes at the end of her term one thereof to be new. Consideration = $81.50.

Fredericca Wolf with her father's consent to go to Deleware State, to Eli Sharp innkeeper, Wilmington, for eight years & six months, to have fifty one weeks schooling & at the end of her term two complete suits of clothes, one to be new. Consideration = $40.75.

Henry Wolf Junior with consent of his father, to John Child, house carpenter, Hammelton Ville, Blockley township, for eight years, to have forty eight weeks schooling & at the end of his two complete suits of clothes, one thereof to be new. Consideration = $81.50.

Henry Wolf Junior at the same time assigned to Clementina Ross, widow, Hammelton Ville, for the remainder of her indenture as above recorded. Consideration = $81.50.

Jacob Nagel to Jacob Preser, baker, Philadelphia for two years & six months, to have at the end of his term two complete suits of clothes one to be new. Consideration = $81.50.

September 14, 1818

John Frederick Heidecke to George & Jacob Peterman, merchants Philadelphia for three years, to have twelve weeks schooling, and at the end of his term two complete suits of clothes, one thereof to be new. Consideration = $81.50.

John Christian Roger to Charles Maysenhoelder, silversmith, Philadelphia for two years, to receive one dollar & 50 cents per week for the first year, & two dollars per week the second year as the same shall come due, in lieu of his washing & clothing. Consideration = $81.50.

Elizabeth Rosina Werthele assigned by David Woelpper, victuler, to her father for the remainder of her indenture recorded page 59. Consideration = $81.50.

Daniel Wethele & wife Walburg with their consent to go to New York State, to James T. Watson, gentleman, City of New York for three years, to have each two complete suits of clothes at the end of their term, one to be new. Consideration = $163.00.

Philip Jacob Werthele willing to go to New York, to the above James T. Watson for three years, to have at the end of his term two complete suits of clothes, one to be new. Consideration = $81.50.

Agnus Magdalena Werthele willing to go to New York, to the above James T. Watson for three years, to have at the end of her term two complete suits of clothes one to be new. Consideration = $81.50.

Rosina Fredericca Werthele with her father's consent to go to New York, to the above James T. Watson, to have twelve weeks schooling, and at the end of her term two complete suits of clothes, one to be new. Consideration = $81.50.

Johanna Dorothea Werthele with her father's consent to go to New York, to the aforesaid James T. Watson for three years, to have eighteen weeks schooling & at the end of her term two complete suits of clothes, one to be new. Consideration = $40.75.

Christianna Walburg Werthele with consent of her father, to the above James T. Watson, for three years to have eighteen weeks schooling & at the end of her term two complete suits of clothes, one to be new. Consideration = $40.75.

John Jacob Staub & wife Maria Barbara willing to go to New York, to the above James T. Watson for three years, to have each two complete suits of clothes at the end of their term, one to be new. Consideration = $163.00.

Gottlieb Frederick Staub with consent of his father, to the above James T. Watson, for three years, to have eighteen weeks schooling, & at the end of his term two complete suits of clothes, one to be new. Consideration = $40.75.

John George Bader & wife Regina Dorothea willing to go to New York, to the above James T. Watson for three years, to have each two complete suits of clothes at the end of their term, one thereof to be new. And their infant child to be fed & clothed & to be free with the parents. Consideration = $163.00.

Elizabeth Bader with consent of her father, to the above James T. Watson for three years, to have twelve weeks schooling & at the end of her term two complete suits of clothes, one thereof to be new. Consideration = $40.74.

Christina Barbara Bader with consent of her father, to the above James T. Watson, to have eighteen weeks schooling & at the end of her term two complete suits of clothes, one to be new. Consideration = $40.75.

John George Bader Junior with consent of his father, to the above James T. Watson for three years, to have eighteen weeks schooling & at the end of his term two complete suits of clothes, one thereof to be new. Consideration = $40.75.

John David Mertz & wife Christina Dorothea willing to go to New York, to the above James T. Watson, for three years, to have at the end of their term each two complete suits of clothes, one to be new, their child to be fed & clothed gratis & free with the parents. Consideration = $160.00.

John David Heisse willing to go to New York, to the above James T. Watson for three years, to have at the end of his term two complete suits of clothes, one to be new. Consideration = $81.50.

John Frederick Burk willing to go to New York, to the above James T. Watson for three years to have at the end of his term two complete suits of clothes, one to be new. Consideration = $81.50.

Christopher Bach to Valintine Phillips, farmer, Upper Mount Bethel township Northampton county, for three years, to have at the end of his term two complete suits of clothes, one to be new & thirty dollars. Consideration = $81.50.

Catharina Batzel with her father's consent, to Nicholas Schultheis, baker, Philadelphia for six years & six months, to have thirty nine weeks schooling, two quarters thereof to be given in the English & one quarter in the German & at the end of her term two complete suits of clothes, one to be new. Consideration = $50.00.

Christina Dorothea Supflein, to William Hurlick, innkeeper, Philadelphia for two years & six months, to have at the end of her term two complete suits of clothes one thereof to be new, & fifteen dollars. Consideration = $77.00.

September 15, 1818

Susana Carien to John Pradel, farmer, Bristol township Bucks county for two years, to have at the end of her term two complete suits of clothes, one to be new. Consideration = $77.00.

Anna Maria Kumlin to Henry Elwell, Southwark blacksmith for three years, to have at the end of her term two complete suits of clothes, one to be new. Consideration = $77.00.

Catharina Magdalena Kauffman assigned by Jacob Ristine to serve her father the remainder of her indenture as recorded in Book B, page 103. Valuable consideration.

John Remele willing to go to New York, to James T. Watson of the City of New York, gentleman, for three years, to have at the end of the term two complete suits clothes, one thereof to be new, & sixteen dollars & fifty cents. Consideration = $63.50.

September 16, 1818

John Frederick Mayer with consent of his father to go to District of Columbia, to Joseph Arny, confectioner, Georgetown, for three years & eight months to have twenty two weeks schooling & at the end of the term two complete suits of clothes, one to be new. Consideration = $81.50.

John Mayer with consent of his father to go to District of Columbia, to Joseph Arny confectioner as above, for seven years five months & twenty three days, to have forty five weeks schooling & at the end of the term two complete suits clothes, one to be new. Consideration = $61.62.

Henry Pitz to David Neff, baker, Moiamensing township Philadelphia county for two years, to have due to him seven dollars per month, out of which his freight is to be repaid to his master. And the servant to find his own clothing. Consideration = $81.50.

September 17, 1818

Dorothea Ulrich with her father's consent, to David Seeger, confectioner, Philadelphia for seven years & seventeen days, to have forty two weeks schooling & at the end of her term two complete suits clothes, one to be new. Consideration = $38.50.

Christian Frederick Knapp with consent of Peter Christian, to William Raster, innkeeper, Philadelphia, for three years & six months, to have four quarters half day schooling & at the end of her term two complete suits of clothes, one to be new. Consideration = $77.00.

64

Anna Dorothea Schenzin to Jacob Steinmetz, gentleman Penn township Philadelphia county for two years & six months, to have two complete suits of clothes at the end of her term, one thereof to be new, to be free at any time within one month if her freight is repaid by her brother within that time. Consideration = $81.50.

Charles Beckhart with consent of Peter Christian, to Hezekiah Buzley & Company for three years, to have six weeks schooling, & at the end of the term two complete suits of clothes, one to be new. Consideration = $81.50.

Ludwig Frederick Braun with consent of Peter Christian, to Samuel Badger, alderman, Philadelphia for three years, to have eighteen weeks schooling, & at the end of the term two complete suits of clothes, one to be new. Consideration = $77.00.

September 18, 1818

Catharina Schafflin with consent of Peter Christian, to Daniel Rubican innkeeper, Philadelphia, for three years, to have one quarter schooling, & at the end of her term two complete suits of clothes, one to be new. Consideration = $77.00.

Barbara Sailerin to William Wray, storekeeper, Philadelphia, for two years to have at the end of the term two complete suits of clothes, one to be new. Consideration = $57.20.

Conrad Kramer with consent of Charles F. Keilig, to Christian G. Smith for three years & six months, to have twelve weeks schooling, & at the end of the term two complete suits of clothes, one to be new. Consideration = $81.50.

September 19, 1818

Jacob Harrer with consent of Jacob Weinman, to Jeremiah Warden Junior merchant Penn township Philadelphia county, for three years to have six weeks schooling & at the end of the term two complete suits of clothes, one to be new. Consideration = $80.00.

Christina Sophia Weinman with her father's consent, to the above Jeremiah Warden for three years, to have fifteen weeks schooling, & at the end of the term two complete suits of clothes, one to be new. Consideration = $80.00.

Christina Gaugerin with consent of her mother, to Amos Hollohan, innkeeper, Philadelphia for three years, to have nine weeks schooling. And at the end of the term two complete suits of clothes, one thereof to be new. Consideration = $80.00.

September 21, 1818

John George Wolf with consent of Jacob Wolf, to Antonio Glz. da Cruz Philadelphia gentleman, for two years, to have twelve weeks schooling & at the end of the term two complete suits of clothes, one to be new. Consideration = $60.00.

Scharlotta Fromeyer to David Woelpper victualer, Penn township for three years, to have at the end of the term two complete suits of clothes, one to be new & twenty dollars. Consideration = $77.30.

Carolina Fromeyer to Thomas Bradley, grazier, Passyunk township Philadelphia county for three years to have at the end of the term two complete suits of clothes, one to be new & twenty dollars. Consideration = $77.30.

Christina Philipina Diesenbach to Margaret Witman, widow Philadelphia for four years, to have twelve weeks schooling & at the end of the term two complete suits of clothes, one to be new & fifteen dollars. Consideration = $77.30.

Jacob Frederick Burger & wife Catharina to Charles Mercier of Philadelphia confectioner they being willing to go to the District of Columbia, for three years, to have at the end of the term two complete suits of clothes, one thereof to be new & sixty dollars. Consideration = $115.00.

Jacob Frederick Burger & wife at the same time assigned to Beeler of Alexandria District of Columbia for the remainder of their indenture as above recorded. Consideration = $115.00.

Frederick Gochler to Adam Breish, farmer of Germantown township, for nine months, at the end of the term to have two complete suits of clothes one to be new. Consideration = $35.00.

September 22, 1818

John Jacob Haberstroh to Charles Ellet of Bristol township Bucks county, farmer, for three years, to have at the end of the term two complete suits of clothes & twenty dollars. Consideration = $57.25.

Johan Georg Lammbach with his father's consent to go to North Carolina to Alexander Graham merchant of Charlotte Mecklenburg county, for twelve years & six months, to be taught the art & mistery of a hatter, to have six weeks schooling for every year of his servitude & at the end of the term two complete suits of clothes, one thereof to be new. Consideration = $40.00.

George Frederick Lammbach with his father's consent to the above Alexander Graham for eleven years & nineteen days, to have at the end of the term two complete suits of clothes, one thereof to be new, also to have during his servitude six weeks schooling for every year. Consideration = $40.00.

Jacob Frederick Sporr with the consent of Jacob Chur to go to Deleware, to John Walke, farmer of Mill Creek hundred New Castle county for three years, to have eighteen weeks schooling & at the end of the term two complete suits of clothes, one thereof to be new. Consideration = $77.00.

Anna Dorothea Schenzin haveing repaid her freight by her brother, her indenture recorded page 64 is by consent of parties canseled & made void.

John Jacob Weimer to Joseph Paul, miller of Germantown township Philadelphia county for three years, to have at the end of the term two complete suits of clothes, one thereof to be new. Consideration = $81.50.

Anna Dorothea Schenzin to Catharine Esslin of Philadelphia widow for three years to have at the end of the term two complete suits of clothes one thereof to be new. Consideration = $81.50.

September 23, 1818

Jacob Frederick Buchtel with consent of Jacob Gilbert, to Christian Scheide of the Northern Liberties baker, for two years & six months, to have fifteen weeks schooling, and at the end of the term two complete suits of clothes, one thereof to be new. Consideration = $41.30.

Charles Frederick Philip Behler with the consent of Jacob Gilbert, to Abraham Kerns of Bedford Pennsylvania merchant for four years, to have to have six weeks schooling, and at the end of the term two complete suits of clothes, one thereof to be new. Consideration = $81.50.

September 24, 1818

Regina Bogerin with her father's consent, to John Dickson of Philadelphia grocer, for three years, to have twelve weeks schooling & at the end of the term two complete suits of clothes, one thereof to be new. Consideration = $80.00.

September 25, 1818

David Melchier Wittel to Jacob Leidy of Francony township Montgomery county, farmer, for three years, to have customary freedoms. Consideration = $81.50.

Frederick Gengenbach with consent of Peter Christian, willing to go to New Jersey to Samuel & Henry Eckel, tanners of Hopewell township Cumberland county for four years, to have twelve weeks schooling & at the end of the term two complete suits of clothes, one thereof to be new. Consideration = $81.50.

September 26, 1818

Christian Ludwig Held to Dietrich Fegenbush of the Northern Liberties, cordwainer, for two years & five months, to have at the end of the term two complete suits of clothes one thereof to be new. Consideration = $53.50.

Johannes Bender willing to go to New Jersey to David Livezey of Evesham township Burlington county for three years, to have at the end of the term two complete suits of clothes, one thereof to be new. Consideration = $81.50.

Magdalena Achenbach with consent of her father, to John Bioren of Philadelphia bookseller for six years, to have at the end of the term two complete suits of clothes, one thereof to be new, to have during the term twelve weeks schooling. Consideration = $100.00.

Wilhelm Treftz to Adam Haydt of Penn township victualar, for three years to have at the end of the term fifty five dollars. Consideration = $44.50.

John Schenck willing to go to North Carolina, to James Cowan, farmer, of Charlotte Meclenburg county, for three years after his arrival at Charlotte, to have at the end of the term two complete suits of clothes, one thereof to be new. Consideration = $81.50.

Andrew Dohinden willing as above, to James Cowan, for three years after his arrival as above, to have at the end of the term the same freedoms. Consideration = $81.50.

Christian Fichtner willing as above, to James Cowan for four years after arrival at Charlotte, to have at the end of the term the same freedoms. Consideration = $81.50.

John Jacob Mayer with his father's consent to go as above to James Cowan for fourteen years & seven months, to have one quarter schooling for every year of his servitude & at the end of the term freedoms as above. Consideration = $40.75.

Jacob Mayer with consent of his father to go as above to James Cowan for nine years & 26 days to have six weeks schooling for every year of his servitude & at the end of the term to have freedom suits as above. Consideration = $61.12.

Francis J. Lehman willing to go to North Carolina, to Wilson & Cowan of Charlotte for two years & three months to have at the end of term freedom suits as above. Consideration = $81.50.

John Dorster willing as above, to William J. Wilson merchant of Meclenburg for three years after his arrival at Charlotte, to have at the end of term freedom suits as above. Consideration = $81.50.

Jacob Berhart willing as above to William J. Wilson, for three years after arrival as above to have at the end of term same freedom suits as above. Consideration = $81.50.

September 28, 1818

Johan George Straub to Daniel Moyer farmer of Maxtany township Berks county for three years to have at the end of his term two complete suits of clothes, one thereof to be new & thirty nine dollars. Consideration = $77.30.

September 29, 1818

Anthony Hohn willing to go to Virginia, to Mark Richard of Philadelphia merchant for three years to have in lieu of cloathing forty dollars per annum & if he conducts himself well pocket mony per week & if convenient to the master some schooling & at the end of the term one complete suit of new clothes. Consideration = $81.50.

Anthony Hohn at the same time assigned to Richard F. Hannon, merchant of Petersburg Virginia for the remainder of his indenture as above recorded. Consideration = $81.50.

Johan Martin Brennenstuhl willing to go to Virginia, to Mark Richards with consent of Peter Christian, for three years to have twelve weeks schooling & at the end of the term two complete suits of clothes, one to be new. Consideration = $81.50.

Johan Martin Brennenstuhl at the same time assigned to the above Richard F. Hannon for the remainder of his indenture as above recorded. Consideration = $81.50.

Emanuel Fegert & wife Barbara willing to go to Alabama teritory to Francis C. Clopper merchant of Philadelphia for three years, to have at the end of the term each two complete suits of clothes, one thereof to be new. Their child Maria Margareta to be fed & clothed gratis, & be free with the parents. And the said Emanuel to be paid one hundred & twenty one dollars 60 cents with legal interest whenever he shall demand the same. Consideration = $64.10.

John Michael Fegert with his father's consent to go to the Alabama territory to Francis C. Clopper for three years to have during his servitude eighteen weeks schooling & at the end of the term clothes as above. Consideration = $16.13.

Philipina Regina Fegert with her father's consent to go as above, to Francis C. Clopper for three years, to have during her servitude eighteen weeks schooling & at the end of the term clothes as above. Consideration = $16.13.

John Martin Stahl & wife Susanna Catharina willing as above, to Francis C. Clopper for three years, to have at the end of the term clothes as above, their children Gottlebin & Frederick to be fed & clothed gratis & be free with the parents. And the said John Martin to be paid one hundred & sixty dollars with legal interest whenever he shall demand the same. Consideration = $64.00.

John Gottlieb Stahl willing as above, to Francis C. Clopper for three years to have at the end of the term clothes as above. Consideration = $32.00.

Catharina Stahl with her father's consent to go as above, to Francis C. Clopper for three years, to have eighteen weeks schooling & at the end of the term clothes as above. Consideration = $16.00.

Martin Stahl with his father's consent as above, to Francis C. Clopper for three years, to have eighteen weeks schooling & at the end of the term clothes as above. Consideration = $16.00.

Jacob Beck willing as above, to Francis C. Clopper for three years to have at the end of term clothes as above. Consideration = $77.25.

Johannes Trautwein willing as above, to Francis C. Clopper for three years, to have at the end of term clothes as above. Consideration = $77.25.

Jacob Frederick Konig willing as above, to Francis C. Clopper for three years, to have at the end of term clothes as above. Consideration = $77.25.

Jacob Frederick Konig Junior willing as above, to Francis C. Clopper for three years to have at the end of term clothes as above. Consideration = $77.25.

John Gottlieb Neubold willing as above with consent of George Abel to Francis C. Clopper for three years, to have eighteen weeks schooling & at end of term clothes as above. Consideration = $77.25.

Jacob Straub willing & with consent as above to Francis C. Clopper for three years, to have six weeks schooling & be paid by his master twenty dollars with interest whenever he shall demand and the same at the end of the term to have clothes as above. Consideration = $37.25.

Jacob Eitel willing & with consent as above to Francis C. Clopper for three years to have twelve weeks schooling & at the end of his term clothes as above. Consideration = $77.25.

Frederick Hassenmeier willing as above to Francis C. Clopper for three years, to have at the end of term clothes as above. Consideration = $77.25.

Gottlieb Frederick Huber willing as above to Francis C. Clopper for three years, to have at the end of term clothes as above & one hundred dollars. Consideration = $69.25.

Johan Jacob Schaubel willing as above to Francis C. Clopper for three years, to have at the end of term clothes as above. Consideration = $77.25.

Jacob Schmidt & wife Maria Elisabetha willing as above to Francis C. Clopper for three years, to have at the end of term each clothes as above. Consideration = $140.00.

Johannes Ritter willing as above to Francis C. Clopper for three years, to have at the end of term clothes as above. Consideration = $70.00.

Anton Schuster & wife Catharina willing as above to Francis C. Clopper for three years, & Anton to be paid forty dollars with interest whenever he demands the same, & at the end of the term to have each clothes as above, their Christina to be fed & clothed & to be free with the parents. Consideration = $140.00.

Johan David Geisser willing as above to Francis C. Clopper for three years to have at the end clothes as above & twenty five dollars. Consideration = $70.00.

September 30, 1818

Christian Daniel Nill to Daniel Dreibelbis, farmer of Richmond township Berks county for two years & six months, to have at the end of his term two complete suits of clothes, one thereof to be new. Consideration = $81.50.

October 1, 1818

Casper Schmidt to John Hollman, clerk of Philadelphia for three years, to have at the end of the term two complete suits of clothes, one thereof to be new. Consideration = $81.50.

Casper Schmidt at the same time transfered to Louisa McIlhany widow of Penn township to serve her or assigns the remainder of his indenture above recorded. Consideration = $81.50.

Charles William Weyhemerger to John Adam Lentner of Philadelphia soapboiler, for three years, to have at the end of his term two complete suits of clothes, one thereof to be new. Consideration = $76.25.

Henrich Schmidt willing to go to the Alabama teritory, to James Brown gentleman of Nashville Tennesee, for three years & six months after his arrival at Hunts Ville Alabama, to have at the end of his term two complete suits of clothes, one thereof to be new. Consideration = $78.00.

Frederick Rapp willing as above to James Brown, for three years & six months after arrival as above, at the end of his term to have clothes as above. Consideration = $78.00.

Johan Samuel Mardini willing as above to James Brown, for three years & six months after arrival as above, at the end of his term to have clothes as above. Consideration = $78.00.

Johannes Schumacher willing as above to James Brown, for three years & six months after arrival as above, at the end of his term to have clothes as above. Consideration = $78.00.

Johannes Miller willing as above to James Brown for three years & six months, after arrival as above, at the end of his term to have clothes as above. Consideration = $78.00.

Friderich Wasman willing as above to James Brown, for three years & six months after arrival as above, at the end of his term to have clothes as above. Consideration = $78.00.

Fransz Spietzl willing as above to James Brown for three years & six months after arrival as above, at the end of his term to have clothes as above. Consideration = $78.00.

Johan Frederick Peisch willing as above to James Brown, for three years & six months after arrival as above, at the end of his term to have clothes as above. Consideration = $78.00.

October 2, 1818

Philip Muller willing & with consent of Peter Christian to go to the Alabama teritory to Francis C. Clopper of Philadelphia merchant for three years, to have eighteen weeks schooling, & at the end of the term two complete suits of clothes one thereof to be new. Consideration = $70.00.

Johan Adam Wolf willing & with consent as above to Francis C. Clopper for three years, to have at the end of the term clothes as above & during the servitude eighteen weeks schooling. Consideration = $70.00.

Johan Jacob Rausch willing as above to Francis C. Clopper for three years to have at the end of the term clothes as above. Consideration = $70.00.

Christian Frederich Kienlen willing as above and with consent of Peter Christian to Francis C. Clopper for three years, to have eighteen weeks schooling & at the end of the term clothes as above. Consideration = $70.00.

October 3, 1818

Christian Frederich Kienlen assigned to Charles G. Braehm of Baltimore confectioner to serve him the remainder of his indenture as above recorded. Consideration = $70.00.

Johan Casper Urban & wife Catharina willing as above to Francis C. Clopper for three years, to have at the end of their term each clothes as above. Consideration = $140.00.

Eva Rosina Mayer with her father's consent to Jacob Epler innkeeper of Bern township Berks county for nine years, to have fifty four weeks schooling & at the end of her term two complete suits of clothes, one thereof to be new. Consideration = $50.00.

Jacob Falkenecker willing to go to New Jersey to Benjamin B. Cooper farmer of New Jersey to have at the end of his term two complete suits of clothes, one thereof to be new & eleven dollars. The term of service to be three years. Consideration = $81.50.

October 6, 1818

John George Greder to David Kreeble farmer of Lower Sulford township Montgomery county for two years & six months, to have at the end of the term two complete suits of clothes, one thereof to be new. Consideration = $60.00.

October 8, 1818

Johannes Mayer & Anna Maria his wife, also their son Wilhelm, to L. H. Voule of Philadelphia merchant for three years, to have each at the end of the their term two complete suits of clothes, one of each to be new, Wilhelm to have during his servitude eighteen weeks schooling. And the infant child Gottlieb to be fed & clothed gratis & be free with the parents. And this indenture to be null & void whenever the passage mony is paid to their master. Consideration = $176.89.

Anna Elisabeth Roy to John Land of Philadelphia hatter for three years & three months from 10th ultimate, to have at the end of the term two complete suits of clothes, one thereof to be new. Consideration = $81.50.

October 10, 1818

Carolina Graff assigned by James Tatham to John Machee of the Northern Liberties upholsterer to serve him the remainder of her indenture recorded page 51. Consideration = $25.00.

October 12, 1818

Catharina Schaufelin to John Hollman clerk of Philadelphia for three years from 12th ultimate to have at the end of her term two complete suits of clothes, one to be new. Consideration = $72.00.

Catharina Schaufelin at the same time assigned to Louisa McIlhany gentlewoman of Penn township to serve her the remainder of her indenture as recorded page 71. Consideration = $72.00.

October 14, 1818

Johannes Bailinger to E. W. Hoskin of Philadelphia merchant for three years to have at the end of his term two complete suits of clothes, one thereof to be new. The servant to be at liberty to seek a place of his own choice & if he shall at any time within one year pay his master the amount of his freight or give approved security for the payment of the same within that time, then this indenture to be null and void. Consideration = $81.50.

October 16, 1818

Rosina Catharina Eberhard to William F. Wolf of Southwark, baker, for one year, her children to be fed & clothed gratis & be free with the mother. Consideration = valuable.

October 17, 1818

Julianna Weisenberger with her father's consent to Isaac Wampole of Philadelphia conveyancer, for seven years & four months, to have six weeks schooling for every year of her term, & at the end thereof two complete suits of clothes one thereof to be new. Consideration = $50.00.

Genevesa Weisenberger, with her father's consent, to Alexander Caldwell of Philadelphia tavernkeeper for four years, to have six weeks schooling, & at the end of her term two complete suits of clothes, one thereof to be new. Consideration = $126.00.

Therese Weisenberger, with her father's consent, to the above Alexander Caldwell for five years, to have twelve weeks schooling, and at the end of her two complete suits of clothes, one thereof to be new. Consideration = $126.00.

Magdelena Wagnerin to the above Alexander Caldwell for three years to have at the end of the term two complete suits of clothes, one thereof to be new. Consideration = $60.00.

Magdelena Wagnerin at the same time assigned to David Starrett of Cumberland county, farmer, to serve him the remainder of her indenture as above recorded. Consideration = $60.00.

Catharina Burkhart to William B. Osman of the Northern Liberties Philadelphia county, mariner, for four years, to have at the end of the term two complete suits of clothes, one thereof to be new. Consideration = $100.50.

Christian Weld with consent of Samuel Wentz & willing to go to New Jersey to Joseph Groff of Woolwich township Gloucester county, farmer, for four years, to have twenty four weeks schooling, and at the end of the term two complete suits of clothes one thereof to be new. Consideration = $30.50.

Catharina Brennin with her father's consent to Abraham Stein of Philadelphia dealer in watches, to have six weeks schooling & at the end of the term two complete suits of clothes, one thereof to be new. The term of her servitude to be three years & six months. Consideration = $70.50.

Anthony Kaiser with consent of his mother to Charles L. Smith of Philadelphia grocer, for ten years & seven months, to have six weeks schooling for every year of his term & at the end thereof two complete suits of clothes one thereof to be new. Consideration = $47.33.

Theresa Kaiserin with her mother's consent, to Isaac Wampole of Philadelphia conveyancer, for three years, to have six weeks schooling, and at the end of the term two complete suits of clothes, one thereof to be new. Consideration = $47.33.

Martin Kisz to Edward Duffield of Moreland township Philadelphia county farmer, for three years, to have at the end of the term two complete suits of clothes, one thereof to be new. Consideration = $70.50.

Marianna Kaiserin with consent of her mother, to Jacob Sulger Junior of Philadelphia merchant, for three years & two months, to have eighteen weeks schooling & at the end of the term two complete suits of clothes, one thereof to be new. Consideration = $47.33.

John George Geiser with consent of his father, to Joseph Taylor of Philadelphia innkeeper, for seven years & six months, to have six weeks schooling for every year of his term & at the end thereof two complete suits of clothes, one whereof to be new. Consideration = $60.50.

Catharina Geiser with her father's consent, to the above Joseph Taylor for six years & two months, to have six weeks schooling for every year of the term & at the end thereof two complete suits of clothes, one whereof to be new. Consideration = $60.50.

October 19, 1818

Agatha Burkhart with consent of her father, to Jacob S. Otto of Philadelphia merchant for six years eight months & eight days, to have six weeks schooling for every year of her term & at the end thereof two complete suits of clothes one whereof to be new. Consideration = $50.50.

Johan Georg Mattmuller & wife Maria to William McClellan Junior of the Borough of Gettysburg Adams county, merchant, for two years & six months to have at the end of the term two complete suits each, one thereof to be new. Consideration = $120.00.

Maria Mattmuller Junior with consent of her father, to the above William McClellan for four years & three months, to have six weeks schooling for every year of her term, & at the end thereof two complete suits of clothes one thereof to be new. Consideration = $30.00.

John George Mattmuller Junior with his father's consent to the above William McClellan, to have six weeks schooling for every year of his term & at the end thereof to have two complete suits of clothes, one thereof to be new and twenty dollars, the term of service nine years. Consideration = $20.50.

Maria Barbara Mattmuller with her father's consent to the above William McClellan, for eight years & three months, to have six weeks schooling for every year of her term & at the end thereof two complete suits of clothes, one thereof to be new, & ten dollars. Consideration = $22.00.

Johan George Mattmuller & wife Maria at the same time assigned to Joseph Thornton of Brownsville, Fayette county, farmer, to serve him the indenture as above recorded on page 73. Consideration = $120.00.

Maria Mattmuller Junior at the same time assigned to the above Joseph Thornton to serve him her indenture as recorded page 73. Consideration = $30.00.

John George Mattmuller Junior at the same time assigned to the above Joseph Thornton to serve him the indenture as above recorded. Consideration = $30.00.

Maria Barbara Mattmuller at the same time assigned to the above Joseph Thornton to serve him her indenture as above recorded. Consideration = $22.00.

Maria Anna Kapp with consent of her father, to James Elliott of Philadelphia currier, for four years & nine months, to have six weeks schooling for every year of the term & at the end thereof two complete suits of clothes, one whereof to be new. Consideration = $50.50.

John Klein with consent of Samuel Wentz, to James S. Ewing of Philadelphia apothocary, to have six weeks schooling for each year of the term, and at the end thereof two complete suits of clothes, one whereof to be new & sixty dollars. The term of servitude to be nine years. Consideration = valuable.

Christian Ott with consent of his wife, to Clement Lee Brady of Philadelphia coachmaker, for two years, his master to pay him one dollar per weeks as the same shall come due, in lieu of apparel. Consideration = $70.00.

Maria Blumin to Thomas Fraley of Oxford township Philadelphia county farmer, for three years, to have at the end of her term two complete suits of clothes one thereof to be new, her son Christian to be fed & clothed gratis, & be free with the the the mother & to have eighteen weeks schooling during the term. Consideration = $60.00.

Magdalena Brennin to Dietrich Dishong of Earl township Lancaster county, storekeeper, for two years & six months, to have at the end of the term two complete suits of clothes, one thereof to be new. Consideration = $60.50.

Frederick Brenn with his father's consent, to William Riehle of Philadelphia tanner, for seven years three months & nineteen days, to have six weeks schooling for each year of the term, & at the end thereof two complete suits of clothes, one thereof to be new. Consideration = $40.50.

Marianna Sutter with consent of her father, to Samuel S. Ewing of Philadelphia apothacary, for three years, to have six weeks schooling, and at the end of the term two complete suits of clothes, one thereof to be new. Consideration = $60.50.

October 20, 1818

Theresa Frederich to George Poppel of Southwark, innkeeper, for three years & six months, to have at the end of the term two complete suits of clothes one whereof to be new. Consideration = $90.75.

Samuel Kople with his father's consent, to Thomas B. Darrach of Philadelphia hatter, for ten years & six months, to have six weeks schooling for each year of the term & at the end thereof two complete suits of clothes, one whereof to be new. Consideration = $50.50.

Maria Barbara Jauchin to Joseph Langer of Philadelphia botler, for three years, to have at the end of the term two complete suits of clothes, one whereof to be new, & ten dollars. Consideration = $80.00.

Elias Kobele with consent of his father, to Benjamin Bear of Conastoga township Lancaster county, farmer, for three years & six months, to have six weeks schooling, & at the end of the term two complete suits of clothes one whereof to be new. Consideration = $90.50.

October 21, 1818

Elisabeth Schneider with consent of her father, to George D. Henck of the Northern Liberties Philadelphia county, baker, to have six weeks schooling for each year of the term, & at the end thereof two complete suits of clothes, one thereof to be new, term of servitude eight years. Consideration = $40.00.

Joseph Bauman & his wife Josepha to David Lightfoot, of Pikeland township Chester county, farmer, for three years, to have at the end of the term each two complete suits of clothes, one of which to be new, their infant to be fed & clothed gratis & be free with the parents. Consideration = $130.00.

Mathias Kobele willing to go to Virginia with his father's consent, to Reeve Lewis of Philadelphia merchant for three years, to have twelve weeks schooling, & at the end of the term two complete suits of clothes, one whereof to be new. Consideration = $70.50.

October 22, 1818

Mathias Kobele assigned to Samuel Forrer of Shenandoah county State of Virginia, farmer, to serve him or assigns the remainder of his indenture as recorded on page 75. Consideration = $70.50.

Martin Kobele willing & with his father's consent to go to Virginia to Reeve Lewis of Philadelphia merchant for five years, to have six weeks schooling for every year of the term, & at the end thereof two complete suits of clothes, one whereof to be new. Consideration = $70.50.

Martin Kobele at the same time assigned to the above Samuel Forrer to serve him or assigns the indenture as above recorded. Consideration = $70.50.

Jacob Kammerle to John Bornman of the Northern Liberties victuler, for three years from 13th ultimate, to have at the end of the term two complete suits of clothes, one whereof to be new & thirty dollars, or fifty dollars at the option of the servant. Consideration = $81.50.

Anna Maria Ott with consent of her husband, to James Fassitt of Philadelphia merchant, for two years, to have at the end of the term two complete suits of clothes, one whereof to be new. And should the servant during the term of her servitude have an offspring then she to serve her master six months longer. Consideration = $55.00.

October 23, 1818

Johan Georg Burgle to John Planck of the Northern Liberties Philadelphia county cooper, for three years & six months, to have at the end of the term two complete suits of clothes, one thereof to be new. Consideration = $70.50.

Johan Friderich with his mother's consent, to the above John Planck for five years one month & ten days, to have six weeks schooling for each year of his term, & at the end thereof two complete suits of clothes, one whereof to be new. Consideration = $70.50.

October 26, 1818

Johan Marlin Konig assigned by Luther Franck to John Mingle of Philadelphia blacksmith, to serve him or assigns the remainder of his indenture recorded Book B, page 202. Consideration = $50.00.

Rosanna Schickin to Alexander Ferguson of Philadelphia merchant for three years, to have at the end of the term two complete suits of clothes one thereof to be new. Consideration = $80.00.

Fredericka Hoffman with her father's consent to Joseph Pyle of Philadelphia storekeeper, for six years, to have thirty weeks schooling, & at the end of the term two complete suits of clothes, one of which to be new. And if she conducts herself well to have the last year of her term relinquished to her by her master. Consideration = $80.00.

October 27, 1818

Johanna Hees to George Nagle of the Northern Liberties, Philadelphia county, storekeeper, for three years, to have no freedoms. Consideration = $99.15.

Pius Zwisele to Ruff & Fisher of Philadelphia, painters & glazers, for three years, to have ten dollars per month paid him by his master, out of which the servant to repay his masters his passage money & provide his own clothing, the servant to have during the term eighteen weeks schooling. Consideration = $85.31.

Anna Maria Schanbacher with consent of George Willig Senior, to William Milnor Junior of Philadelphia attorney at law for four years one month & ten days, to have three months schooling, & at the end of the term two complete suits of clothes, one of which to be new. Consideration = $102.79.

October 28, 1818

Johan Georg Meier with consent of his wife to Jacob Musser of Buffalo township Union county, farmer, for one year & nine months, the servant to be free at any time if he shall give the master a reasonable compensation for the remainder of his term. Consideration = $61.92.

Margareta Meier with consent of her husband, to the above Jacob Musser for one year & nine months, to be free at any time upon the above conditions. Consideration = $61.92.

Dothothea Wagnerin with consent of Jacob Emhardt, to Peter Lex of Philadelphia merchant for three years, to have fifteen weeks schooling & at the end of the term two complete suits of clothes, one whereof to be new. Consideration = $80.00.

Melchier Kraus willing to go to New Jersey, to Joshua Folwell of Springfield township Burlington county, farmer, for three years & six months, to have at the end of the term two complete suits of clothes, one whereof to be new. And if he is honest & faithful to have six months of his time of servitude relinquished by his master. Consideration = $102.85.

October 29, 1818

Fransz Joseph Weber to John Benethum of Heidelberg township, Berks county, farmer, for three years & three months, to be taught the art trade & mistery of a tanner. And give him at the end of the term ten dollars. Consideration = $70.50.

78

Friderika Kunzler to Jacob Boller of Philadelphia merchant for four years & six months, to have at the end of the term two complete suits of clothes, one of which to be new. And in case of the repayment of $9.10 mentioned in the receipt for charges made by the Sweedish Government being repaid, then the servant to serve only four years. Consideration = $117.26.

Christianna Catharina Palmer to John King of Chambergsburg, merchant for three years, to have at the end of the term two complete suits of clothes one whereof to be new. Consideration = $80.00.

Jacob Wilhelm Palmer with his mother's consent, to the above John King for twelve years eight months & fifteen days, to have six weeks schooling for each year of his term & be taught the art of a merchant or a tanner, to have at the end of the term two complete suits of clothes, one whereof to be new. Consideration = $20.00.

October 30, 1818

Catharina Schanbacher, willing to go to New Jersey, to John Aelurns of New Hanover township Burlington county storekeeper for four years, to have at the end of the term two complete suits of clothes, one of which to be new. Consideration = $102.79.

Johan Israel Hees with consent of his father, to Henry Volkner Philadelphia sheetiron worker, for five years & six months, to have six weeks schooling for each year of the term, to be taught the art trade & mistery of a stove finisher, & at the end of the term to have two complete suits of clothes, one of which to be new, or thirty dollars, at the option of the servant. Consideration = $99.15.

Johan Friderich Jenewein willing to go to the Alabama teritory, to James Brown of Nashville Tennesee, gentleman, for three years & five months from his arrival in Alabama teritory, to have at the end of the term two complete suits of clothes one whereof to be new, the servant is not bound to go out of the above teritory. Consideration = $60.00.

Johan Gold willing to go to Alabama territory, with consent of his wife, to the above James Brown, for three years & five months from his arrival as above, to have at the end of the term clothes as above, and not bound to go out of Alabama territory. Consideration = $60.00.

Elisabetha Gold willing as above with her husband's consent, to the above James Brown for three years & five months from arrival as above, to have at the end of the term clothes as above, not bound to go out of Alabama territory. Consideration = $60.00.

Carl Zimmerman willing as above, to the above James Brown for three years & five months from arrival as above, to have at the end of the term clothes as above, not bound to go out of Alabama territory. Consideration = $60.00.

Jacob Fohr willing as above, to the above James Brown for three years & five months after arrival as above, to have at the end of the term clothes as above, & not bound to go out of said teritory. Consideration = $60.00.

Johan Beck with his wife's consent, willing as above, to the above James Brown for three years & five months after arrival as above, to have at the end of the term clothes as above, & not bound to go out of said teritory. Consideration = $60.00.

Magdalena Beck with her husband's consent, willing as above, to the above James Brown for three years & five months after arrival as above, to have at the end of the term clothes as above, & not bound to go out of said territory. Consideration = $60.00.

Lorensz Beck with his father's consent, willing as above to said James Brown for three years & five months after arrival as above, to have twelve weeks schooling & at the end of the term clothes as above, & not bound to go out of said teritory. Consideration = $60.00.

Johan Wurtzburger with his wife's consent willing as above, to said James Brown for three years & five months after arrival as above, his infant to be fed & clothed gratis & be free with the parent, the servant at the end of the term to have clothes as above & is not bound to go out of said teritory. Consideration = $60.00.

Maria Wurtzburger with her husband's consent, willing as above to said James Brown for three years & five months after arrival as above, her infant to be fed & clothed gratis & be free with the parent, the servant to have at the end of the term clothes as above & is not bound to go out of said teritory. Consideration = $60.00.

Fransz Anton Klohr willing as above to said James Brown for three years & five months after arrival as above, to have at the end of the term clothes as above & is not bound to go out of said teritory. Consideration = $60.00.

Anton Freytag with consent of his wife, willing as above to said James Brown for three years & five months after arrival as above, to have at the end of the term clothes as above, his infant to be fed & clothed gratis & be free with the parent, not bound to go out of said teritory. Consideration = $60.00.

Anna Maria Freytag with consent of her husband, willing as above to said James Brown for three years & five months after arrival as above, to have at the end of the term clothes as above, her infant to be fed & clothed gratis & be free with the parent, & not bound to go out of said teritory. Consideration = $60.00.

Sebastian Hog willing as above, to said James Brown for three years & five months after arrival as above, to have at the end of the term clothes as above & is not bound to go out of said teritory. Consideration = $60.00.

Christian Scherrer willing as above, to said James Brown for three years & five months after arrival as above, to have at the end of the term clothes as above, & not bound to go out of said teritory. Consideration = $60.00.

Ferdinand Bengle willing as above, to said James Brown for three years & five months after arrival as above, to have at the end of the term clothes as above & is not bound to go out of said teritory. Consideration = $60.00.

John Hell with consent of his wife & willing as above to said James Brown for three years & five months after arrival as above, to have at the end of the term clothes as above & not bound to go out of said teritory, his infant to be fed & clothed gratis & be free with the parent. Consideration = $60.00.

Seolastico Hell with consent of her husband & willing as above to said James Brown for three years & five months from arrival as above, to have at the end of the term clothes as above & not bound to go out of said territory, her infant to be fed & clothed gratis & be free with the parent. Consideration = $60.00.

Jacob Kopp with consent of his wife & willing as above to said James Brown for three years & five months from arrival as above, to have at the end of the term clothes as above & not bound to go out of said teritory. Consideration = $60.00.

Agatha Kopp with consent of her husband & willing as above, to said James Brown for three years & five months after arrival as above, to have at the end of the term clothes as above & not bound to go out of said teritory. Consideration = $15.00.

Joseph Geiser with consent of his wife & willing as above to said James Brown for three years & five months from arrival as above, to have at the end of the term clothes as above & not bound to go out of said teritory, his infant to be fed & clothed gratis & be free with the parent. Consideration = $60.00.

Carolina Geiser with consent of her husband & willing as above to said James Brown for three years & five months after arrival as above, to have at the end of the term clothes as above & not bound to go out of said territory, her infant to be fed & clothed gratis & be free with the parent. Consideration = $60.00.

Christianna Hees with consent of her father, to Jacob F. Riley of Philadelphia baker, for three years, to have six weeks schooling. Consideration = $99.15.

Gottfried Hees with consent of his father, to Tobias Riley of Philadelphia baker, for eight years & four months, to have six weeks schooling for each year of the term & to be taught the art trade & mistery of a baker, to have at the end of the term two complete suits of clothes, one whereof to be new. Consideration = $50.17.

October 31, 1818

Tobias Brenn & his wife Sarah willing to go to Maryland, to Emalls Martin Junior of Talbot county Eastern Shore Maryland farmer, for four years, to have at the end of the term two complete suits of clothes, one of each to be new. Consideration = $131.00.

November 2, 1818

Johan Georg Ott with consent of his father, to George Willig of Philadelphia storekeeper for twelve years & eleven months, to have six weeks schooling for each year of the term & at the end thereof two complete suits of clothes, one of which to be new. Consideration = $10.00.

Frederick Weiss assigned by George Steiner to Henry Goldenpenny of Philadelphia baker, to serve him or assigned the remainder of his indenture recorded page 36. Consideration = $55.00.

November 3, 1818

Johannes Muhlhauser with his father's consent, to William Bishop of Edgemont township Deleware county, farmer, for ten years, to have six weeks of schooling for each year of the term & at the end thereof two complete suits of clothes, one of which to be new. Consideration = $85.00.

Christianna Kunzler to Rachel Steinmetz of Penn township Philadelphia county, widow, for four years, to have at the end of her term two complete suits of clothes, one of which to be new. Consideration = $105.69.

Johannes Koch to William Means of Townday township Bradford county farmer, for three years & three months, to have at the end of their term two complete suits of clothes, one of which to be new. Consideration = $90.79.

Anna Maria Koch to the above William Means for three years & three months, to have at the end of the term two complete suits of clothes one of which to be new. Consideration = $90.79.

Catharina Waiblin with consent of her stepfather, to William Wallace of Philadelphia storekeeper for four years, to give her occational oppertunity of working at the Bonnet making, & at the end of the term two complete suits of clothes, one whereof to be new. Consideration = $101.19.

November 4, 1818

Barbara Fiedler with consent of her father, to Christlieb Bartling of the Northern Liberties Philadelphia county gentleman for seven years & nine months to have six weeks schooling for each year of her term & at the end thereof two complete suits of clothes, one of which to be new. Consideration = $70.00.

Dorothea Hoffman with consent of her father, to Anthony Antelo of Philadelphia mariner for seven years, to have six weeks schooling for each year of the term & at the end thereof two complete suits of clothes, one of which to be new. Consideration = $61.19.

Joseph Barthema & wife Kresen, to Samuel Emery of Philadelphia shipbroker for three years, to have at the end of the term two complete suits of clothes each, one of each to be new, their infant to be fed & clothed gratis & be free with the parent. Consideration = $131.00.

November 6, 1818

Jacob Gaupp willing to go to Virginia, to Nathaniel Chauncey of Philadelphia merchant for three years, to have at the end of the term two complete suits of clothes, one of which to be new. Consideration = $91.19.

Jacob Gaupp at the same time assigned to Archibald Baugh esquire of Petersburg Virginia to serve him or assigned the remainder of his indenture as above recorded. Consideration = $91.19.

Daniel Linsenmeier willing to go to Deleware State, to Hugh Harbson of Philadelphia grocer for three years & six months, to have six weeks schooling & at the end of the term two complete suits of clothes, one thereof to be new. Consideration = $91.19.

Daniel Linsenmeier at the same time assigned to George Hickman of Lewis town State of Deleware storekeeper, to serve him or assigns the remainder of indenture as above recorded. Consideration = $91.19.

November 9, 1818

Johannes Lentz willing to go to Virginia, to Nathaniel Chauncey of Philadelphia merchant for four years & six months, to have at the end of the term two complete suits of clothes, one of which to be new. Consideration = $136.19.

Johannes Lentz at the same time assigned to Archibald Baugh esquire of Petersburg Virginia to serve him or assigns the remainder of indenture above recorded. Consideration = $136.19.

Daniel Weimer assigned by Henry Weaver to William Lamb of Chilicothe, Ohio, graser, to serve him or assigns the remainder of his indenture recorded page 56. Consideration = $81.50.

Christina Margaretha Muhlhauser with her father's consent, to Daniel Lefever of Strasburg township, Lancaster county, farmer for four years & one month, to have six weeks schooling, and at the end of the term two complete suits of clothes one of which to be new. Consideration = $96.19.

November 12, 1818

Jacob Schninger with his father's consent, to George Krum of Heidelberg township Lebenon county, farmer, for seven years three months & eighteen days, to have six weeks schooling for each year of the term, and at the end thereof two complete suits of clothes, one whereof to be new. Consideration = $90.00.

November 13, 1818

Christina Hofman to George Hoffmeister of Manheim township Lancaster county farmer for three years & six months, to have at the end of the term two complete suits of clothes, one of which to be new. Consideration = $84.39.

Christina Hofman at the same time assigned to Jacob Ehresman of Manheim township Lancaster county, farmer, to serve him or assigns the remainder of indenture recorded on preceding page. Consideration = $84.39.

Johan Georg Kunzler with his mother's consent to go to New Jersey to William Keyser & John Rink of Sweedes Borough, Gloucester county, New Jersey, storekeeper, for four years & three months, to have three months schooling, and at the end of the term two complete suits of clothes, one of which to be new. Consideration = $106.78.

George Michael Kunzler with his mother's consent, to Daniel H. Miller of Philadelphia ironmonger for six years, to have thirty weeks schooling & at the end of the term two complete suits of clothes, one whereof to be new. Consideration = $105.59.

November 16, 1818

Catharina Achenbach with consent of her father, to Daniel Adgate of Philadelphia grocer for five years, to have six weeks schooling for each year of the term, & at the end thereof two complete suits of clothes, one of which to be new. Consideration = $50.00.

November 19, 1818

Anna Maria Hasertin with consent of her mother to go to New Jersey, to Michael Taylor of Chesterfield township Burlington county New Jersey, farmer, for four years, to have six weeks schooling and at the end of the term two complete suits of clothes, one of which to be new. Consideration = $81.20.

Christina Vogt with consent of her father, to William M. Evans of Hammeltonville clock & watchmaker, for eight years five months & ten days, to have six weeks schooling for each year of the term & at the end thereof two complete suits of clothes, one of which to be new. Consideration = $61.19.

Christina Vogt at the same time assigned to Clementine Ross of Hammiltonville Philadelphia county, widow, to serve her or assigns the remainder of her indenture above recorded. Consideration = $61.19.

November 20, 1818

Christina Barbara Eitelbussin with consent of her father, to Jacob Heyn of Philadelphia, drover, for five years one month & twenty days, to have six weeks schooling for each year of the term, and at the end thereof two complete suits of clothes, one of which to be new. Consideration = $70.00.

November 21, 1818

Johan Frederick Gudbrodt with his father's consent, to Francis Ingraham of Philadelphia, gentleman, for three years, to have eighteen weeks schooling, and at the end of the term two complete suits clothes one to be new. Consideration = $80.82.

Daniel Koch with consent of Johannes Schiller, to John McCormick of Summerset township, Washington county, farmer, for four years, to have eighteen weeks schooling, and at the end of the term two complete suits of clothes, one of which to be new. Consideration = $80.00.

November 23, 1818

Margareta Vogt with consent of her father, to John Rudy of Philadelphia combmaker, for five years three months & fifteen days, to have six weeks schooling for each year of the term, and at the end thereof two complete suits of clothes, one of which to be new. Consideration = $61.19.

Gottlieb Schiller with his consent to go to Virginia, to Charles F. Keilig of Philadelphia storekeeper, for three years, to have at the end of the term two complete suits of clothes, one of which to be new. Consideration = $91.19.

Gottlieb Schiller at the same time assigned to John L. Schedlice of Fredericksburg, Virginia baker, to serve him or assigns the indenture above recorded. Consideration = $91.19.

Jacob Fredler with his father's consent to go to Virginia, to Charles F. Keilig of Philadelphia storekeeper, for nine years, to have six weeks schooling for each year of the term & at the end thereof two complete suits of clothes, one of which to be new. Consideration = $71.19.

Jacob Fredler at the same time assigned to James Williams of Fredericksburg Virginia merchant to serve him or assigns the remainder of indenture above recorded. Consideration = $71.19.

November 28, 1818

Christina Schiller to Gottfried Weber of Philadelphia merchant for three years, to have at the end of the term two complete suits of clothes, one to be new. Consideration = $80.00.

Gottlieb Schiller with consent of his father, to John Jordan of Philadelphia merchant for five years ten months & twenty days, to have six weeks schooling for each year of the term & at the end thereof two complete suits of clothes, one of which to be new. Consideration = $81.19.

December 2, 1818

Michael Flosch & his wife Christina to George Devries of Moyamensing township Philadelphia county, innkeeper, for three years, to have at the end of the term two complete suits of clothes, each, one of each to be new. Consideration = $130.00.

Jacob Brenn with consent of his father, to George Kline of Greenwich township Berks county, farmer, for three years & six months, to have twelve weeks schooling, & at the end of the term two complete suits of clothes one of which to be new. Consideration = $70.00.

December 4, 1818

Catharina Lentzin willing to go to Virginia, to Nathaniel Chauncey of Philadelphia merchant for one year & six months. Consideration = $46.19.

Catharina Lentzin at the same time assigned to Archibald Baugh esquire of Petersburg, Virginia, to serve him or assigns indenture as above recorded. Consideration = $46.19.

Daniel Lentz willing & with his mother's consent, to the above Nathaniel Chauncey for four years & six months, to have six weeks schooling for each year of his term & at the end thereof two complete suits of clothes one thereof to be new. Consideration = $91.19.

Daniel Lentz at the same time to before named Archibald Baugh to serve him or assigns the indenture above recorded. Consideration = $91.19.

December 5, 1818

Susanna Catharina Noll assigned by Margaret Quig, administrator to the estate of John Quig deceased, to Daniel Streeper of Norinton township Montgomery county to serve him or assigns the remainder of indenture recorded page 48. Consideration = $15.00.

December 11, 1818

Christianus Muhlhauser & Rosina Regina his wife to John Brindle of Munsey Creek township Lycoming county, storekeeper, for four years, to have at the end of their term two complete suits of clothes each, one of each to be new, & their child Elena to be fed & clothed gratis & be free with the parents. Consideration = $177.00.

John Burkle haveing by his sister paid John Borman eighty five 50/100 dollars he is discharged from any further servitude of his indenture recorded Book B, page 112.

December 17, 1818

Johan Georg Geiser & Regina his wife willing to go out of Pennsylvania, to George Devries of Moyamensing township Philadelphia county, innkeeper, for three years, to be paid at the end of the first year fifty dollars, and at the end of each succeeding year of their term one hundred & fifty dollars in lieu of apparel and at the end of their term to have twenty acres of land given them by their master without any cost or charges, their infant child to be fed & clothed gratis & be free with the parents. Consideration = $70.00.

December 18, 1818

Sebastian Friderich & Rosina his wife willing as above, to the above George Devries for three years, to be paid at the end of each year of their term twenty five dollars in lieu of clothing. And at the end of the term to have five acres of land without any cost or charge which they may possess for ten years, when a price shall be paid for it as the parties may agree on, their infant to be provide for & be free with the parents. Consideration = $130.00.

Joseph Sutter & Fransiska his wife willing as above to said George Devries for three years, to be paid at the end of each year of their term twenty five dollars in lieu of clothing & at the end of the last year ten dollars addition, to have at the end of their term five acres of land upon conditions as next above. Consideration = $130.00.

December 22, 1818

Johannes Gudbrodt willing to go to New Jersey to Elijah Carman of Anvil township Hunterdon county New Jersey, farmer, for four years, to have at the end of the term two complete suits of clothes, one to be new, & thirty dollars. Consideration = $91.19.

Johan George Vogt with consent of his father to go out of Pennsylvania to John Biddle of Philadelphia major United States service, for seven years, to have six weeks schooling for each year of the term & at the end thereof two complete suits of clothes, one of which to be new. Consideration = $70.00.

January 14, 1819

Margaretha Harlein (with her own consent) assigned by George Alcorn to Jonas Miller of Little Egg Harbor township Burlington county New Jersey, innkeeper, to serve him or assigns the remainder of her indenture recorded in Book B, page 194. Consideration = $20.00.

January 24, 1819

Anna Maria Kallenburn assigned by Jacob Peterson to serve herself the remainder of her indentured recorded Book B, page 129. Valuable consideration.

March 6, 1819

Christian Wahl & wife Magdalena willing to go to New Jersey to Thomas Wilson of Greenwich township Gloucester county, farmer, for three years, to have at the end of their term two complete suits of clothes each, one of each to be new. Their infant child to be fed & clothed gratis & be free with the parents. Consideration = $178.00.

March 17, 1819

John Frederick Heidecke assigned by George & Jacob Peterman to serve himself the remainder of his indenture recorded page 61, in consideration of his promisery note of this date at twelve months for one hundred dollars.

April 21, 1819

Carolina Graff assigned by John Macke to Jacob Agster of Upper Milford township Lehigh county, farmer, to serve him or assigns the remainder of her indenture recorded page 8. Consideration = $25.00.

April 26, 1819

Anna Maria Ott assigned by James Fossett to William Warren of Philadelphia coachmaker to serve him or assigns the remainder of indenture recorded page 76. Consideration = $30.00.

May 1, 1819

Philip David Dingeswith, with consent of Martin Lauber, to George Bird of the Northern Liberties Philadelphia county, mariner, for two years & six months to have at the end of the term thirty dollars. Consideration = $124.00.

May 3, 1819

Catharina Maria Lenz, with consent of her father, to John Roland of Philadelphia merchant, for three years eight months & twenty five days, to have six months half day schooling, & at the end of her term two complete suits of clothes, one of which to be new. {Cancelled by mutual consent June 8, 1821.} Consideration = $70.00.

May 5, 1819

Johan George Ott assigned by George Willig to Simon Phillipson of Philadelphia merchant to serve him or assigns the remainder of his indenture recorded page 81. Consideration = $20.00.

May 25, 1819

Catharina Schanbacher assigned by Thomas Sexton, by virtue of a power of attorney bearing date 22 April 1819 to him given by John Adams, to Joseph Langer of Philadelphia suspendermaker, to serve him or assigns the remainder of her indenture recorded page 78. Consideration = $95.00.

May 29, 1819

Adam Diehr haveing fully sattisfied his servant Andreas Heinz the indenture recorded page 315 Book B is by consent of parties canseled & made void.

May 31, 1819

Anna Elizabeth Ray assigned by John Land to herself. Consideration = valuable.

June 7, 1819

Wilhelmina Bogger, with consent of her mother, to William K. Hamilton of Philadelphia stablekeeper for six years, to have six weeks schooling for each year of her term, and at the end thereof two complete suits of clothes, one of which to be new. Consideration = $40.00.

June 9, 1819

George Henry Lochner assigned by Luther Franck to himself. Consideration = $1.00.

June 18, 1819

Jacobina Rost assigned by Adam Everly to herself. Consideration = $1.00.

June 25, 1819

Frederick Knoderer, with consent of his Uncle, to John Planck of the Northern Liberties oak cooper for two years & six months, to have fifteen weeks schooling, and at the end of the term two complete suits of clothes, one of which to be new. And to be free if he shall at any time within one month repay his master the passage money with reasonable expenses. Consideration = $50.00.

July 9, 1819

Genevesa Weisenberger assigned by Alexander Caldwell to John Stock of Philadelphia painter & glazier to serve him or assigns the remainder of her indenture recorded page 72. Consideration = $100.00.

July 27, 1819

Rosina Elisabetha Behner, with consent of her father, to Curtis Cavender, of Philadelphia storekeeper, for nine years & 6 months, to have six weeks schooling for each year of the term, & at the end thereof two complete suits of clothes, one of which to be new. Consideration = $40.00.

Elisabetha Grossmannin to John Rea of Philadelphia upholsterer for four years, to be paid by her master twenty five dollars for the last year of her servitude and give her at the end of the term two complete suits of clothes, one of which to be new. Consideration = $80.00.

Friderich Adam Dorner, with consent of his father, to John Folwell of Philadelphia merchant, for eleven years, to have six weeks schooling for each year of the term, and at the end thereof two complete suits of clothes, one of which to be new. Consideration = $60.00.

Sophia Magdalena Heinrichin to Thomas Ogle of Philadelphia coachmaker for two years to have at the end of the term two complete suits of clothes, one of which to be new, & twenty dollars. Consideration = $31.00.

July 28, 1819

Louisa Wilhelmina Holzingerin to George Pepper of Philadelphia brewer, for three years & six months, to have at the end of the term two complete suits of clothes, one of which to be new. Consideration = $80.00.

Catharina Beckin to Francis Pott of Pesyunk township Philadelphia county, farmer, for three years, to have at the end of the term two complete suits of clothes, one of which to be new. Consideration = $80.00.

Christina Eitel to George Breidenhart of Philadelphia upholster for three years & six months, to have at the end of the term two complete suits of clothes, one of which to be new. Consideration = $80.00.

July 29, 1819

Elisabetha Frida Jauszin to Adam Guier of Kingsessing township Philadelphia county, gentleman, for three years, to have at the end of the term two complete suits of clothes one of which to be new. Consideration = $80.00.

Rosina Magdelena Ehretin, with consent of her father, to the above Adam Guier, for three years, to have twelve weeks schooling and at the end of the term two complete suits of clothes, one of which to be new. Consideration = $80.00.

July 30, 1819

Dorothea Dornerin, with consent of her father, to Manuel Pries of Southwark Philadelphia county corker, for six years, to have six weeks schooling for each year of the term, and at the end thereof give her two complete suits of clothes one of which to be new. Consideration = $65.00.

July 31, 1819

Regina Zahnin, with consent of Gottlieb Albrecht, to Augustus L. Baumfort Germantown township Philadelphia county, professor of mathematics, for three years, to have twelve weeks schooling, and at the end of the term two complete suits of clothes, one of which to be new, and fifteen dollars. Consideration = $70.00.

Regina Zahnin at the same time assigned to P. F. B. Constant of Mount Airy Germantown to serve him or assigns the indenture above recorded. Consideration = $70.00.

Dorothea Burklin, with consent of Gottlieb Albrecht, to the above Augustus L. Baumfort, for three years, to have twelve weeks schooling and at the end of the term two complete suits of clothes, one of which to be new. Consideration = $80.00.

Dorothea Burklin at the same time assigned to the above P. F. B. Constant, to serve him or assigns, the above indenture. Consideration = $80.00.

Rosina Holzhainin to the above Augustus L. Baumfort, for three years, to have at the end of the term two complete suits of clothes, one of which to be new. Consideration = $80.00.

Philipina Heinrichin to James Arbuckle of Philadelphia grocer, for four years, to be paid twenty dollars for the last year of her term, & have two complete suits of clothes, one of which to be new. Consideration = $80.00.

Johan Michael Ehret with consent of his father, to John Singer of Philadelphia merchant for seven years nine months & seventeen days, to have six weeks schooling for each year of his term, and at the end thereof two complete suits of clothes, one of which to be new. Consideration = $70.00.

Sabina Catharina Gotzin, with consent of John Beer, to the above John Singer, for three years, to have six weeks schooling and the end of the term two complete suits of clothes, one of which to be new. Consideration = $80.00.

August 2, 1819

Friderika Eitel to Charles W. Bazeley of Philadelphia keeper of female seminary, for three years, to have at the end of the term two complete suits of clothes, one of which to be new. Consideration = $80.00.

August 3, 1819

Catharina Humerlin to William Steel of Philadelphia flower merchant for three years, to have at the end of the term two complete suits of clothes, one of which to be new, and ten dollars. Consideration = $70.00.

Regina Wurtembergerin to Jacob Sperry of Philadelphia merchant for three years, to have at the end of the term two complete suits of clothes, one of which to be new. Consideration = $80.00.

Sophia Schulz to Magdalen Ewing of Philadelphia, widow, for three years, to have at the end of the term two complete suits of clothes, one of which to be new. Consideration = $80.00.

Regina Buchmanin, with consent of Henry Shell, to John Mingle of Philadelphia, blacksmith, for four years, to have six weeks schooling for each year of the term, and at the end thereof two complete suits of clothes, one of which to be new & nineteen dollars. Consideration = $40.00.

August 4, 1819

Christina Konigin, with consent of Peter Field, to John Carter of Philadelphia stablekeeper, to have six weeks schooling, and at the end of the term two complete suits of clothes, one of which to be new, & be paid fifteen dollars, term of servitude four years. Consideration = $80.00.

Barbara Edlin to James L. Duval of Philadelphia merchant for three years, to have at the end of the term two complete suits of clothes, one of which to be new. Consideration = $77.20.

August 5, 1819

Jacob Rieth willing to go to North Carolina to James Cowin of Charlotta Mecklenburg county North Carolina farmer, for four years, to be paid at any time during his servitude if demanded eight dollars, and give him at the end of the term two complete suits of clothes, one of which to be new. And give him such compensation for the last year of his term as his master shall think his service merits. Consideration = $65.00.

John Friderick Rebman, (willing as above) with consent of John Rees, to the above James Cowin for four years, to have twelve weeks schooling & be paid eighteen dollars when demanded, to have at the end of the term two complete suits of clothes, one of which to be new, and give him compensation as above for last year. Consideration = $53.00.

Conrad Looser, willing as above and with consent of John Rees, to the above James Cowin, for four years, to have twelve weeks schooling and at the end of the term clothes and compensation as above. Consideration = $77.00.

Christian Friderick Wagner, willing as above and with consent of John Rees, to the above James Cowin for four years, to have twelve weeks schooling, and at the end of the term clothes & compensation as above. Consideration = $77.00.

Christoph Elsasser, willing as above & with consent of John Rees, to the above James Cowin, to have six weeks schooling, and be paid twenty five dollars whenever demanded, and at the end of the term to have clothes & compensation as above stipulated, term of servitude four years. Consideration = $45.00.

Henrich David Keil, willing as above to the above James Cowin, for four years, to have at the end of the term clothes & compensation as above stipulated. Consideration = $77.00.

Philip Bernhard Treffinger willing to go to Hillsborough, Jasper county, Georgia, to the above James Cowin for four years, to have at the end of the term clothes & compensation as above stipulated. Consideration = $77.00.

George Philip Schauffele willing as above to go to Georgia to the above James Cowin, for four years to have at the end of the term clothes & compensation as above stipulated. Consideration = $77.00.

August 6, 1819

Catharina Dillmanin to John Conard esquire of the Northern Liberties for three years, to have at the end of the term two complete suits of clothes, one of which to be new & twenty five dollars. Consideration = $60.00.

Philip Heison, with consent of William Space, to John Vernon, of Philadelphia hairdresser, for three years, to have at the end of the term two complete suits of clothes, one of which to be new. Also during the term six weeks schooling. Consideration = $81.20.

Elisabetha Hensin to Sebastian Schnatz of Philadelphia baker for three years to have at the end of the term two complete suits of clothes, one of which to be new. Consideration = $77.20.

Barbara Schwartz to John Marbacher of the Northern Liberties, brewer, for three years, to have at the end of the term two complete suits of clothes, one of which to be new. Consideration = $77.20.

August 7, 1819

Simon Walter, with consent of his father, to Thomas & William H. Hart of the Northern Liberties grocers, to have eighteen weeks schooling, and at the end of the term two complete suits of clothes one to be new. Consideration = $77.20.

Barbara Langin to Christopher Steinmetz of Northern Liberties innkeeper, for three years, to have at the end of the term two complete suits of clothes, one of which to be new. Consideration = $77.20.

August 9, 1819

Johannes Fuchs, with consent of Jacob Lichet, to Jacob Osterman of Philadelphia victuler for five years, to have six weeks schooling for each year of the term, and at the end thereof two complete suits of clothes one of which to be new and be paid twenty seven dollars. Consideration = $81.25.

Johannes Fuchs at the same time assigned to Daniel Benzinger from New McKeansburg Schuylkill county, tavernkeeper, to serve him or assigns the remainder of the above indenture. Consideration = $81.25.

August 10, 1819

Augustin Wandel, with consent of James Smith, to Thomas Stewart of New Britton township Bucks county, farmer, for five years, to have twenty four weeks schooling, and at the end of the term two complete suits of clothes one of which to be new, and forty dollars. Consideration = $81.25.

August 11, 1819

Johan Friderick Schuhurt with consent of Jacob Beidelman, to Frederick A. Kochlin, of the Northern Liberties, baker, to have six weeks schooling, & at the end of his term two complete suits of clothes, one of which to be new, term of servitude three years. Consideration = $81.25.

Sophia Graussin to John Ross esquire president of court of common pleas Montgomery county, for three years, to have at the end of the term two complete suits of clothes, one of which to be new. Consideration = $80.00.

Sophia Christina Eglerin to Jacob Nitzell of Kingsessing township Philadelphia county, farmer, for three years, to have at the end of the term two complete suits of clothes, one of which to be new. Consideration = $80.00.

August 12, 1819

Charles Wilhelm Weyhenmeyer assigned by Adam Lentner to serve himself the remainder of his indenture, recorded page 70. Consideration = $40.00.

August 13, 1819

Sabina Baderin, with consent of Daniel Lebo, to George Hoppel of Penn township Philadelphia county, victuler, for three years, to have twelve weeks schooling, and at the end of the term two complete suits of clothes, one of which to be new. Consideration = $80.00.

August 14, 1819

George Jacob Enz & his wife Christina willing to go to New Jersey to John Pissant of Woolwich township, Gloucester county, farmer, for two years, to have at the end of the term two complete suits of clothes each, one of each to be new, or each fifteen dollars, at the option of the servant. And should they become parents during their servitude then to serve their master six months longer. Consideration = $100.00.

Margaretha Enz, willing to go to New Jersey, to the before named John Pissant, for three years & six months, to have at the end of the term two complete suits of clothes, one of which to be new, or fifteen dollars at the option of the servant and ten dollars. Consideration = $67.00.

August 16, 1819

Casper Walter, with consent of his father, to Jacob Hoffman of Rockland township Berks county, farmer, for four years, to have twenty four weeks schooling, and at the end of the term two complete suits of clothes, one to be new. Consideration = $77.20.

August 18, 1819

Bardina Hussing, willing to go to Deleware State, to Hugh Harbison of Philadelphia grocer, for three years & six months, to have at the end of the term two complete suits of clothes, one to be new. Consideration = $81.20.

Bardina Hussing at the same time assigned to George Hickman of Lewistown, State of Deleware, farmer, to serve him or assigns the above indenture. Consideration = $81.20.

August 21, 1819

Mathias Spittelmeisler to Jesse Grim of Macunsey township Lehigh county, farmer, for three years, to have at the end of the term two complete suits of clothes, one to be new, & fifteen dollars. Consideration = $65.00.

Rosina Heinrichin to John Harman of Lampeter township Lancaster county, farmer, for three years, to have at the end of the term two complete suits of clothes, one to be new. Consideration = $80.00.

August 23, 1819

Catharina Groszin to Anthony Taylor of Bristol township Bucks county for four years, to have at the end of the term two complete suits of clothes, one to be new, & sixteen dollars. Consideration = $80.00.

Johannes Haussel, with consent of Gottlieb Kletz, to Jacob Geitner of Warwick township Lancaster county tanner, for four years three months & fifteen days, to have six weeks schooling for each year of the term and at the end thereof two complete suits of clothes, one to be new. Consideration = $80.00.

August 24, 1819

Carl Ollie, with consent of John Kline, to Jacob Keely of Douglass township Berks county, farmer, for three years, to have eighteen weeks schooling and at the end of the term two complete suits of clothes, one to be new. Consideration = $81.20.

Gottfried Straub, with consent of Jacob Keely, to John Kline of Emmety township Berks county, farmer, for three years & three months to have six weeks schooling for each year, and at the end of the term two complete suits of clothes, one of which to be new. Consideration = $81.20.

Jacob Friderich Ehret, with consent of his father, to John Hart of Philadelphia drugist, for five years five months & eleven days, to have six weeks schooling for each year of the term, and at the end thereof two complete suits of clothes, one to be new. Consideration = $50.00.

Charles Kim & wife Christina willing to go to New Jersey, to Benjamin W. Richards of Philadelphia merchant, for one year, to be paid during their servitude twenty dollars in lieu of clothing. Consideration = $100.00.

Charles Kim & wife Christina at the same time assigned to William Richards esquire of Mount Holly New Jersey, to serve him or assigns the above indenture. Consideration = $100.00.

August 25, 1819

Rosina Catharina Motz assigned by Ebenezer McCutchen to Conrad Ripperger of Philadelphia, bleecher, to serve him or assigns the remainder of her indenture recorded page 56. Consideration = $40.00.

August 28, 1819

David Schilling to Jacob Nitzell of Kingsessing township Philadelphia county, farmer, for three years to have at the end of the term two complete suits of clothes one of which to be new. Consideration = $70.00.

August 30, 1819

Johan Georg Freck & his wife Anna Maria to Jacob Sperry of Philadelphia merchant, for three years, to have at the end of the term two complete suits of clothes each, one of each to be new, & fifty dollars. Consideration = $80.00.

Margaretha Kuhnlerin, with consent of her father, to William Mandry of Philadelphia health officer, for seven years, to have six weeks schooling each year and at the end of the term two complete suits of clothes, one to be new. Consideration = $35.00.

August 31, 1819

Dorothea Kuhnlerin, with consent of her father, to Joseph Stouse of Northern Liberties Philadelphia county physician, for three years to have at the end of the term two complete suits of clothes, one to be new. Consideration = $77.00.

Michael Hohl & wife Catharina, willing to go to Alabama, to Amand Pfister of Eagle Ville Maringo county, Alabama, for three years to have at the end of the term two complete suits of clothes each, one of each to be new. And their child Rosina to be fed & clothed & be free with the parents. Consideration = $77.00.

Johan Georg Hohl, willing as above, to the above Amand Pfister for three years, to have at the end of the term two complete suits of clothes, one of which to be new. Consideration = $77.00.

Margaretha Hohl, willing as before, to the said Amand Pfister, for three years, to have at the end of the term clothes as before. Consideration = $77.00.

Christianna Hohl, willing as before & with consent of her father, to said Amand Pfister, for six years, to have six weeks schooling for each year of the term, and at the end thereof clothes as before. Consideration = $38.00.

Catharina Hohl, willing as above & with consent of her father, to the above Amand Pfister, for ten years, to have six weeks schooling for each year of the term, and at the end thereof clothes as above. Consideration = $38.00.

Franz Krucker to Leonard Nutz Junior of Germantown Philadelphia county, tanner, for two years, to have at the end of the term two complete suits of clothes, one of which to be new. Consideration = $53.20.

September 1, 1819

Johan Friderich Gudeman, with consent of Jacob Beidelman to go to Alabama, to Julius Alexander Fournier, of Eagle Ville, Maring county, Alabama for three years, to have twelve weeks schooling. And at the end of the term two complete suits of clothes, one of which to be new. Consideration = $81.20.

September 2, 1819

Rosina Kuhnlerin to Henry Lelar of Philadelphia merchant for three years, to have at the end of the term two complete suits of clothes, one of which to be new. Consideration = $77.00.

Johan Friderich Bossert, with consent of William Lecompt to go to Maryland to Greensburg L. Rauleig of Dorchester county State of Maryland, planter, for four years to have 24 weeks schooling, and at the end of the term two complete suits of clothes, one of which to be new. Consideration = $80.00.

Christina Loreherin, with consent of her father, to John Heyl of the Northern Liberties Philadelphia county brushmaker, for five years 9 months & 22 days to have 6 weeks schooling for each year, and at the end of the term two complete suits of clothes, one of which to be new. Consideration = $38.00.

September 3, 1819

Catharina Staub to Thomas Sterrett of Rapho township Lancaster county, farmer, for three years to have at the end of the term two complete suits of clothes, one of which to be new. Consideration = $77.25.

Catharina Staub at the same time assigned to Sarah Sterrett of the same township & county, widow, to serve her indenture as above recorded. Consideration = $77.20.

Mathias Friderich Loreher, with consent of his father, to the above Thomas Sterrett, for eleven years one month & 18 days, to have 6 weeks schooling for each year of the term and at the end thereof two complete suits of clothes, one of which to be new. Consideration = $38.00.

Johan Adam Bernhart assigned by Charles B. Rees, attorney for Catharina Stall, executor of the estate of F. Stall died, to himself. Consideration = $1.00.

Maria Rosina Hering, with consent of her father, to James Way of Philadelphia merchant, for six years six months & 20 days, to have 6 weeks schooling for each year of the term and at the end thereof two complete suits of clothes, one of which to be new. Consideration = $38.50.

Gottfried Knoll to Catharina Waltman of Moyamansing township Philadelphia county, widow, for 6 months, the servant to be paid six dollars per month as the same shall come due, the mistress first reducing there from his passage mony, the servant to find his own clothing. Consideration = $17.25.

September 5, 1819

Anton Vonbun, willing to go to Deleware State, to Samuel P. Davis of Philadelphia gentleman, for two years, to have at the end of the term two complete suits of clothes, one of which to be new. Consideration = $81.20.

Xavier Vonbun, willing as above, to the same for two years, to have at the end of the term same as above. Consideration = $81.20.

Maria Rosina Hering assigned by James Way to Jacob Beck of Northern Liberties tobacconist, to serve him or assigns the remainder of her indenture recorded above. Consideration = $38.50.

September 6, 1819

Gottlieb Wilhelm to Jacob Stern of Penn township Philadelphia county, victuler, for one year & six months, the servant to find his own apparel. Consideration = $81.25.

September 7, 1819

Maria Witmanin to Frederick Gaul of Philadelphia brewer, for three years, to have at the end of the term two complete suits of clothes one of which to be new, or fifteen dollars at the option of the servant. Consideration = $77.20.

Jacob Walter, with consent of his father, to Thomas Boyd of Douglas township Montgomery county, papermaker, for five years 7 months & 25 days, to have six weeks schooling for each year of the term, and at the end thereof two complete suits of clothes, one of which to be new. Consideration = $77.20.

September 8, 1819

Johannes Sulzer, with consent of Daniel Lebo, to Adam Dux of the Northern Liberties Philadelphia county, whitesmith, for five years & six months, to have six weeks schooling for each year of the term, and at the end thereof two complete suits of clothes, one of which to be new. Consideration = $50.00.

Johannes Sulzer at the same time assigned to Michael Diehr of Tyoga county Pennsylvania farmer, to serve him or assigns the remainder of his indenture before recorded page 96. Consideration = $50.00.

September 10, 1819

Johan David Wohrle, willing to go to New Jersey, to Benjamin B. Cooper of Waterford township, Gloucester county, New Jersey farmer, for one year & six months, the servant to find his own apparel. And to be paid at the end of the term fifteen dollars. Consideration = $34.87.

September 15, 1819

Elisabetha Eitelin to Henry Boraef of Penn township Philadelphia county Pennsylvania victuler, for three years, to have at the end of the term two complete suits of clothes, one of which to be new. Consideration = $76.00.

September 16, 1819

Abraham Knaur, with consent of M. Baker, to William Haverstick Junior of Philadelphia merchant, for four years & six months, to have six weeks schooling for each year of the term, and at the end thereof two complete suits of clothes, one of which to be new or be paid thirty dollars at the option of the servant. Consideration = $81.25.

Johan Martin Bronni, with consent of Daniel Lebo, to James Jefferies of East Bradford township Chester county Pennsylvania farmer, for three years & 3 months to have at the end of the term two complete suits of clothes, & be paid twenty six dollars 40 cents. Consideration = $41.33.

September 17, 1819

Margaretha Barbara Aisenbrey, with consent of her father, to Conrad Lohrer of the Northern Liberties Philadelphia county, whitesmith, for four years & five months, to have six weeks schooling for each year of the term, & at the end thereof give her two complete suits of clothes, one of which to be new. Consideration = $40.00.

September 20, 1819

Johan Georg Kastenbader, with consent of his father, to Joseph Taylor of Philadelphia innkeeper, for three years & three months, to have six weeks schooling for each year of the term, & at the end thereof two complete suits of clothes, one of which to be new, & be paid thirty nine dollars. Consideration = $36.00.

September 23, 1819

Johan Georg Weller, with consent of his father, to John Krause of Bethahem Northampton county Pennsylvania victuler, for five years & three months, to have six weeks schooling for each year of the term, and be taught the art trade & mistery of a victuler. And at the end of the term give him two complete suits of clothes, one of which to be new. Consideration = $70.00.

September 24, 1819

Rosalia Schneider, with consent of her father, to Peleg Hall of Philadelphia mariner, for three years & six months, to have during the term eighteen weeks schooling & at the end thereof of two complete suits of clothes, one of which to be new. Consideration = $65.00.

Henrietta Hayn to Peter Bachman of Philadelphia baker, for three years, to have at the end of the term two complete suits of clothes, one of which to be new. Consideration = $81.85.

September 27, 1819

Friderich Schmidt, willing to go to New Jersey, to John Browning of Waterford township Gloucester county New Jersey farmer, for four years, to have three months schooling, and at the end of the term two complete suits of clothes, one which to be new & be paid twenty dollars. Consideration = $77.20.

Elisabeth Gallmeyer, with consent of her father, to Abraham Raiguel of Amwell township, Lebanon county, Pennsylvania, miller, for eight years & three months, to have six weeks schooling for each year, and at the end of the term to have two complete suits of clothes, one of which to be new. Consideration = $38.00.

By virtue of power vested in Jasper Cole by Jane Shoemaker, he has assigned Anna Maria Dower to herself for valuable consideration the remainder of indenture recorded page 53.

Catharina Kiks, willing to go to Illinois, to John Grant of the town of Carmi, White county, Illinois, merchant, for five years, to have at the end of the term two complete suits of clothes, one of which to be new, & be paid twenty six dollars. Consideration = $67.20.

Anna Elisabeth Straatman, willing as above to the above John Grant, for five years, to have at the end of the term clothes as above & be paid twenty six dollars. Consideration = $67.20.

Jeremiah Hartenbauer, willing as above, with consent of Daniel Lebo, to the above John Grant, for four years, to have eighteen weeks schooling, & at the end of the term two complete suits of clothes, one of to be new. Consideration = $67.20.

Ludwig Henrich Buhner, willing as above, to said John Grant for four years, to have at the of the term clothes as above. Consideration = $67.20.

Magdalena Schneider, with consent of her father to said John Grant for eleven years, to have six weeks schooling for each year of the term, and at the end thereof clothes as above. Consideration = $33.60.

Fransiscus Schneider, with consent of his father, to the said John Grant for ten years & six months, to have six weeks schooling for each of the years & at the end thereof clothes as above. Consideration = $33.60.

Xaverius Schneider, with consent of his father, to the said John Grant for nine years, to have six weeks schooling for each year of the term, & at the end thereof clothes as above. Consideration = $34.20.

Catharina Schneider, with consent of her father, to the said John Grant for six years & three months, to have at the end of the term clothes as above & be paid ten dollars. Consideration = $134.40.

Maria Anna Schneider, to the said John Grant, willing as before, for seven years, to have at the end of the term clothes as above & be paid ten dollars. Consideration = $134.40.

Johan Georg Steinbran, with consent of Daniel Lebo, to Enos Reece, of Upper Darby township, Delaware county, Pennsylvania storekeeper, for three years three months & twenty four days, to have six weeks schooling for each year of the term, and at the end thereof two complete suits of clothes, one of which to be new. Consideration = $70.00.

September 28, 1819

Catharina Schaffer to George Gesner, of Kingsess township, Philadelphia county, farmer, for four years, to have at the end of the term two complete suits clothes, one of which to be new. Consideration = $109.00.

September 29, 1819

Maria Schroeder, with consent of her father, to Joseph H. Dullis, of Philadelphia merchant, for seven years four months, to have six weeks schooling for each year of the term, & at the end thereof two complete suits of clothes, one of which to be new. Consideration = $37.00.

Johannes Stierlen, with consent of Daniel Lebo, to Henry Haas of Conastoga township, Lancaster county, Pennsylvania farmer, for three years, to have six weeks schooling, and at the end of the term two complete suits of clothes, one of which to be new. Consideration = $78.00.

Johan Gotthard Reyher, with consent of Daniel Lebo, to John Buchalder of Conastoga township, Lancaster county, Pennsylvania farmer for three years, to have six weeks schooling, and at the end of the two complete suits of clothes, one of which to be new, & be paid thirty five dollars 80 cents. Consideration = $43.20.

Susanna Weberin to George Eckhart, of Strasburg township Lancaster county, Pennsylvania farmer, for four years, to have at the end of the term two complete suits of clothes, one of which to be new. Consideration = $77.25.

Henrich Buhler, with consent of Daniel Lebo, to Carl Taschner, of Philadelphia farmer, for three years, to have twelve weeks schooling, and at the end of the term two complete suits of clothes, one of which to be new. Consideration = $67.20.

Maria Witmanin, assigned by Frederick Gaul to herself. Consideration = $81.88.

Justus Mohl, with consent of his father, to George Rex, of Willow Grove, Montgomery county, Pennsylvania farmer, for seven years & six months to have six weeks schooling for each year. And at the end of the term two complete suits of clothes, one of which to be new. Consideration = $40.00.

Henrich Hauser, with consent of Daniel Lebo, to Jacob Marckle, of Strasburg township, Lancaster county farmer for two years & six months to have at the end of the term two complete suits of clothes, one of which to be new. Consideration = $77.20.

September 30, 1819

Johan Ulrich Marsch, with consent of Johan George Lutz, to Conrad Hess of the Northern Liberties, Philadelphia county, shoemaker, for three years & five months, to have five months schooling during the term, & be taught the art trade & mistery of a shoemaker. Consideration = $30.00.

Maria Catharina Mohl, willing to go to Deleware State, to James Canby of Wilmington, Deleware, miller, for three years, to have at the end of the term two complete suits of clothes, one of which to be new. Consideration = $77.00.

Hadwig Sophia Mohl, with consent of her father, to the above James Canby, for three years, to have at the end of the term two complete suits of clothes, one of which to be new. Consideration = $77.00.

Rosina Lorcher, with consent of her father, to Henry Davis of the Northern Liberties Philadelphia county, farmer, for ten years & three months, to have six weeks schooling for each year of the term, and at the end thereof two complete suits of clothes, one of which to be new. Consideration = $30.00.

Margaretha Baumann, with consent of her father, to Daniel Smith Junior of Philadelphia merchant, for five years, to have six weeks schooling for each year, and at the end of the term two complete suits of clothes, one of which to be new. Consideration = $40.00.

Christina Baumann, with consent of her father, to Joseph Johnson, of Philadelphia, shipchandler, for six years & eight months, to have six weeks schooling for each year of the term, and at the end thereof two complete suits of clothes, one of which to be new. Consideration = $40.00.

October 1, 1819

Jacob Hoffman, with consent of his father, to George H. Krug of Lancaster, Pennsylvania tanner, for eight years & eight months, to have six weeks schooling for each year of the term, and at the end thereof two complete suits of clothes, one of which to be new. And be taught during his servitude the art trade & mistery of a tanner. Consideration = $38.00.

Elisabeth Hoffman, with consent of her father, to William Haverstick Junior, of Philadelphia merchant for nine years one month & fourteen days, to have six weeks schooling for each year of the term, and at the end thereof two complete suits of clothes, one of which to be new. Consideration = $38.00.

Elisabeth Hoffman at the same time assigned to George Musser, of Lancaster, Pennsylvania, tanner, to serve him or assigns the the indenture above recorded. Consideration = $38.00.

Christina Pleyfus to George Willig, of Philadelphia storekeeper, for three years, to have at the end of the term two complete suits of clothes, one of which to be new. Consideration = $76.00.

Louisa Eckhart to Daniel Bickley, of the Northern Liberties, Philadelphia county, grocer, for three years, to have at the end of the term two complete suits of clothes, one of which to be new. Consideration = $77.20.

Rosina Schelling, with consent of Friderich Storr, to Clayton Earl, of Philadelphia merchant, for three years to have at the end of the term two complete suits of clothes, one of which to be new, and paid ten dollars. Consideration = $50.00.

October 2, 1819

Anna Maria Geisser to Johannes Wahly, of Philadelphia, weaver, for four years, to have at the end of the term two complete suits of clothes, one of which to be new. Consideration = $110.

Friderich Hoffman, with consent of his father, to James Teisseire, of Philadelphia merchant, for six years & five months, to have six weeks schooling for each year of the term, and at the end thereof give him two complete suits of clothes, one of which to be new. Consideration = $40.00.

Elisabeth Margaretha Heinrich to Cadwaleder Evans Junior of Philadelphia merchant, for seven years, to have six weeks schooling for each year of the term. And at the end thereof two complete suits of clothes, one of which to be new. Consideration = $70.00.

Elisabeth Mantoft, willing to go to South Carolina, to Joseph Madia, of Charleston, South Carolina, merchant, for four years, to have at the end of the term two complete suits of clothes, one of which to be new, & paid fifteen dollars. Consideration = $50.00.

Anna Catharina Heinrichin, with consent of her mother, to John Wilbank of Philadelphia, brassfounder, for three years & 2 months, to have six weeks schooling and at the end of the term two complete suits of clothes, one of which to be new. Consideration = $66.50.

Eva Margaretha Ziegler to Chandler Price of Philadelphia merchant for three years, to have at the end of the term two complete suits of clothes, one of which to be new. Consideration = $50.00.

Eva Catharina Pfluger, with consent of her father, to George W. Morgan of Philadelphia, gentleman, for four years one month & seventeen days, to have six weeks schooling for each years of the term, and at the end thereof two complete suits of clothes one of which to be new. Consideration = $45.00.

October 4, 1819

Margareta Nagele to Louis Desauge, of Philadelphia merchant, for three years, to have at the end of the term two complete suits of clothes, one of which to be new. Consideration = $50.00.

Wilhelmina Mohl, with consent of her father, to go to Deleware, to Samuel Canby Junior, of Philadelphia merchant, for seven years & ten months, to have six weeks schooling for each year of the term, & at the end thereof two complete suits of clothes, one of which to be new. Consideration = $40.00.

Wilhelmina Mohl at the same time assigned to Margaret Marshall of Willmington, Deleware, widow, to serve her or assigns the indenture above recorded. Consideration = $40.00.

Elisabeth Mohl, with consent of her father as above, to the above Samuel Canby Junior, for six years, to have six weeks schooling for each year of the term, and at the end thereof two complete suits of clothes, one of which to be new. Consideration = $40.00.

Elisabeth Mohl, at the same time assigned to Jeremiah Woolston of Willmington, Deleware, gentleman, to serve him or assigns the indenture above recorded. Consideration = $40.00.

Paul Klingelberg & his wife Susanna, willing to go to New Jersey to Benjamin B. Cooper, of Waterford township, Gloucester county, New Jersey farmer, to have at the end of the term two complete suits of clothes each, one of each to be new, & be paid each ten dollars. The term of servitude to be five years & four months. Consideration = $144.40.

Peter Klingelberg, with consent of his father, to the above Benjamin B. Cooper, for five years & four months, to have six weeks schooling for each year of the term, & at the end thereof two complete suits of clothes, one of which to be new, & be paid ten dollars. Consideration = $38.55.

Margaretha Heinrich to Sarah Musser of Philadelphia widow, for three years & three months, to have at the end of the term two complete suits of clothes, one of which to be new. Consideration = $70.00.

Gottlieb Schiller assigned to his father by John Jordan to serve him the remainder of his indenture recorded page 84. Consideration = $85.00.

Friderica Aldinger with consent of her father, to Samuel Gilbert, of the Northern Liberties Philadelphia county, tobacconist, for five years and four months, to have six weeks schooling for each year of the term and at the end thereof two complete suits of clothes, one of which to be new. Consideration = $77.20.

Sarah Reichardin to William Montgomery Junior, of Philadelphia merchant, for four years, to have at the end of the term two complete suits of clothes, one of which to be new. Consideration = $40.00.

Friderica Weinmanin assigned by Jacob Zell to herself. Consideration = $1.00.

Rosina Catharina Spadin to Frederick Osterheldt, of Penn township Philadelphia county, victuler, for one year, to have no freedom suits. Consideration = $25.00.

Christina Ziegler, with consent of her father, to Charles Brugier, of Philadelphia merchant, for three years & six months, to have twelve weeks schooling and at the end of the term two complete suits of clothes, one of which to be new. Consideration = $50.00.

October 5, 1819

Christian Ott, assigned by Clement Lee Brady, to John Kohler, of Philadelphia, wheelwright, to serve him or assigns the remainder of his indenture recorded page 74. Consideration = $40.00.

Catharina Elisabeth Diefenbach to Jacob Sommer esquire, of Moreland township, Philadelphia county, for four years, to be paid fifty cents per week for the last six months of her term if she behaves herself well, & have at the end of the term two complete suits of clothes, one of which to be new. Consideration = $50.00.

Regina Catharina Munzunger to Edward Russell, of Philadelphia merchant, for four years, to have at the end of the term two complete suits of clothes, one of which to be new. Consideration = $50.00.

Catharina Ellenweinin to Henry Yourhaus, of Southwark Philadelphia county, baker, for four years, to be paid fifty cents per week for the last six months of her term. And it is further agreed that she be paid one dollar in place of fifty cents above stated if she behaves herself well, also to have customery freedoms. Consideration = $45.00.

Margaretha Elisabeth Kinichin to James Way, of Philadelphia merchant, for three years, to have at the end of the term two complete suits of clothes, one of which to be new. Consideration = $77.00.

October 6, 1819

Conrad Doringer, with consent of his father to go to New Jersey, to Alexander McKenzie, of Cape Island, Cape May county, New Jersey innkeeper, for nine years, to have six weeks schooling for each year of the term, & at the end thereof two complete suits of clothes, one of which to be new & be paid twenty dollars. Consideration = $51.25.

Maria Elisabeth Doringer, with consent of her father, as above, to the above Alexander McKenzie, for four years, to have six weeks schooling for each year of the term, & at the end thereof two complete suits of clothes, one of which to be new. Consideration = $30.00.

Friderica Barbara Foll, with consent of her father to go to New Jersey, to Joseph D. Drinker, of Willenburra township, Burlington county, New Jersey, for eight years, to have six weeks schooling for each year of the term, & at the end thereof two complete suits of clothes, one of which to be new. Consideration = $60.00.

Johan Ludwig Foll, with his father's consent as above, to the above Joseph D. Drinker, for ten years & two months, to have six weeks schooling for each year of the term, & at the end thereof two complete suits of clothes, one of which to be new. Consideration = $60.00.

October 7, 1819

Jacob Becker, willing to go to New Jersey, to Benjamin B. Cooper, of Waterford township, Gloucester county, New Jersey farmer, for three years & six months, to have at the end of the term two complete suits of clothes, one of which to be new, & be paid fifteen dollars. Consideration = $77.20.

Johan Michael Dietlein, willing as above, to the above Benjamin B. Cooper for two years, to have at the end of the term two complete suits of clothes, of which to be new, & be paid ten dollars. Consideration = $37.20.

Johan Georg Bebion, willing as above, to the above Benjamin B. Cooper, for two years, to have at the end of the term two complete suits of clothes, one of which to be new, & be paid fifteen dollars. Consideration = $29.20.

Jacob Becker assigned to Nathan Cooper, of Greenwich township Gloucester county New Jersey farmer, to serve him or assigns the indenture above recorded. Consideration = $77.20.

October 8, 1819

Maria Heinrich, with consent of her mother, to Sarah Connelly, of Philadelphia, widow, for nine years, to have six weeks schooling for each year of the term, & at the end thereof two complete suits of clothes, one of which to be new. Consideration = $40.00.

Johan Dietrich Feth, with consent of Christian Wentzel, to James Moore, of Southwark, Philadelphia county, bottler, for four years, to have six weeks schooling for each year of the term, & at the end thereof two complete suits of clothes, one of which to be new. Consideration = $55.00.

Jacob Friderich Apfel, willing to go to New Jersey, to Benjamin B. Cooper, of Waterford township, Gloucester county, New Jersey farmer, for four years, to be paid two dollars in hand, & have at the end of the term two complete suits of clothes, one of which to be new & be paid twenty dollars. Consideration = $77.20.

Gottfried Simon assigned by Adam Everly, to serve himself the remainder of his indenture recorded Book B, page 280. Valuable consideration.

Johan Dietrich Dingwerth, to C. Biddle & M. Canby, of Philadelphia sugar refiners, for one year & six months, to have at the end of the term two complete suits of clothes, one of which to be new. Consideration = $65.00.

October 9, 1819

Elisabeth Schiffin, with consent of Daniel Lebo, to John Brock, of Northern Liberties, Philadelphia county, storekeeper, for five years & nine months, to have six weeks schooling for each year of the term, & at the end thereof two complete suits of clothes, one of which to be new. Consideration = $78.67.

Margaretha Barbara Schacherlin, with consent of C. V. Hagner, to Henry Downar, of Lampeter township Lancaster county, Pennsylvania farmer, for three years, to have at the end of the term two complete suits of clothes, one of which to be new. Consideration = $77.20.

Magdalena Lofflerin, with consent of Daniel Lebo, to John Flower, of Southwark Philadelphia county, gentleman, for four years, to have six weeks schooling for each year of the term & at the end thereof two complete suits of clothes, one of which to be new. Consideration = $50.00.

Anna Maria Herneisin, with consent of her father, to Christopher Fritz, of Philadelphia, baker, for six years & eleven months, to have six weeks schooling for each year of the term, & at the end thereof two complete suits of clothes, one of which to be new. Consideration = $39.20.

October 11, 1819

Carl Ludwig Lauffer, willing to go to New Jersey, to Benjamin B. Cooper, of Waterford township, Gloucester county, New Jersey farmer, for four years, to have at the end of the term two complete suits of clothes, one of which to be new, & be paid twenty dollar. And if he shall return one half of his passage mony to his master at the expiration of two years of the term, then he to be free he relinquishing his freedom dues & the twenty dollars mentioned above. Consideration = $77.20.

Christian Sturm, willing as above, to the above Benjamin B. Cooper, for four years to have the same terms as above. Consideration = $77.20.

Friderich Taubenhein willing as above, to the above Benjamin B. Cooper, for four years, to have at the end of the term two complete suits of clothes one of which to be new, & be paid twenty dollars. Consideration = $77.20.

Johan Georg Maier, willing as above, to the above Benjamin B. Cooper, for four years, the same terms as the first above. Consideration = $77.20.

Johan Georg Kummerlein, willing as above, to the above Benjamin B. Cooper, for four years, to have the same terms as above. Consideration = $77.20.

Michael Fah, willing as above to the above Benjamin B. Cooper for four years, to have the same terms as above. Consideration = $77.20.

Georg Franze Klee to Jacob Lichtel, of the Northern Liberties, Philadelphia county, porter, for three years, to have at the end of the term two complete suits of clothes, one of which to be new. Consideration = $77.20.

October 12, 1819

Elisabeth Margaretha Weller to Margaretha Jones, of Southwark, Philadelphia county, widow, for four years, to have at the end of the term two complete suits of clothes, one of which to be new. Consideration = $80.00.

Anna Catharina Lang to the above Margaretha Jones, for four years, to have at the end of the term clothes as above. Consideration = $80.00.

Anna Maria Heinrich, with consent of her mother, to John Myer of Lancaster, Pennsylvania merchant for six years & three months & 19 days, to have six weeks schooling for each year of the term and at the end thereof two complete suits of clothes one of which to be new. Consideration = $40.00.

October 13, 1819

Elisabeth Wentzel, with consent of her father, to Samuel Newbold, of Philadelphia merchant, for four years, to have six weeks schooling for each year of the term & at the end thereof two complete suits of clothes, one of which to be new. Consideration = $65.00.

Christian Wentzel, with consent of his father, to go to New Jersey, to John Earl of Springfield township, Burlington county, New Jersey farmer, for eight years & seven months, to have six weeks schooling for each year of the term & at the end thereof two complete suits of clothes, one of which to be new, & be paid ten dollars. Consideration = $50.00.

Peter Wentzel, with consent of his father, to Clayton Earl of Philadelphia merchant for five years four months & fourteen days, to have six weeks schooling for each year of the term, & at the end thereof two complete suits of clothes, one of which to be new, & be paid ten dollars. Consideration = $50.00.

October 14, 1819

Johan Georg Scharr, with consent of George A. Trefts, to George D. Henck, of the Northern Liberties Philadelphia baker, for four years & two months, to have six weeks schooling for each year of the term & at the end thereof two complete suits of clothes, one of which to be new. Consideration = $34.00.

Anna Margaret Weller, with consent of her father, to Samuel Hollingsworth of Philadelphia merchant, for five years eleven months & nineteen days, to have six weeks schooling for each year of the term & at the end thereof two complete suits of clothes, one of which to be new. Consideration = $50.00.

Waldburg Heimin to Philip Eisenbrey of Philadelphia coach painter, for two years, to have at the end of the two complete suits of clothes, one of which to be new. Consideration = $41.45.

October 15, 1819

Andreas Scheel, willing to go to New Jersey to Benjamin B. Cooper, of Waterford township Gloucester county, New Jersey farmer, for four years, to have at the end of the term two complete suits of clothes one of which to be new, & be paid twenty dollars. Consideration = $77.20.

Andreas Eiszle willing as above with consent of L. McDonald, to the above Benjamin B. Cooper to have twelve weeks schooling during the term & at the end thereof two complete suits of clothes, one of which to be new, & be paid twelve dollars. Consideration = $61.70.

David Beck, willing as above with consent of L. McDonald, to the above Benjamin B. Cooper, for two years, to have at the end of the term clothes as above & paid ten dollars. Consideration = $36.70.

Albert Stracker, willing as above, to the above Benjamin B. Cooper, for four years, to have at the end of the term clothes as above & be paid nineteen dollars. Consideration = $77.20.

Jacob Wagner, willing as above with consent of L. McDonald, to the above Benjamin B. Cooper, for four years, to have six weeks schooling during the term, & at the end thereof clothes as above & be paid nineteen 50/100 dollars. Consideration = $77.20.

Joseph Blenckner, willing to go to the Island of Cuba, to George Bartlett of the Island of Cuba, planter, for two years, to have at the end of the term two complete suits of clothes, one of which to be new. And be paid one hundred dollars, if he conducts himself to the satisfaction of his master. Consideration = $77.20.

Burckhardt Herdle, willing as above with consent of L. McDonald to the above George Bartlett for two years, to have six weeks schooling, & at the end of the term clothes as above, & be paid one hundred upon the same conditions as above. Consideration = $70.00.

Johan Georg Gron, willing as above, with consent of L. McDonald, to the above George Bartlett, for two years, to have twelve weeks schooling, & at the end of the term clothes as above, & one hundred dollars upon the same conditions as above. Consideration = $77.20.

Anna Maria Kurz, with consent of Daniel Lebo, to John Goodman of the Northern Liberties, Philadelphia county esquire for four years, to have six weeks schooling, & at the end of the term two complete suits of clothes, one of which to be new. Consideration = $77.45.

Maria Ellinger, to James Worth, of Middletown township, Bucks county, Pennsylvania farmer, for three years, to have at the end of the term two complete suits of clothes, one of which to be new. Consideration = $77.20.

October 16, 1819

Eberhart Walch, with consent of David Lust, to Jacob Peiffer, of Germantown township, Philadelphia county, farmer, for two years, to have during the term six weeks schooling, & at the end thereof two complete suits of clothes, one of which to be new. Consideration = $36.00.

Georg Michael Diem, willing to go to New Jersey, to Benjamin B. Cooper, of Waterford township, Gloucester county, New Jersey farmer, for four years, to have at the end of the term two complete suits of clothes, one of which to be new, & be paid twenty dollars. Consideration = $77.20.

Georg Steinman, willing as above, to the above Benjamin B. Cooper, for four years, to have at the end of the term clothes as above, & be paid twenty dollars. Consideration = $77.20.

Johan Jacob Wurster, willing as above, to the above Benjamin B. Cooper, for four years, to have at the end of the term clothes as above & be paid twenty dollars. Consideration = $77.20. Afternote: Five 50/100 dollars now paid Colonel Egmond being a debt due him, leaving fourteen 50/100 comeing to servant.

Catharina Doringer, to Stacy Gillingham, of Franckford, Philadelphia county, tanner, for three years & six months, to have at the end of the term two complete suits of clothes, one of which to be new. Consideration = $75.00.

Casper Fischer with consent of G. Wile, to Anthony Tay of Bristol township, Bucks county, Pennsylvania farmer, for four years, to have eighteen weeks schooling during the term & at the end thereof two complete suits of clothes, one of which to be new, & be paid twenty dollars. Consideration = $77.20.

Georg Jacob Gantzhorn, with consent of his father, to John F. Steinman Junior, of Lancaster, Pennsylvania merchant, for nine years & three months, to have six weeks schooling for each year of the term, & at the end thereof two complete suits of clothes, one of which to be new. Consideration = $40.00.

October 18, 1819

Johan Steinman, willing to go to New Jersey, to Benjamin B. Cooper, of Waterford township, Gloucester county, New Jersey farmer, for four years, to have at the end of the term two complete suits of clothes, one of which to be new, & be paid twenty dollars. Consideration = $77.20.

Johannes Belz, willing as above, to the above Benjamin B. Cooper, for four years, to have at the end of the term clothes as above & be paid twenty dollars. And be free at any time he shall pay his master his passage mony. Consideration = $77.20.

Friderich Bohrer, willing to go to New Jersey, to Joseph Marshall, of the township & county of Gloucester, New Jersey farmer, for three years, to have at the end of the term two complete suits of clothes, one to be new, & be paid fifteen dollars. Consideration = $77.20.

Sophia Urban, with consent of her father, to Lewis Davis, of Haverford township Deleware county, farmer, for four years six months & twenty days, to have six weeks schooling for each year of the term, & at the end thereof two complete suits of clothes, one of which to be new. Consideration = $40.00.

Sophia Urban at the same time assigned to Hanah Davis, of the same township & county, single woman, to serve her or assigns the indenture recorded before. Consideration = $40.00.

Rosina Durr willing to go to New Jersey, to John Stevenson, of Mannington township Salem county, New Jersey farmer, for four years, to have at the end of the term two complete suits of clothes, one of which to be new, & be paid seventy five cents per week for the last six months of her term if she conducts herself well. Consideration = $77.45.

October 20, 1819

Anna Maria Schott, with consent of her father to go to New Jersey, to John L. Whiteall, of Woodbury, New Jersey farmer, for eleven years & seven months, to have six weeks schooling for each year of the term, & and at the end thereof two complete suits of clothes, one of which to be new. Consideration = $20.00.

Elisabeth Schott, with consent of her father to go to New Jersey, to Samuel Murdoch, of Philadelphia mariner, for nine years & six months, to have six weeks for each year of the term, & at the end thereof two complete suits of clothes, one of which to be new. Consideration = $20.00.

Johannes Rummel, with consent of Daniel Lebo, to Anthony Kennedy, of the Northern Liberties, Philadelphia county, farmer, for three years ten months & fourteen days, to have six weeks schooling for each year of the term, & at the end thereof two complete suits of clothes one of which to be new. Consideration = $60.00.

Joseph Brosey, willing to go to Allabama, to Edward Clark of Philadelphia gentleman, agent to N. Farrow, for two years two months & ten days, to be paid at the end of the term fifty dollars if he conducts himself well. Consideration = $70.00.

Johan Jacob Kamp, willing as above, to the above Edward Clark, agent to N. Farrow, for two years two months & ten days, to have at the of term fifty dollars, if he conducts himself well. Consideration = $70.00.

Carl Buhn, willing as above to Edward Clark, agent to N. Farrow, for two years, two months, & ten days, to be paid at the end of the term fifty dollars if he conducts himself well. Consideration = $70.00.

Georg Michael Schmidt, with consent of his wife & willing as above to Edward Clark, agent to N. Farrow, for two years two months & ten days, to be paid at the end of the term fifty dollars if he conducts himself well. Consideration = $70.00.

Barbara Schmidt, with consent of her husband & willing as above to Edward Clark, agent for N. Farrow, for two years, two months, & ten days, to be paid at the end of the term fifty dollars if she conducts herself well. Consideration = $70.00.

Conrad Schliphach, willing to go to Allabama, to Edward Clark agent for N. Farrow for two years two months & ten days, to be paid at the end of the term fifty dollars if he conducts himself well. Consideration = $70.00.

Johan Geschroindt, willing as above, to Edward Clark agent for N. Farrow, for two years two months & ten days, to be paid in hand eight dollars & forty five dollars 60 cents to him his heirs or assigns at the end of the term, being a part of his passage mony paid at Amsterdam, with legal interest thereon. Also to be paid fifty dollars if he conducts himself well. Consideration = $28.00.

Ludwig Fisher, willing as above, to Edward Clark, agent to N. Farrow, for two years two months & ten days, to be paid at the end of the term fifty dollars if he conducts himself well. Consideration = $70.00.

Christian Schliphack, willing as above, with consent of G. Wile, to Edward Clark, agent to N. Farrow, for two years two months & ten days, to have twelve weeks schooling, & be paid at the end of the term fifty dollars if he conducts himself well. Consideration = $70.00.

David Stampfle, willing as above, to Edward Clark, agent to N. Farrow, for two years two months & ten days, to be paid him his heirs or assigns at the end of the term twenty four dollars 10 cents being the amount with interest by him paid on his passage. Also pay him fifty dollars as above. Consideration = $48.00.

Gottlieb Brulling willing as above with consent of G. Wile to Edward Clark, agent for N. Farrow, for two years two months & ten days, to have twelve weeks schooling, & be paid at the end of the term fifty dollars as above. Consideration = $70.00.

Jacob Rauber, willing as above to Edward Clark, agent to N. Farrow, for two years two months & ten days to be paid at the end of the term fifty dollars as above. Consideration = $70.00.

Michael Maszne willing as above, to Edward Clark agent for N. Farrow, for two years two months & ten days, to be paid at the end of the term fifty dollars, as above. Consideration = $70.00.

Urich Walter, willing as above, to Edward Clark, agent to N. Farrow, for two years two months & ten days, to be paid to him his heirs or assigns at the end of the term twenty seven 42/100 being the amount with interest by him paid on his passage. Also to be paid fifty dollars as above. Consideration = $46.00.

Carl Breton, willing as above to Edward Clark, agent to N. Farrow, for two years two months & ten days, to be paid at the end of the term fifty dollars as above. Consideration = $70.00.

Johannes Schaufele, willing as before, to Edward Clark, agent to N. Farrow, for two years, two months, & ten days, to be paid to him his heirs or assigns at the end of the term thirty eight 76/100 dollars being the amount with interest by him paid on his passage, also pay him fifty dollars as before stated. Consideration = $36.00.

Jacob Leeroix, willing as above, to Edward Clark, agent for N. Farrow, for two years two months & ten days, to be paid at the end of the term fifty dollars as above stated. Consideration = $70.00.

Johan Georg Herman, willing as above, to Edward Clark, agent to N. Farrow, for two years two months & ten days, to be paid to him his heirs or assigns at the end of the term twenty two 80/100 dollars, being the amount with interest by him paid on his passage, also pay him fifty dollars as above stated. Consideration = $50.00.

Friderich Lenberger, willing as above, to Edward Clark, agent for N. Farrow, for two years two months & ten days, to be paid to him his heirs or assigns at the end of the term seven 16/100 dollars, being the amount with interest by him paid on his passage, also pay him fifty dollars as above stated. Consideration = $63.60.

Jacob Melchier Feigel, willing as above, to Edward Clark, agent to N. Farrow, for two years two months & ten days, to be paid at the end of the term fifty dollars if he conducts himself well. Consideration = $77.20.

Andreas Schmidt, willing as above, to Edward Clark, agent to N. Farrow, for two years two months & ten days, to be paid at the end of the term fifty dollars as before stated. Consideration = $77.20.

Johannes Schwager & his wife Elisabeth, willing as above, to Edward Clark, agent to N. Farrow, for two years two months & ten days, to be paid at the end of the term forty eight 76/100 dollars, being the amount with interest by them paid on his passage, in case of the death of either, to be paid to the survivor, & in case of the death of both servants to be paid to their heirs or assigns. Also pay each of them fifty dollars as above stated. Their infant to be provided for during their servitude & be free with the parent. Consideration = $97.20.

Maria Lego, willing as above, to Edward Clark, agent for N. Farrow, for two years two months & ten days, to be paid at the end of the term fifty dollars as before stated. Consideration = $70.00.

Friderich Zoller, willing as above, to Edward Clark, agent for N. Farrow, for two years two months & ten days, to be paid at the end of the term fifty dollars as before stated. Consideration = $70.00.

Johannes Blasz, willing as above, to Edward Clark, agent to N. Farrow, for two years two months & ten days, to be paid at the end of the term fifty dollars as before stated. Consideration = $70.00.

Johan Georg Henning, willing as above, to Edward Clark, agent to N. Farrow, for two years two months & ten days, to be paid at the end of the term fifty dollars as before stated. Consideration = $70.00.

Victor Kuny & his wife Anna Maria, willing as above, to Edward Clark, agent to N. Farrow, for two years two months & ten days, to be paid at the end of the term fifty dollars each as before stated. Consideration = $140.00.

Julianna Graussin, willing as above, to Edward Clark, agent for N. Farrow, for two years two months & ten days, to be paid at the end of the term fifty dollars as before stated. Consideration = $70.00.

Wilhelmina Benekendorferin, willing as above, to Edward Clark, agent to N. Farrow, for two years two months & ten days, to be paid at the end of the term fifty dollars as before stated. Consideration = $70.00.

Wilhelmina Hohnin, willing as above, to Edward Clark, agent to N. Farrow, for two years two months & ten days, to be paid at the end of the term fifty dollars as before stated. Consideration = $70.00.

Barbara Hohnin, willing as above, to Edward Clark, agent to N. Farrow, for two years two months & ten days, to be paid at the end of the term fifty dollars as before stated. Consideration = $70.00.

Friderich Schmolin, willing as above, to Edward Clark, agent to N. Farrow, for two years two months & ten days, to be paid at the end of the term fifty dollars as before stated. Consideration = $70.00.

Andrea Imle, willing as above with consent of G. Wile, to Edward Clark, agent to N. Farrow, for two years two months & ten days, to have twelve weeks schooling. And be paid at the end of the term fifty dollars as before stated. Consideration = $70.00.

Jacob Friderich Mayer, willing as above, to Edward Clark, agent to N. Farrow, for two years two months & ten days, to be paid at the end of the term fifty dollars as before stated. Consideration = $77.00.

Johannes Eisenbrey, willing as above, to Edward Clark, agent to N. Farrow, for two years two months & ten days, to be paid at the end of the term fifty dollars as before stated. Consideration = $70.00.

Johan Georg Hiller, willing as above & with consent of his wife, to Edward Clark, agent to N. Farrow, for two years two months & ten days, to be paid at the end of the term fifty dollars as before stated. Consideration = $70.00.

Sabina Catharina Hiller, with consent of her husband to Edward Clark, agent to N. Farrow, for two years two months & ten days, to be paid at the end of the term fifty dollars as before stated. Consideration = $70.00.

Gottlieb Supfle, willing as above, to Edward Clark, agent for N. Farrow, for two years two months & ten days, to be paid at the end of the term fifty dollars as before stated. Consideration = $70.00.

Johan Seiz, willing as above with consent of G. Wile, to Edward Clark, agent to N. Farrow, for two years two months & ten days, to have twelve weeks schooling, and at the end of the term be paid fifty dollars as before stated. Consideration = $70.00.

Johan Manner, willing as above, to Edward Clark, agent to N. Farrow, for two years two months & ten days, to be paid at the end of the term fifty dollars as before stated. Consideration = $70.00.

Carl Limbech, willing as above, to Edward Clark, agent to N. Farrow, for two years two months & ten days, to be paid at the end of the term fifty dollars as before stated. Consideration = $70.00.

Johan Jacob Kienast, willing as above, to Edward Clark, agent to N. Farrow, for two years two months & ten days, to be paid at the end of the term fifty dollars as before stated. Consideration = $70.00.

Friderich Werohe, willing as above, to Edward Clark, agent to N. Farrow, for two years two months & ten days, to be paid at the end of the term fifty dollars as before stated. Consideration = $70.00.

Francis Joseph Ripberger, willing as above with consent of G. Wile, to Edward Clark, agent to N. Farrow, for two years two months & ten days, to be paid at the end of the term fifty dollars as before stated. Consideration = $70.00.

October 21, 1819

Catharina Seuterin, willing to go to New Jersey, to William Newbold of Springfield township, Burlington county New Jersey for three years, to have at the end of the term two complete suits of clothes, one to be new. Consideration = $60.00.

Ceron Stern, willing to go to Georgia & with consent of Daniel Lebo, to C. H. Gundelach, of Philadelphia merchant, for three years five months & fifteen days, to have six weeks schooling for each year of the term. And at the end thereof two complete suits of clothes one of which to be new. Consideration = $77.20.

Ceron Stern at the same time assigned by C. H. Gundelach, to ... Sturgis, of Savannah, Georgia, merchant to serve him or assigns the remain of the indenture above recorded. Consideration = $77.20.

Jacob Friderich Walbold, with consent of John Notton to John Borman, of Penn township Philadelphia county, victuler, to have twelve weeks schooling during the term. And at the end thereof two complete suits of clothes, one of which to be new, & be paid twenty dollars, the term of servitude two years & six months. Consideration = $33.00.

October 22, 1819

Christianna Aldinger, with consent of her father to John P. Shott, of Philadelphia custom house officer, for four years three months & seventeen days, to have six weeks schooling for each year of the term, & at the end thereof two complete suits of clothes, one to be new. Consideration = $40.00.

October 23, 1819

Friderich Nithhammer with consent of C. H. Gundelach to Gottlieb Gross, of Spring Garden, Philadelphia county, victuler, for six years, to have six weeks schooling for each year of the term, to be taught the art trade & mistery of a victuler. And at the end of the term to have two complete suits of clothes, one of which to be new. Consideration = $50.00.

Gottfried Friderich Nithhammer to John Philip Lotz, of Spring Garden, Penn township, Philadelphia county, victuler, for three years & six months, to be taught the art trade & mistery of a victuler, & have at the end of the term two complete suits of clothes, one of which to be new, or twenty dollars at the option of the servant. Consideration = $70.00.

Catharina Knotz to John Plank of the Northern Liberties Philadelphia county, oak cooper, for three years, to have at the end of the term two complete suits of clothes, one of which to be new, & be paid fifteen dollars. Consideration = $70.00.

Catharina Rillinger to John Warner of Spring Garden, Penn township, Philadelphia county, victuler, for three years, to have at the end of the term two complete suits of clothes, one to be new. Consideration = $50.00.

Wilhelm Urban, with consent of his father, to go to New Jersey, to Samuel Lippincott, of Springfield township, Burlington county, New Jersey, for four years, to have six weeks schooling for each year of the term, & at the end thereof two complete suits of clothes, one of which to be new, & be paid twenty dollars. Consideration = $76.20.

Carlina Urban, with consent of her father, to the above Samuel Lippincott, for twelve years & eleven months, to have six weeks schooling for each year of the term, & at the end thereof two complete suits of clothes one to be new. Consideration = $1.00.

Johan Jost Althaus, with consent of G. Wile, to the above Samuel Lippincott, for five years & two months to have six weeks schooling for each year of the term & at the end thereof two complete suits of clothes, one to be new. Consideration = $76.20.

Henrich Hackenbracht, with consent of G. Wile, to go to New Jersey, to Benjamin B. Cooper, of Waterford township, Gloucester county, New Jersey farmer, for three years, to have six weeks schooling. And at the end of the term two complete suits of clothes, one of which to be new, & be paid twenty nine 60/100 dollars with interest. Consideration = $43.60.

October 25, 1819

Johan Gottfried Scherner, willing as above to the above Benjamin B. Cooper, for three years, to have at the end of the term two complete suits of clothes, one of which to be new. Consideration = $77.20.

Georg Bader, willing as above, to the above Benjamin B. Cooper, for three years, to have at the end of the term two complete suits of clothes, one of which to be new. Consideration = $77.20.

Jacob Althaus, with consent of C. H. Gundelach to go to New Jersey, to Benjamin B. Cooper above mentioned, for three years, to have six weeks schooling, & at the end of the term two complete suits of clothes, one to be new, & be paid four dollars, & should he at any time return to his master his freight then this indenture to be void. Consideration = $77.20.

Joseph Schott & his wife Elisabeth, willing as above, to the above Benjamin B. Cooper, for three years, to have each at the end of the term two complete suits of clothes, one of each to be new. And be paid to them their heirs or assigns forty two 40/100 dollars with interest, the interest to be paid annually. And their children Johan Georg, & Osgood, to be fed & clothed during the servitude of the parents & be free with them. Consideration = $112.40.

Georg Knochel & his wife Salome, willing as above, to the above Benjamin B. Cooper, for three years, to have at the end of the term two complete suits of clothes each, one of each to be new. And be paid them their heirs or assigns eighty 40/100 dollars with interest, their infant Philip Georg to be fed & clothed during the servitude of the parents & be free with them. Consideration = $66.00.

Christian Katz & wife Barbara, willing as above to Benjamin B. Cooper, for three years, to have at the end of the term two complete suits of clothes each, one of each to be new. Consideration = $154.40.

Conrad Ziegle, willing as above to the above Benjamin B. Cooper, for two years, to provide his own Sunday clothes, to have at the end of the term two complete suits of clothes one to be new & be paid six dollars if he serves his time out, to be free at any time if he shall return his master his passage mony. Consideration = $60.00.

Kraft Weder & his wife Maria, willing as above, to the above Benjamin B. Cooper for three years, to have each at the end of the term two complete suits of clothes, one of each to be new, & be paid to them their heirs or assigns fifty two 20/100 dollars with interest, their infant to be fed & clothed during the servitude of the parents, & be free with them. Consideration = $101.20.

Anton Petter, willing as before, to the aforesaid Benjamin B. Cooper, for three years, to have at the end of the term two complete suits of clothes one to be new. And be paid thirty three 20/100 dollars with interest. Consideration = $44.00.

October 26, 1819

Henrich Adler, willing as above, to Benjamin B. Cooper, for three years, to have at the end of the term clothes as above. Consideration = $77.20.

Christian Reisz & his wife Barbara, willing as above, to Benjamin B. Cooper, for three years, to have each at the end of the term clothes as above. Consideration = $154.40.

Joseph Lang, willing as above to Benjamin B. Cooper, for three years, to have at the end of the term clothes as above. Consideration = $77.20.

Adam Wieland, with consent of C. H. Gundelach, & willing as above to Benjamin B. Cooper, for three years, to have at the end of the term clothes as above, to have during the term eighteen weeks schooling. Consideration = $77.20.

Ludwig Koch, with consent of C. H. Gundelach, & willing as above, to Benjamin B. Cooper, for three years, to have during the term fifteen weeks schooling, & at the end thereof clothes as above. Consideration = $77.20.

Ferdinand Carl August Sauter, with consent of C. H. Gundelach to go to New Jersey to John A. Crane of Camden New Jersey printer for four years to have six weeks schooling for each year of the term & be taught the art trade & mistery of a printer, & have at the end of the term two complete suits of clothes, one to be new. Consideration = $77.20.

Agatha Schachterlin, with consent of C. H. Gundelach, to Abraham Schrack, of Philadelphia innkeeper, for four years, to have six weeks schooling, & at the end of the term two complete suits of clothes, one to be new. Consideration = $70.00.

Joseph Ridder, willing to go to New Jersey to Benjamin B. Cooper, of Waterford township, Gloucester county, New Jersey farmer, for three years, to have at the end of the term two complete suits of clothes one to be new. Consideration = $77.20.

Dorothea Beck to Robert B. Belville of Warwick township Bucks county, Pennsylvania, minister of the gospel, for four years, to have at the end of the term two complete suits of clothes, one of which to be new. And if she conducts herself well to have six months of her term relinquished to her. Consideration = $76.00.

October 27, 1819

Eva Haisch, with consent of her father, to Isaac Cooper, of Philadelphia, gentleman, for four years six months & eighteen days, to have six weeks schooling for each year of the term & at the end thereof two complete suits of clothes, one of which to be new. Consideration = $77.20.

John Foll, with consent of his father, to Christopher Vanarsdalen, of Northampton township, Bucks county, Pennsylvania farmer, for six years, to have six weeks schooling for each year of the term, & at the end thereof two complete suits of clothes, one of which to be new. Consideration = $50.00.

October 28, 1819

Daniel Herneisen, with consent of his father, to George Schott, of Philadelphia physicion, for six years, to have six weeks schooling for each year of the term, & at the end thereof two complete suits of clothes, one of which to be new. Consideration = $40.00.

Carl Ludwig Schenck, with consent of his father, to Henry Rush of Leacock township, Lancaster county, Pennsylvania farmer, for three years & nine months, to have six weeks schooling for each year of the term, & at the end thereof twenty dollars in lieu of freedoms. Consideration = $76.00.

Simon Mesner, to Thomas Thompson, of Philadelphia mariner, for two years, to have at the end of the term two complete suits of clothes, one to be new. Consideration = $77.20.

October 29, 1819

Anna Herneisen, with consent of her father, to Martin Dubs, of Philadelphia merchant, for five years, to have eighteen weeks schooling during the term, & at the end thereof two complete suits of clothes, one to be new. Consideration = $77.20.

Johan Wildemuth, with consent of C. H. Gundelach to go to New Jersey, to Benjamin B. Cooper, of Waterford township Gloucester county, New Jersey farmer, for three years, to be paid in hand three dollars, to have during the term six weeks schooling, to be placed at the trade of a saddler, he professing to have learnt that art, & have at the end of the term two complete suits of clothes, one to be new. Consideration = $78.00.

Peter Pflugfelder, willing as above, to the above Benjamin B. Cooper, with consent of C. H. Gundelach, for three years, to be paid in hand two dollars, to have six weeks schooling during the term, & at the end thereof two complete suits of clothes, one to be new, and be free at any time if he shall pay his master his freight or passage mony. Consideration = $78.00.

Catharina Weidlin, willing to go to New Jersey, to the before named Benjamin B. Cooper, for three years, to be paid one dollar 12/100 in hand, and have at the end of the term two complete suits of clothes, one to be new. Consideration = $77.20.

Johannes Fischer, willing as above, to the above Benjamin B. Cooper, for three years, to be paid in hand two dollars, to be placed with a tanner, to have at the end of the term two complete suits of clothes, one to be new. And if he conducts himself well to be paid at the end of the term twenty five dollars. Consideration = $77.20.

Catharina Wolf to Joseph Siddons, of Philadelphia biscuit baker, for four years, to have at the end of the term two complete suits of clothes, one to be new. Consideration = $77.20.

October 30, 1819

Jacob Hohn, willing to go to New Jersey, to Benjamin B. Cooper, of Waterford township Gloucester county, New Jersey farmer, for three years to have at the end of the term two complete suits of clothes, one to be new, & be paid twenty five dollars. Consideration = $77.20.

November 2, 1819

Christian Heimerdinger, with consent of his brother, to Nicholas Schultheis, of Philadelphia baker, for three years, to have six weeks schooling for each year of the term, to be taught the art trade & mistery of a baker & be paid at the end of the term twenty five dollars. Consideration = $10.00.

November 3, 1819

Maria Margaretha Schenck, with consent of her father to go with her master to any part of the United States, to Henry Riesh, of Philadelphia groecer, for five years, to have fifteen weeks schooling & at the end of the term two complete suits of clothes, one to be new. Consideration = $77.20.

Jacob Friderich Machtle to Henry Pratt, of Philadelphia merchant, for three years, to have at the end of the term two complete suits of clothes, one to be new. Consideration = $81.20.

November 4, 1819

Conrad Dornis & his wife Anna Maria, willing to go to New Jersey, to Benjamin B. Cooper, of Waterford township Gloucester county, New Jersey farmer, for three years, to be paid to them their heirs or assigns at the end of the term ninety six dollars, with interest, & to have each two complete suits of clothes, one of each to be new. The parents not to be separated from their children without their consent. Consideration = $85.00.

Wilhelm Dornis, with consent of his father, to the above Benjamin B. Cooper, for three years, to have eighteen weeks schooling, not to be separated from his parents without the consent of parties, & have at the end of the term two complete suits of clothes, one to be new. Consideration = $1.00.

Anna Catharina Dornis, with consent of her father, to the above Benjamin B. Cooper, upon the same terms & conditions as before. Consideration = $1.00.

Anna Sabina Weidlein, with consent of her mother to go to New Jersey, to Benjamin B. Cooper, of Waterford township, Gloucester county New Jersey farmer, for eleven years, to have six weeks schooling for each year of the term, and at the end thereof two complete suits of clothes, one to be new, her mother, her heirs or assigns to be paid by the master at the end of three years twenty dollars, if the servant shall live. Consideration = $1.00.

November 6, 1819

Heinrich Buttell to Henry Rush, of Conastoga township, Lancaster county, Pennsylvania farmer, for three years, to have at the end of the term two complete suits of clothes, one to be new. Consideration = $71.60.

Anna Maria Michlen, willing to go to New Jersey, to John Dobbins, of Northampton township, Burlington county, New Jersey storekeeper, for three years & six months, to have at the end of the term two complete suits of clothes, one to be new. Consideration = $77.20.

Georg Friderich Benz, willing to go to New Jersey, to James Lippincott, of Greenwich township, Gloucester county, New Jersey storekeeper, for three years, to be paid two dollars in hand. And at the end of the term have two complete suits of clothes, one to be new, & be paid twenty five dollars. Consideration = $77.20.

Regina Friderica Frechin, willing to go to New Jersey to Benjamin B. Cooper of Waterford township Gloucester county New Jersey farmer, for four years to have at the end of the term two complete suits of clothes, one to be new. Consideration = $77.00.

Regina Barbara Kromerin, willing as above, to the above Benjamin B. Cooper, for four years, have at the end of the term clothes as above & be paid thirty two dollars with interest. Consideration = $35.00.

Johan Georg Weber, willing as above, to the above Benjamin B. Cooper, for three years to be paid two dollars in hand, to have at the end of the term clothes as above, & be paid ten dollars. Consideration = $80.00.

Johan Georg Reiner, willing as above with consent of Daniel Lebo to the above Benjamin B. Cooper, for three years & six months, to have six weeks schooling for each year, to be paid two dollars in hand & have at the end of the term clothes as above & be paid eight dollars. Consideration = $80.00.

Johan Kucherer, willing as above, to the above Benjamin B. Cooper, for three years, to be paid in hand two dollars. And have at the end of the term clothes as above & be paid eight dollars. Consideration = $80.00.

November 11, 1819

Georg Henrich Bute to Henry Pratt, of Philadelphia merchant, for three years, to have at the end of the term two complete suits of clothes, one to be new. Consideration = $81.20.

November 16, 1819

Regina Ackerman to Mathew Law, of Vincent township, Chester county farmer, for nine years, to have at the end of the term two complete suits of clothes, one to be new, her infant to be fed & clothed gratis & be free with the mother. Consideration = $65.00.

Maria Catharina Weidleinin, willing to go to New Jersey to Benjamin B. Cooper of Waterford township, Gloucester county, New Jersey farmer, for three years, to have at the end of the term two complete suits of clothes, one to be new, & be paid fifteen dollars. Consideration = $77.20.

November 18, 1819

Barbara Mayerin to William Horstmann, of Philadelphia lace weaver, for three years & four months, to have six months of the term relinquished to her if she conducts herself well. And be paid during the servitude twenty five cents per week in lieu of apparel. And be paid at the end of the term twelve dollars in lieu of freedoms. Consideration = $77.25.

November 20, 1819

Georg William Miller, willing to go to New Jersey with consent of C. H. Gundelach, to Benjamin B. Cooper, of Waterford township Gloucester county New Jersey farmer, for three years, to have at the end of the term two complete suits of clothes, one to be new & be paid ten dollars, to have six weeks schooling. Consideration = $81.20.

Johan Jacob Starck, willing as above, to Benjamin B. Cooper, for three years, to have at the end of the term clothes & cash as above. Consideration = $81.20.

Friderich Ellinger to Jacob Janney, of Newtown township, Bucks county, Pennsylvania farmer, for three years, to have at the end of the term two complete suits of clothes & be paid ten dollars. Consideration = $65.00.

November 29, 1819

Gottlieb Neithhammer to John Warner, of Penn township Philadelphia county, victuler, for three years & six months, to have at the end of the term two complete suits of clothes, one to be new, or twenty five dollars at the option of the servant. Consideration = $50.00.

Johannes Wizeman, with consent of Daniel Lebo, to Jacob Franz Gausz, of Philadelphia baker, for four years, to have six weeks schooling for each year of the term, to be taught the art trade & mistery of a baker, to have at the end of the term two complete suits of clothes, one to be new. Consideration = $75.00.

November 30, 1819

Anna Maria Ott assigned by William Warrance to John Kohler of Philadelphia coach wheel wright, to serve him or assigns the remainder of her indenture recorded page 76. Consideration = $20.00.

Christian Ott & his Anna Maria, haveing paid the above John Kohler thirty six dollars in consideration of the remainder of their indentures, they are both discharged from any further obligations containd therein & the indentures made null & void.

December 1, 1819

Jacob Mark, with consent of his father, to Henry Swertzer, of Bronville, Pennsylvania merchant, for six years & nine months, to have six weeks schooling for each year of the term & at the end thereof two complete suits of clothes, one to be new. Consideration = $72.00.

Jacob Mark at the same time assigned to Jacob Bowman, of the before mentioned place, esquire, to serve him or assigns the remainder of his indenture before recorded. Consideration = $72.00.

December 27, 1819

Christian Kattz & his wife Barbara, assigned by Benjamin B. Cooper to Henry Kattz, of Whitemarsh township Montgomery county, Pennsylvania papermaker, to serve him or his assigns the remainder of their indenture recorded page 115. Consideration = $156.65.

January 22, 1820

Pius Zwisele assign by Ruff & Fisher to himself. Consideration = $40.00.

January 27, 1820

Friderick Hoffman, assigned by James Tiessiere to his father Christoph Hoffman to serve him the remainder of his indenture recorded page 101. Consideration = $40.00.

February 12, 1820

Frederica Hoffman assigned by Joseph Pyle to her father to serve him the remainder of her indenture recorded page 77. Consideration = $82.00.

Sophia Schulz, assigned by Magdalen Ewing to Peter Fayssoux, assistant commisary United States Army, of St. Louis Missouri teritory to serve him or assigns the remainder of her indenture recorded page 90. Consideration = $15.00.

February 26, 1820

Anna Dietiker, assigned by Charles Bird, to her father to serve him the remainder of her indenture recorded in Book B, page 251. Consideration = $40.00.

March 30, 1820

Margaretha Kleindienst, assigned by Robert Pearpoint to herself. Consideration = $1.00.

April 1, 1820

John Weiss, assigned by Richard Peters esquire to Bastian Weiss of Lancaster to serve him the remainder of his indentured recorded in Book B, page 255. Consideration = $1.00.

April 11, 1820

Jacob Friderick Gogel, & wife Dorothea Margaretha to James McIlvain, of Ridly township Deleware county, farmer for two years to have at the end of the term two complete suits of clothes each, one of each to be new. Their infant Anna Maria to be fed & clothed during the term & be free with the parents. Consideration = $98.20.

Johan Michael Gogel, with consent of his father, to the above James McIlvain for two years, to have twelve weeks schooling during the term & at the end thereof two complete suits of clothes one to be new. Consideration = $15.00.

Gottlieb Friderick Gogel, with consent of his father, to the before named James McIlvain, for eight years nine months & 21 days to have six weeks schooling for each year of the term & at the end thereof two complete suits of clothes, one of which to be new & be paid twenty dollars. Consideration = $15.00.

Carl Christian Gogel, with consent of his father, to Jesse J. Maris of Chester township Deleware county farmer for eleven years & three months, to have six weeks schooling for each year of the term & at the end thereof two complete suits of clothes, one of which to be new, & be paid twenty dollars. Consideration = $10.00.

April 22, 1820

John Christian Roger assigned by Charles Maysenhoelder to himself. Consideration = $1.00.

April 24, 1820

Johan Ulrich Maisch assigned by Conrad Hess, to Michael Stoltz of the Northern Liberties, cordwainer, to serve him or assigns the remainder of his indenture recorded page 100. Consideration = $30.00.

May 2, 1820

Jacob Friderich Bauman, assigned by August Gabrael Thommisont, administrator to the estate of Anthony Ratshiller deceased, to himself. Consideration = $1.00.

May 13, 1820

Catharina Lingg assigned by Peter Hahn to herself he relinquishing all further claims contained in her indenture recorded Book B, page 144. Consideration = $1.00.

May 23, 1820

Christianna Huhnle, with consent of her mother, to Henry Lelar of Philadelphia merchant for eight years & one month, to have six weeks schooling for each year of the term, and at the end thereof two complete suits of clothes one of which to be new. Consideration = $20.00.

June 8, 1820

A. M. C. Rosina Troxler, assigned by Jacob Reindollar, to her father. Consideration = $1.00.

July 1, 1820

Johannes Wizeman, assigned by Jacob Fransz Gausz, to his brother Jacob Wizeman, of Philadelphia distiller, to serve him the remainder of his indenture recorded page 120. Consideration = $75.00.

July 8, 1820

Henry Gottfried Klinck, with consent of Christian Leicht, to Michael Stoltz of the Northern Liberties cordwainer for three years two months & 7 days to have six weeks schooling for each year of the term and be taught the art & mistery of a cordwainer. At the end of the term to have two complete suits of clothes one of which to be new. Consideration = $60.00.

July 13, 1820

Frederick Kingeter, assigned by Jacob Benner to Michael Benner, of Moreland township Philadelphia county, farmer, to serve him or assigns the remainder of his indenture recorded page 32. Consideration = $50.00.

September 11, 1820

Marianna Sutter assigned by James S. Ewing to her father Joseph Sutter, to serve him remainder of indenture recorded page 75. Consideration = $30.00.

John Klein, assigned by James S. Ewing, to Joseph Sutter of Allintown, Northampton county, to serve him or assigns the remainder of his indenture recorded page 74. Consideration = $1.00.

October 2, 1820

By consent of parties, the indenture between Sarah Reichardin & William Montgomery Junior recorded page 103 is canseld & the servant set free.

November 8, 1820

H. R. Wegman, willing to go to New Jersey, to Benjamin Reeves, of Camdon New Jersey ferry keeper for three years, to have at the end of the term two complete suits of clothes, one of which to be new. Consideration = $62.45.

November 14, 1820

Elisabeth Schimmern to Frederick Gaul, of Philadelphia brewer, for four years, to have at the end of the term two complete suits of clothes, one of which to be new. Consideration = $71.25.

Elisabeth Schimelin, to John D. Campbell of Philadelphia taylor for three years, to have at the end of the term two complete suits of clothes, one of which to be new. Consideration = $71.25.

November 15, 1820

Catharina Geiser, assigned by Joseph Taylor to her father John George Geiser, to serve him the remainder of her indenture recorded page 73. Consideration = $60.00.

November 18, 1820

Casper Henrich Behring, to David Landis of Philadelphia sugar boiler, for three years, to have at the end of the term two complete suits of clothes, one of which to be new. And if he conducts himself well to be paid twenty dollars. Consideration = $80.25.

November 22, 1820

Christina Wilhelmina Tiedemann, to Peter Hertzog of Philadelphia sugar boiler, for three years, to have at the end of the term two complete suits of clothes, one of which to be new. Consideration = $90.00.

November 29, 1820

Jacob Brandsteller with consent of Samuel Wentz, to T. Hope of Philadelphia exchange broker, for three years, to have six weeks schooling for each year of the term, and at the end thereof two complete suits of clothes, one of which to be new. Consideration = $80.00.

November 30, 1820

Joseph Lotze & his wife Margareth, willing to go to New Jersey, to Mesheck Fish, of Gloucester county, New Jersey for three years, to have at the end of the term two complete suits of clothes each, one of each to be new. Consideration = $152.00.

Geneveva Weisenberger, assigned by John Stock to herself. Consideration = $100.00.

Lazerus Ulman to Lazerus Mentzenheimer, of Harford township Berks county, dealer, for one year & six months, to have at the end of the term two complete suits of clothes one of which to be new. Consideration = $64.00.

December 6, 1820

Peter Mathias Paulsen to Henry Dietrich of Conastoga township, Lancaster county, farmer, for three years, to have at the end of the term two complete suits of clothes, one of which to be new. Consideration = $80.00.

January 7, 1821

Eva Wagner, with consent of her father to John M. Brown of the Northern Liberties, Philadelphia county, riger, for five years, to have six months schooling. And at the end of the term two complete suits of clothes, one of which to be new, also one straw bed, one cott bedstead, one blanket, one pillow, & one sheet. Consideration = $70.00.

January 30, 1821

Regina Bogerin, assigned by Levy Taylor, one of the executors of the estate of John Dickson deceased, to her father. Consideration = $15.00.

February 3, 1821

Anna Margaret Weller, assigned by Samuel Hollingsworth to her father. Consideration = $25.00.

February 9, 1821

Catharina Genth, assigned by Abraham Stein to Charles F. Kerly of Philadelphia merchant, to serve or assigns the remainder of her indenture recorded page 139, Book B. Consideration = $30.00.

February 13, 1821

Catharina Kopp, assigned by George W. Mentz, to her father to serve him the remainder of her indenture recorded in Book B, page 125. Consideration = $1.00.

March 12, 1821

Elisabeth Wagner, with consent of her father, to John Mingle Junior of Penn township Philadelphia county, smith, for five years from 22nd January last past, to have six weeks schooling for each year of the term. And at the end thereof two complete suits of clothes, one of which to be new. Also one straw bed, one cott bedstead, one blanket, one pillow & one sheet. Consideration = $40.00.

March 20, 1821

By mutual consent of parties in the indenture between Jacob Nitzel and Sophia Christina Eglerin recorded page 92, all claims containd therein are relinquished and the indenture made null & void.

March 29, 1821

Christina Barbara Eickelbuss with consent of her father John Eickelbuss, to Elizabeth Philler living in Front Street no. 429, for four years from the 29th March 1821, & at the expiration of four years two complete suits of clothes one of which to be new. Consideration = $68.00.

April 3, 1821

Francis Leelenfrid with his own consent to Mr. John Zimmerman, for two years beginning the 9th December 1820 to pay him weekly twenty five cents pocket money and when free ten dollars. Consideration = $80.00.

July 14, 1821

Mary Ann Hufnagle with consent of her father Caspar Hufnagle to Michael Brown for 4 years beginning the 14th July 1821, & at the expiration of 4 years 2 suits of clothes one to be new & six weeks schooling yearly. Note. The father if he choses may at the expiration of 2 years make her free by paying the difference between 30 & 50 dollars. Consideration = $50.00.

July 25, 1821

Dorothea Dornerin with her consent is assigned by Manuel Priess to Lambert Keatting tavernkeeper to serve him or assigned the remainder of her indentured recorded page 88. Consideration = $1.00.

August 2, 1821

Mary Meyer with her consent to Jacob David for eighty six weeks & five days beginning from the 2nd of August, at 75 cents per week. Consideration = $65.00.

August 3, 1821

Maria Ursula Spat with her consent is assigned by John Clopp to William Esher to serve him or his assigns the remainder of her indenture recorded page 207, Book B.

November 24, 1821

By consent of parties the indenture between Christina Ziegler & Charles Brugiere as recorded page 103 is cancelled & the servant set free.

April 29, 1822

By consent of parties the indenture between Doris Neff & John Pemberton as recorded page 241, Book B is transferred to William Henniker for consideration of one dollar.

May 11, 1822

By consent of the parties the indenture between Regina Catharina Muazungerin & Josiah R. Evans as administrator to Edward Russel as recorded page 103 is cancelled & the servant set free.

June 22, 1822

By mutual consent of parties in the indenture between John Warner & Catherina Rilliger recorded page 114 all claims contained therein are relinquished & the indenture made null & void.

August 1, 1822

By consent of parties the indenture between Philipina Heinrichin & James Arbuckle as recorded page 89 is cancelled & the servant set free.

November 14, 1822

By consent Wilhelmina Bogger is willing to serve the remainder of her time as recorded page 87 with Tobias Beekler for the consideration of $35.00, he has to pay to William K. Hamilton her former master.

October 18, 1823

Catherina Guntherin with her own consent bound herself for 3 years to Michael Weaver Cohockson Penn township, Consideration = $100.00, fifty of which have been paid by said Weaver to her & the other to be paid when free, besides two suits of clothes one to be new.

October 20, 1823

By consent of parties the indenture between Frederick Brenn & William Rickle as recorded page 75 is transferred to Gottlieb Sheerer shoemaker.

February 18, 1824

John Henry Keiser, with his own, & the consent of his mother is assigned by Joseph & George M. Elkinton, administrators of Asa Elkinton deceased to Charles Eckhardt of Northern Liberties, soap & candle manufacturer, to serve the remainder of the term of his indenture recorded in Book B, page 145. Consideration = $20.00.

May 19, 1824

Susanna Herbster of her own free will, and consent of her father Laurence Herbster, to Christian Schenck of the Northern Liberties shoemaker for six years, and also give her six months schooling. And within the first three years of the term to have her confirmed at the German Lutheran Church in Philadelphia, and attend the lectures of the minister, and at the expiration of her term to have two complete suits of clothes, one thereof to be new, also a good bed, bolster pillow & blanket worth at least twenty five dollars.

September 13, 1824

John Frederick Hueter with his own, & the consent of his father George M. Hueter, bound himself to Daniel Wolff of the Northern Liberties cordwainer, for five years and twenty seven days, to have three months night schooling for every year of the term of his service, to be taught the trade of a boot & shoe maker, and at the expiration of his term to have two complete suits of clothes one whereof to be new.

October 1, 1824

Henry Snyder, with his own consent, assigned by Dr. Elijah Griffith to Erhart Snyder of Lancaster county coverlit weaver, to serve the remainder of the term of his indenture recorded in Book B, page 267. This assignment being made for the express purpose that the said Henry may learn a trade.

October 27, 1824

Elizabeth Schifferin, with her own consent, assigned by John Brock to George Ziegler of the Northern Liberties, storekeeper, to serve the remainder of the term of her indenture, recorded in Book B, page 105. He the said George Ziegler performing the covenants contained on the part of the said John Brock his executors, from and since the sixteenth day of June last, at which time the said servant was sold to the said George Ziegler.

George Ziegler, assignee of John Brock, released unto Elizabeth Schifferin all his right and claim to her service during the remainder of the term of her indenture, recorded in Book B, page 105. And the said Elizabeth Schifferin at the same time voluntarily releasing the said George Ziegler from the performance of the covenants contained in the said indenture on the part of the said John Brock his executors administrators & assigns and also releasing the said John Brock his executors &.

Barbara Heinrich of her own free will, and in consideration of 41 dollars paid by John G. Foley of Southwark Philadelphia county baker to H. R. Packard for her passage from Rotterdam and as also for other causes and considerations, bound to John Foley for two years and six months, to have fifteen weeks schooling, and at the expiration of her term two complete suits of clothes, one whereof to be new.

December 4, 1824

Caroline Miller with her own, and, consent of her father John Miller, in consideration of the sum of seventy dollars paid by John Singer of the city of Philadelphia merchant to the said John Miller, bound herself servant to the said John Singer for three years and six months, at the expiration of the term to have two complete suits of clothes one whereof to be new.

September 16, 1825

John Jatzge with his own, and consent of his father George Jatzge in consideration of the sum of forty dollars paid by Frederich Renz of the Northern Liberties baker at the execution of the indenture, and the like sum of forty dollars at the expiration of two years from the date hereof, unto the said George Jatzge, bound himself servant to the said Frederich Renz for four years, to be taught the art and trade of a baker, & at the expiration of the term to have a new suit of clothes.

January 5, 1826

Henry Urspruch Junior with his, and consent of his father Henry Urspruch bound himself to Daniel Wolff of the Northern Liberties cordwainer for five years, to have three months English schooling for every year of the term of his service, to be taught the art and trade of a boot and shoe maker, and to be confirmed at church, and at the expiration of his term to have two complete suits of clothes, one of which to be new.

January 9, 1826

Charles Frederick Wohrer, with his own, and consent of his father Christian Frederick Wohrer bound himself to William H. Horstmann of the city of Philadelphia lace and fringe weaver for two years, to pay to the said servant the sum of two dollars and fifty cents per week in lieu of board &, to be paid at the expiration of the said term, calculating the wages earned by the said servant the last year of his term and deducting the same two dollars and fifty cents per week from such wages and paying him the balance thereof if any. And to be taught the trade of a coach lace and fringe weaver. Consideration = eighty dollars heretofore paid by the said William H. Horstmann for his passage from Havre.

June 20, 1827

John Nicholas Tietjens of his own free will and accord bound himself servant to John Maull of the city of Philadelphia sail maker for five years, wearing apparel of servant to be suitable for working in only, and to teach or cause to be taught the said servant the art and trade of a sail maker.

September 10, 1827

Jacob Schaeffer of his own free will and consent of Frederick Zechele, bound himself servant to Jacob Sheerer of Penn township baker for seven years seven months & fourteen days, to have six weeks schooling for every year of the term of his servitude, to be confirmed at church, and to be taught the art and trade of a baker, and at the expiration of his term to have two complete suits of clothes one whereof to be new, and if the said servant behaves himself well the said master agrees to relinquish the last year of his term and pay him wages. Consideration twenty four dollars paid by the said Jacob Sheerer to the said Frederick Zechele which he paid for the passage of the said Jacob Schaeffer from Graventiel.

October 15, 1828

Eve Smith, of her own free will and consent of her father Jacob Smith, in consideration of the sum of fourteen dollars paid to the said Jacob Smith, by John Johnston of the city of Philadelphia merchant, bound herself servant to the said John Johnston for eight years seven months and twenty one days, to have six weeks schooling for every year of her term of servitude, one half in the English, and the other half in the German language. And during her term to have her confirmed at the German Presbyterian Church, and to attend the preparatory lectures of the minister, and at the expiration of her term to have two complete suits of clothes, one of which to be new, and ten dollars in cash.

August 14, 1829

Jacob Frederick Reichmann of his own free will and consent of Jacob D. Scheerer bound himself servant to Frederick Snyder of the city of Philadelphia baker for five years six months & two days, to teach the said servant the trade of a baker to have six weeks schooling for every year of the term of his servitude, at the expiration of the first four years and six months to give the said servant a complete new suit and for the remaining one year to pay the said servant eight dollars per month in lieu of clothing. Consideration = $40.00.

November 24, 1831

Barbara Witmire of her own free will bound herself servant to John Seiser of the city of Philadelphia tailor for two years, at the expiration of the term to have two complete suits of clothes one whereof to be new. Consideration = $40.00.

November 28, 1831

Fredericka Witmire of her own free will bound herself servant to Frederick Snyder of the city of Philadelphia baker for two years, at the expiration of the term to have two complete suits of clothes one whereof to be new. Consideration = $45.00.

December 1, 1831

Jacob Schaeffer, with his own consent, assigned by Jacob Sheerer to Frederick Snyder of the city of Philadelphia baker to serve the remainder of the term of his indenture, recorded page 129. Consideration = $24.00.

END

INDEX OF PERSONS

A

Abel, Catharina 42
Abel, George 69
Abercromby, James Junior 54
Achenbach, Catharina 83
Achenbach, Magdalena 66
Ackerman, Regina 119
Adam, Anton 34
Adam, Rosa 34
Adam, Serafin 34
Adams, Daniel 34
Adams, John 87
Adgate, Daniel 83
Adler, Henrich 116
Aelurns, John 78
Agnew, Doctor 59
Agster, Jacob 86
Aisenbrey, Margaretha Barbara 97
Albert, John 48
Albrecht, Gottlieb 89
Alcorn, George 86
Aldinger, Christianna 114
Aldinger, Frederica 102
Allebough, David 34
Almendinger, Frederick 57
Alter, Maria Dorothea 43
Alter, Maria Juliana 50
Althaus, Jacob 115
Althaus, Johan Jost 114
Amholtz, Jacob Friedrick 46
Andrew, Jacob 29
Angue, John 53
Antelo, Anthony 81
Apfel, Jacob Friderich 104
Arbuckle, James 89, 126
Arnold, Barbara 21, 29
Arnold, Frederick 21
Arnold, George 21, 29
Arnold, Jacob 21, 29
Arnold, Ludwig 22
Arny, Joseph 63
Ashhurst, Richard 2
Aughinbauch, Peter 39
Aughinbaugh, Peter 40
Auig, John 48

B

Babcock, Robert 11, 37
Bach, Christopher 63
Bache, Richard 16
Bachman, Peter 97
Bader, Christina Barbara 62
Bader, Elizabeth 62
Bader, Georg 115
Bader, John George 62
Bader, John George Junior 62
Bader, Regina Dorothea 62
Bader, Sibila Catharina 36
Baderin, Sabina 92
Badger, Samuel 64
Bailinger, Johannes 72
Baker, Fred D. 43

Baker, M. 97
Baker, Margareth 43
Barnes, Joseph 10
Barthema, Joseph 81
Barthema, Kresen 81
Bartlett, George 107
Bartling, Christlieb 81
Basseler, Franz 32, 33
Batzel, Catharina 63
Bauer, Barbara 7
Bauer, David 52
Bauer, John Christoph 7
Bauer, Margretta 7
Baugh, Archibald 82, 84, 85
Bauman, Henry 40
Bauman, Jacob Frederick 58
Bauman, Jacob Friderich 122
Bauman, Joseph 75
Bauman, Josepha, 75
Baumann, Christina 100
Baumann, Margaretha 100
Baumfort, Augustus L. 89
Baumgartner, Anthon 44
Baumgartner, Joseph Mehchior 43
Bazeley, Charles W. 89
Bear, Benjamin 75
Beard, Captain 29
Beasley, Charles W. 16
Bebion, Johan Georg 104
Bechtel, Issac 40
Bechtel, John A. 40
Bechtel, John M. 40
Bechtle, Peter 44
Beck, Anna Maria 22
Beck, David 107
Beck, Dorothea 116
Beck, Jacob 52, 68, 96
Beck, Johan 79
Beck, John George 4, 22
Beck, John Michael 4
Beck, Lorensz 79
Beck, Magdalena 79
Beck, Nicholas 55
Becker, Jacob 104
Beckhart, Charles 64
Beckin, Catharina 88
Beekler, Tobias 127
Beeler, ? 65
Beeler, Louis 42
Begert, Maria 43
Behler, Charles Frederick Philip 66
Behner, Rosina Elisabeth 88
Behring, Casper Henrich 123
Beidelman, Jacob 92, 95
Beiler, Baltasar 40
Bell, Charles 30, 31
Belville, Robert B. 116
Belz, Johannes 108
Bender, Johannes 66
Benekendorferin, Wilhelmina 112
Benethum, John 77
Bengle, Ferdinand 80
Benner, George 32
Benner, Jacob 31, 32, 123

Benner, Michael 123
Benneville, Nathan De 43
Benz, Georg Friderich 119
Benzinger, Daniel 92
Berhart, Jacob 67
Bernhard, John Adam 31
Bernhart, Johan Adam 96
Betz, Philipina 10
Betz, Susanna Magdelena 10
Bickley, Daniel 101
Biddle, C. 105
Biddle, John 86
Bioren, John 66
Bird, Charles 121
Bird, George 86
Bishop, William 81
Bisschopf, Frederick 25
Blank, George 32
Blasz, Johannes 111
Blenckner, Joseph 107
Bletscher, Barbara 13
Bletscher, Elizabeth Junior 13
Bletscher, Martin 8
Bletscher, Zacharias 13
Blumin, Maria 74
Boal, John 42
Boeam, Ignats 9
Bogerin, Regina 124
Bogerin, Regina 66
Bogger, Wilhelmina 87, 127
Bohrer, Friderich 108
Boller, Jacob 78
Bollinger, Jacob 23, 24, 25, 26
Bollinger, Samuel 53
Boraef, Henry 97
Borie, Joseph 54
Borman, John 85, 114
Bornman, John 76
Bossert, Johan Friderich 95
Boutiere, Jean Claude Benoit 10
Bowman, Jacob 121
Bowman, Jesse 45
Bowman, John 45
Boyd, Parkes 5, 41
Boyd, Thomas 96
Bradley, Thomas 65
Brady, Clement Lee 74, 103
Braehm, Charles G. 71
Brandsteller, Jacob 124
Braun, Christian 57
Braun, Ludwig Frederick 64
Brechbill, Philip 47
Breidenhart, George 35, 88
Breish, Adam 65
Breitenstein, Eva 16
Brenn, Frederick 75, 127
Brenn, Jacob 84
Brenn, Sarah 80
Brenn, Tobias 80
Brennenstuhl, Johan Martin 67
Brennin, Catharina 73
Brennin, Magdalena 75
Breton, Carl 110
Brindle, John 85
Brock, John 105, 128
Bronni, Johan Martin 97

Brosey, Joseph 109
Brosse, Charles de 10
Brown, James 70, 78, 79, 80
Brown, John M. 124
Brown, Michael 125
Browning, John 98
Brugier, Charles 103
Brugiere, Charles 126
Brulling, Gottlieb 110
Brunin, Anna Maria 59
Brunner, John 53, 57
Bryan, James 43
Buchalder, John 99
Buchmanin, Regina 90
Buchtel, Jacob Frederick 66
Budd, Wesley 8, 13
Buehrer, Ludwig 8
Buhl, Gotlib 54
Buhler, Henrich 99
Buhn, Carl 109
Buhner, Ludwig Henrich 98
Buhrer, Francis 18
Buhrer, Ignatius 18
Buhrer, Joseph 18
Buhrer, Maria Franzisca 18
Buhrer, Othilia 18
Bull, John G. 29
Burckhart, Barbara 11
Burckhart, Samuel 11
Burge, John 55
Burger, Catharina 65
Burger, Jacob Frederick 65
Burger, John 3
Burgle, Johan Georg 76
Burk, John Frederick 62
Burkhart, Agatha 73
Burkhart, Catharina 72
Burkle, John 85
Burklin, Dorothea 89
Bury, Barbara 33
Bury, Jacob 33
Buser, John Jacob 10
Bute, Georg Henrich 119
Buttell, Heinrich 119
Buzley, Hezekiah 64

C

Caldwell, Alexander 72, 87
Campbell, John D. 123
Canby, James 100
Canby, M. 105
Canby, Samuel Junior 102
Carien, Susana 63
Carman, Elijah 85
Carter, John 90
Casselly, Michael P. 5, 6
Cavender, Curtis 88
Charles, Jacob 35
Charles, John 35
Chattin, Chester 53
Chauncey, Nathaniel 82, 84, 85
Child, John 61
Christian, Peter 57, 63, 64, 66, 67, 70, 71
Chur, Jacob 65
Clark, Edward 109, 110, 111, 112, 113

Clayton, Thomas 38, 39
Clopp, John 126
Clopper, Francis C. 68, 69, 70, 71
Coats, Thomas Junior 42
Cohockson, Michael Weaver 127
Cole, Jasper 98
Coleman, Margaretta 33
Conard, John 91
Connelly, Sarah 104
Constant, P. F. B. 89
Contoit, John H. Junior 39
Cooch, Fancis L. 38
Cooper, Benjamin B. 71, 97, 102, 104,
    105, 107, 108, 115, 116, 117,
    118, 119, 120, 121
Cooper, Isaac 117
Cooper, Nathan 104
Cowan, James 66, 67
Cowin, James 90, 91
Cox, Gideon 11
Craighead, George 29
Crane, John A. 116
Creigh, John 10
Crist, Daniel 2
Cruz, Antonio Glz. da 64

D

Dachtler, John 2
Dachtler, John Jacob 3
Dachtler, John Michael 2
Dachtler, Maria Barbara 3
Daniel, Joseph 41
Darrach, Thomas B. 75
David, Jacob 126
Davis, Hanah 109
Davis, Henry 100
Davis, John M. 1
Davis, Lewis 108
Davis, Samuel P. 96
Debold, Jacob 44
Debolt, Christian 47
Deery, George 39
Deery, Peter 39
Denger, John Jacob 22
Denz, Joseph 43
Deppeler, Anna Maria 38, 47
Deppeler, Barbara 36
Deppeler, Ferena 35
Deppeler, Jacob 44
Deppeler, John 47
Deppeler, Rudolph 44
Deppeler, Ursula 36
Desauge, Louis 102
Dethier, Francis Nicolas 4
Dettweiler, Abraham 22
Devries, George 23, 24, 25, 26, 50, 84, 85
Dickson, John 66, 124
Diefenbach, Catharina Elisabeth 103
Diehr, Adam 87
Diehr, Michael 97
Diem, Georg Michael 108
Dieringer, John 46
Dieringer, John Junior 47
Diesenbach, Christina Philipina 65
Dietiker, Anna 121

Dietlein, Johan Michael 104
Dietrich, Henry 124
Digel, Martin 57
Diller, Frederick 1
Dillmanin, Catharina 91
Dingeswith, Philip David 86
Dingwerth, Johan Dietrich 105
Dishinger, John Albrecht 58
Dishong, Dietrich 75
Dobbins, John 119
Dohinden, Andrew 66
Doringer, Catharina 108
Doringer, Conrad 103
Doringer, Maria Elisabeth 103
Dorner, Friderich Adam 88
Dornerin, Dorothea 88, 125
Dornis, Anna Catharina 118
Dornis, Anna Maria 118
Dornis, Conrad 118
Dornis, Wilhelm 118
Dorster, John 67
Dower, Anna Maria 53, 98
Downar, Henry 105
Downing, Joseph M. 38
Dreer, Frederick 56
Dreibelbis, Daniel 69
Drinker, Joseph D. 104
Dubs, Martin 117
Duffield, Edward 73
Dullis, Joseph H. 99
Dulmer, John 58
Durr, Rosina 109
Duval, James L. 90
Duwe, Catharina 35
Duwe, Henry Ludwig 35
Dux, Adam 96

E

Earl, Clayton 22, 101, 106
Earl, John 106
Eberhard, Jacob 57
Eberhard, Rosina Catharina 72
Eberle, Henry 8
Eckel, Henry 66
Eckel, Samuel 66
Eckhardt, Charles 127
Eckhart, George 99
Eckhart, Louisa 101
Eddows, Ralph Junior 43
Edlin, Barbara 90
Egart, Mathew 60
Egger, John 23
Eglerin, Sophia Christina 92, 125
Egmond, Colonel 108
Ehlers, John 32, 33, 41, 42
Ehresman, Jacob 83
Ehret, Jacob Friderich 94
Ehret, Johan Michael 89
Ehretin, Rosina Magdelena 88
Eichelberger, Albrecht 27, 29
Eichelberger, Margaretta 27, 29
Eickelbuss, Christina Barbara 125
Eickelbuss, John 125
Eisenbraun, John Daniel 17
Eisenbrey, Johannes 112

Eisenbrey, Philip 107
Eisenhun, John D. 54
Eiszle, Andreas 107
Eitel, Christina 88
Eitel, Frederika 89
Eitel, Jacob 69
Eitelbussin, Christina Barbara 83
Eitelin, Elisabeth 97
Elkinton, Asa 127
Elkinton, George M. 127
Elkinton, Joseph 127
Ellenweinin, Catharina 103
Ellet, Charles 65
Ellinger, Friderich 120
Ellinger, Maria 107
Elliott, James 74
Ellis, Charles 9
Ellwanger, John George 52
Elsasser, Christoph 91
Elwell, Henry 63
Emery, Samuel 81
Emhardt, Jacob 53, 77
Emhart, Jacob 55
Engelhardt, John 26
Enz, Christina 92
Enz, George Jacob 92
Enz, Margaretha 93
Epler, Jacob 71
Erb, Christian 32
Erb, David 32
Ernst, Jacob 56
Esher, William 126
Esslin, Catharina 65
Evans, Cadwaleder Junior 101
Evans, Josiah R. 126
Evans, William M. 83
Everly, Adam 29, 87, 104
Ewing, James S. 74, 123
Ewing, Magdalen 90, 121
Ewing, Mrs. 30
Ewing, Samuel S. 75

F

Fah, Michael 105
Fahnestock, Charles 58
Falkenecker, Jacob 71
Farrow, N. 109, 110, 111, 112, 113
Fassitt, James 59, 76
Fayssoux, Peter 121
Fegenbush, Dietrich 66
Fegert, Barbara 68
Fegert, Emanuel 68
Fegert, John Michael 68
Fegert, Maria Margareta 68
Fegert, Philipina Regina 68
Feigel, Jacob Melchier 111
Fell, Jonathan Junior 3
Ferguson, Alexander 76
Feth, Johan Dietrich 104
Fichtner, Christian 67
Fiedler, Barbara 81
Field, Peter 90
Fillar, Elizabeth 16
Fischer, Casper 108
Fischer, Johannes 118

Fish, Mesheck 124
Fisher, ? 77, 121
Fisher, Frederick 12
Fisher, Ludwig 110
Flosch, Christina 84
Flosch, Michael 84
Flower, John 105
Foering, Frederick 16, 56
Fogel, Benjamin 1
Fogt, John 6
Fohr, Jacob 79
Foley, John G. 128
Foll, Friderica Barbara 104
Foll, Johan Ludwig 104
Foll, John 117
Folwell, John 88
Folwell, Joshua 77
Forrer, Samuel 76
Fossett, James 86
Fournier, Julius Alexander 95
Fox, Edward 57
Fraley, Christian 74
Fraley, Thomas 74
Franck, Luther 76, 87
Frank, Luther 52
Frechin, Regina Friderica 119
Freck, Anna Maria 94
Freck, Johan Georg 94
Frederich, Theresa 75
Fredler, Jacob 84
Freed, Henry 34
Freidiger, Samuel 4
Frey, Frederick 22
Frey, Mathias 25
Freytag, Anna Maria 79
Freytag, Anton 79
Fricke, Henry 51
Friderich, Johan 76
Friderich, Rosina 85
Friderich, Sebastian 85
Fries, John 59
Fritz, Anna Maria 12, 19
Fritz, Christopher 105
Fritz, Daniel 19
Fritz, George 19
Fritz, Jacob 19
Fritz, John 19
Fritzinger, Catharina 36
Fritzinger, George 47
Fritzinger, Margarette Elizabeth 38
Fritzinger, Michael 38
Froelich, Elizabeth 59
Froelich, Jacob 59
Fromeyer, Carolina 65
Fromeyer, Scharlotta 64
Fruh, Dorothea 14, 29
Fruh, Dorthea Junior 14
Fruh, Mathias 14, 29
Fuchs, Caspar 22
Fuchs, Johannes 92
Fuchs, Margaretta 22
Furt, Richard 7, 9

G

Gaissert, John Andrew 58

Gallmeyer, Elisabeth 98
Gamp, Aloise 35, 38
Gamp, John 36
Gantzhorn, Georg Jacob 108
Gaugerin, Christina 64
Gaul, Frederick 54, 96, 99, 123
Gaupp, Jacob 82
Gausz, Jacob Franz 120, 122
Gehle, John George 55
Gehring, Andrew 57
Geiger, Conrad 42
Geiger, Henry 8
Geiser, Carolina 80
Geiser, Catharina 73, 123
Geiser, Johan Georg 85
Geiser, John George 73, 123
Geiser, Joseph 80
Geiser, Regina 85
Geisinger, John 41
Geiss, William 54
Geisser, Anna Maria 101
Geisser, Johan David 69
Geitner, Jacob 93
Gender, Joseph 25
Gengenbach, Frederick 66
Genth, Catharina 124
Gerber, John 57
Gerhardt, George 43
Gerock, Jacob Frederick 4
Gerockin, Catharina 4
Gerockin, Fredericca 4
Gerspach, Leonzy 37
Geschroindt, Johan 110
Gesner, George 99
Gessenheimer, Henry 23
Gessenheiner, Henry 51
Gest, John 1
Geyer, John 55
Gilbert, Jacob 66
Gilbert, Samuel 102
Gile, John 47
Gillingham, Stacy 108
Gilman, Nathaniel 8
Gising, Elizabeth 55
Glaser, John L. 42, 43, 50, 51
Glohr, John 32
Gochler, Frederick 65
Goetsche, Michael 24
Goetz, Jacob Frederick 58
Gogel, Anna Maria 121
Gogel, Carl Christian 122
Gogel, Dorothea Margaretha 121
Gogel, Gottlieb Friderick 122
Gogel, Jacob Friderick 121
Gogel, Johan Michael 121
Gohl, Christian 9
Gold, Elisabeth 78
Gold, Johan 78
Goldenpenny, Henry 81
Goodman, John 107
Gotz, Henry 45
Gotzin, Sabina Catharina 89
Grabial, John Junior 44
Graff, Carolina 8, 51, 71, 86
Graham, Alexander 65
Graham, John K. 56

Graham, Thomas 56
Grant, John 98
Grauser, Christian 32
Graussin, Julianna 112
Graussin, Sophia 92
Gray, Richard 36
Greder, John George 71
Green, E. 9
Greverson, Jacob 57
Grevison, Jacob 35
Gries, Susanna 56
Griffith, Elijah 127
Grim, Jesse 93
Groff, Joseph 35, 72
Groh, John 47
Grohe, Magdalena 3
Gron, Johan Georg 107
Gross, Gottlieb 114
Grossmannin, Elisabetha 88
Groszin, Catharina 93
Grundelock, Gottlieb 32
Grupp, John 60
Gruver, John 3
Gudbrodt, Johan Frederick 83
Gudbrodt, Johannes 85
Gudeman, Johan Friderich 95
Guier, Adam 88
Gullarowitch, Ferdinand 26
Gundelach, C. H. 113, 114, 115, 116, 117, 120
Gunther, John L. 58
Guntherin, Catherina 127
Gyger, Jesse 37

H

Haas, Henry 99
Haas, Norbert 31
Haberstroh, John Jacob 65
Hackenbracht, Henrich 115
Hadiamont, Emanuel De 4
Hagner, C. V. 105
Hahn, Barbara 21
Hahn, John George 20
Hahn, Peter 122
Haimbach, David 36, 37
Haisch, Eva 117
Haldeman, Jacob M. 2, 3
Haldeman, John 3
Hall, Peleg 97
Haman, John Samuel 50
Hamilton, William K. 87, 127
Hampff, Jacob 9
Hampff, Rosina 9
Hancock, Joseph 3
Handle, Baltus 17
Handle, Gottlieb 17, 52
Handle, Johanna 17, 52
Handle, Johanna Junior 17, 52
Handle, John 17
Handle, Maria 17
Hannon, Richard F. 67
Hantle, Margaretta 13
Harbison, Hugh 93
Harbson, Hugh 82
Hardorfer, Fredericka Catharina 42

Harlein, Margaretha 86
Harman, Andreas 32
Harman, John 59, 93
Harrer, Jacob 64
Harris, Edward 22
Hart, John 94
Hart, Thomas 91
Hart, William H. 91
Hartenbauer, Jeremiah 98
Hartman, Elizabeth 27, 30
Hartman, John Jacob Junior 27, 30
Hartman, John Jacob Senior 27, 30
Hartzel, Henry Junior 6
Hasertin, Anna Maria 83
Hassenmeier, Frederick 69
Hassinger, Jacob 1, 8, 49
Hassinger, Valentine 8
Hauser, Henrich 99
Hauser, Jacob 23
Hausman, George 46
Hausman, Maria Magdalena 46
Haussel, Johannes 93
Haverstick, William Junior 97, 100
Haydt, Adam 66
Hayes, William 2
Hayn, Henrietta 97
Heberling, George 16
Hees, Christianna 80
Hees, Gottfried 80
Hees, Johan Israel 78
Hees, Johanna 77
Heidecke, John Frederick 61, 86
Heidlauf, Christian 58
Heimedinger, John George 8
Heimerdinger, Christian 118
Heimin, Walburg 107
Heinrich, Anna Maria 106
Heinrich, Barbara 128
Heinrich, Elisabeth Margaretha 101
Heinrich, Margaretha 102
Heinrich, Maria 104
Heinrichin, Anna Catharina 101
Heinrichin, Philipina 89, 126
Heinrichin, Rosina 93
Heinrichin, Sophia Magdalena 88
Heinz, Andreas 87
Heison, Philip 91
Heisse, John David 62
Held, Christian Ludwig 66
Hell, John 80
Hell, Seolastico 80
Henck, George D. 75, 106
Henniker, William 126
Henning, Johan Georg 112
Henry, Joseph 52
Hensin, Elisabetha 91
Herbster, Laurence 127
Herbster, Susanna 127
Herdle, Burckhardt 107
Hering, Maria Rosina 96
Herman, Johan Georg 111
Herman, Will 30
Herneisen, Anna 117
Herneisen, Daniel 117
Herneisin, Anna Maria 105
Hershberger, John 46

Hershberger, Samuel 46
Hertzog, Peter 58, 123
Herzog, Lambert 45, 54
Herzog, Rosanna 54
Herzog, Rosina 45
Hess, Christian 12
Hess, Conrad 100, 122
Hess, David 42
Hess, Henry 2
Hetz, Frederick 10
Heyl, John 95
Heyll, Henry O. 46
Heyn, Jacob 83
Hickman, George 82, 93
Hiller, Johan Georg 112
Hiller, Sabina Catharina 113
Hinman, E. 57, 58
Hitz, John 2
Hitz, Melcher 8
Hochstrasser, Henry 22
Hocker, Adam 12
Hodge, Andrew 36
Hodiamont, Emanuel De 5
Hoeckley, Frederick 3
Hoerper, Michael 54
Hofer, Barbara 50
Hoffman, Catharina 54
Hoffman, Christoph 121
Hoffman, Dorothea 81
Hoffman, Elisabeth 100
Hoffman, Frederica 121
Hoffman, Fredericka 77
Hoffman, Friderich 101, 121
Hoffman, Jacob 93, 100
Hoffman, Ludwig 2
Hoffman, Nicholas 54
Hoffman, Philip 54
Hoffmeister, George 82
Hofman, Christina 82, 83
Hog, Sebastian 79
Hohl, Catharina 94, 95
Hohl, Christianna 95
Hohl, Johan Georg 94
Hohl, Margaretha 95
Hohl, Michael 94
Hohl, Rosina 94
Hohn, Anthony 67
Hohn, Jacob 118
Hohnin, Barbara 112
Hohnin, Wilhelmina 112
Hollingsworth, Samuel 106, 124
Hollman, John 69, 71
Hollmann, John 60
Hollmann, Thees 48
Hollmann, Theese 52
Hollohan, Amos 64
Holzhainin, Rosina 89
Holzingerin, Lousia Wilhelmina 88
Hope, T. 124
Hope, Thomas 57
Hoppel, George 92
Horst, Joseph 12
Horstmann, William 120
Horstmann, William H. 129
Hoskin, E. W. 54, 72
Houck, George 58

Houssel, John Conrad 54
Howell, Joshua L. 33, 38, 39
Howell, Samuel L. 31, 33
Huber, Carolina 3
Huber, Gottlieb Frederick 69
Huber, Jacob Adam 39
Hueter, George M. 127
Hueter, John Frederick 127
Hufnagle, Caspar 125
Hufnagle, Mary Ann 125
Huhnle, Christianna 122
Humerlin, Catharina 89
Hunter, Jacob V. 13
Hunziker, John Rudolph 46
Hurlick, William 55, 63
Hurst, Michael 38
Hurtzler, Felix 10
Hussing, Bardina 93
Hutz, Catharina 27
Hutz, Lontze 27
Hutz, Lonzi 46
Hutz, Mariana 37
Hutz, Philip 28, 34

I

Imle, Andrea 112
Ingraham, Francis 83
Irwin, John 4

J

Jack, John 50
Jack, Maria Ursula 50
Jack, Mary Ann 42
Janney, Jacob 120
Jatzge, George 128
Jatzge, John 128
Jauchin, Maria Barbara 75
Jauszin, Elisabetha Frida 88
Jefferies, James 97
Jenewein, Johan Friderich 78
Jenner, Dorothea 2
Johnson, Joseph 100
Johnson, William 22
Johnston, John 129
Jones, Margaretha 106
Jones, Thomas 55
Jones, Thomas Junior 55
Jordan, John 84, 102
Jost, Jacobina 29
Justice, Philip 3, 50

K

Kachel, Jacob 40
Kagi, John 48
Kagi, Simon 48
Kaiser, Anthony 73
Kaiserin, Marianna 73
Kaiserin, Theresa 73
Kalender, Fredericca 61
Kallenburn, Anna Maria 86
Kammerle, Jacob 76
Kamp, Johan Jacob 109
Kapp, Leonard 30

Kapp, Maria Anna 74
Karmone, Henry 13
Kaser, Barbara 3
Kaser, Conrad 1
Kaser, Elizabeth 3
Kaser, Hans Ulrich 1, 49
Kastenbader, Johan Georg 97
Kattz, Barbara 121
Kattz, Christian 121
Kattz, Henry 121
Katz, Barbara 115
Katz, Christian 115
Kauffman, Catharina Magdalena 63
Kayser, Barbara 52
Kayser, Benedict 42
Kayser, Samuel 40
Keatting, Lambert 125
Keely, Jacob 93
Kegh, John 10
Keil, Henrich David 91
Keilig, Charles F. 52, 64, 84
Keim, Catharina 47
Keim, Paul 42, 47
Keiser, John Henry 127
Kembach, George Michael 8
Kennedy, Anthony 109
Ker, William Junior 15
Kerly, Charles F. 124
Kerns, Abraham 66
Keyser, William 83
Kienast, Johan Jacob 113
Kienlen, Christian Frederich 71
Kientzle, George 48
Kiks, Catharina 98
Kim, Charles 94
Kim, Christina 94
King, John 78
Kingeter, Dorothea 19, 32
Kingeter, Frederick 19, 32, 123
Kingeter, John 19, 31
Kinichin, Margaretha Elisabeth 103
Kintzle, Gottlieb 9
Kirkhoven, Maria 60
Kisz, Martin 73
Klee, Georg Franze 106
Klein, John 74, 123
Kleindienst, Margaretha 121
Kleist, George 4
Klepser, Andreas 15
Klepser, Andreas Junior 15
Klepser, Jacob 15
Klepser, Jeremias 15
Klepser, Johanna Elizabeth 15
Kletz, Gottlieb 93
Klinck, Gottlieb 12
Klinck, Henry Gottfried 122
Klinck, John 12
Klinck, Rosina 4
Kline, George 84
Kline, John 93
Klingelberg, Paul 102
Klingelberg, Peter 102
Klingelberg, Susanna 102
Klingler, Catharina 1
Klingler, Christian 23, 51
Klingler, George 10

Klingler, John 23, 51
Klingler, John David 7
Klingler, Judith 23, 51
Klohr, Fransz Anton 79
Knapp, Christian Frederick 63
Knapp, John 7
Knapp, Peter 7
Knaur, Abraham 97
Knochel, Georg 115
Knochel, Philip Georg 115
Knochel, Salome 115
Knoderer, Frederick 87
Knoll, Gottfried 96
Knotz, Catharina 114
Kobele, Elias 75
Kobele, Martin 76
Kobele, Mathias 75, 76
Kober, Catharina 4, 18, 44
Kober, Christina 18, 44
Kober, Christoph 18, 44
Kober, John Mathias 11
Kober, Juliana 18
Kober, Philip 18, 44
Koch, Anna Maria 81
Koch, Daniel 83
Koch, Johannes 81
Koch, Ludwig 116
Kochenburger, Catharina 20, 30
Kochenburger, Elizabeth 20, 30
Kochenburger, Eva 20, 30
Kochenburger, Henry 20, 30
Kochenburger, Martin 20
Kochlin, Frederick A. 92
Koepfler, Jacob 25
Kohler, Henry 27
Kohler, Jacob 7
Kohler, John 103, 120
Kohler, John Ulrich 27
Kohr, Michael 48
Konig, Christian 2
Konig, Jacob Frederick Junior 68
Konig, Jacob Fredrick 68
Konig, Johan Marlin 76
Konigin, Christina 90
Kople, Samuel 75
Kopp, Agatha 80
Kopp, Catharina 124
Kopp, Gottlieb 52
Kopp, Jacob 80
Kopp, John 52
Kramer, Catharina 39
Kramer, Conrad 64
Kraus, Melchier 77
Krause, John 97
Kraut, Jacob 13
Krayl, Ludwig Frederick 7, 8
Kreeble, David 71
Kreh, William Frederick 5
Kreider, Christian 37
Kreiner, Philip 24
Krieger, John 31
Kromer, John George 9
Kromerin, Regina Barbara 119
Krucker, Franz 95
Krug, George H. 100
Krum, George 82

Kubler, Jacob 57
Kucherer, Johan 119
Kuern, Elizabeth Barbara 12
Kuhn, Adam 11
Kuhn, Anna Maria 56
Kuhn, Benedict 11
Kuhn, Josiah 11
Kuhn, Ludwig 56
Kuhn, Sophia 55
Kuhne, Franz Ludwig 20
Kuhne, Teresia 20
Kuhnle, John Ernst 57
Kuhnlerin, Dorothea 94
Kuhnlerin, Margaretha 94
Kuhnlerin, Rosina 95
Kumlin, Anna Maria 63
Kummerlein, Johan Georg 105
Kuny, Anna Maria 112
Kuny, Victor 112
Kunzler, Christianna 81
Kunzler, Friderika 78
Kunzler, George Michael 83
Kunzler, Johan Georg 83
Kurn, Catharina 12
Kurz, Anna Maria 107
Kurz, Fredericca 29

L

Lakasin, Johanna 30
Lamb, William 82
Lammbach, George Frederick 65
Lammbach, Johan Georg 65
Land, John 71, 87
Landis, David 123
Lane, William M. 53
Lang, Anna Catharina 106
Lang, Joseph 116
Langer, Joseph 29, 75, 87
Langin, Barbara 91
Langstroth, John 55
Lapp, Michael 11
Lardner, John 4
Lardner, William 59
Larer, Melchior 56
Laube, Joseph 28
Laube, Theresa 28
Lauber, Martin 86
Lauffer, Carl Ludwig 105
Law, Mathew 119
Lebo, Daniel 92, 96, 97, 98, 99, 105, 107,
    109, 113, 119, 120
Lecompt, William 95
Leelenfrid, Francis 125
Leeroix, Jacob 111
Lefever, Daniel 82
Lego, Maria 111
Lehman, Francis J. 67
Lehman, Joseph 30
Leibfried, Maria Dorethea 54
Leicht, Christian 122
Leidy, Jacob 66
Lelar, Henry 95, 122
Lemle, Jacob 50
Lenberger, Friderich 111
Lentner, Adam 92

Lentner, John Adam 70
Lentz, Daniel 85
Lentz, Johannes 82
Lentzin, Catharina 84
Lenz, Catharina Maria 87
Leuthweiller, Jacob 10
Leuthweiller, Maria 10
Lewis, Henry 9
Lewis, Reeve 75, 76
Lex, Peter 77
Ley, Mathias 13
Lichet, Jacob 92
Lichtel, Jacob 106
Light, Martin 10
Lightfoot, David 75
Lim, James 57
Limbech, Carl 113
Lindsay, Andrew 40, 41
Lindsay, John 39
Lindsay, Thomas 39, 40, 41, 52
Lingg, Catharina 122
Linsenmeier, Daniel 82
Lippincott, James 119
Lippincott, Samuel 114
Livezey, David 66
Lloyd, Ephraim 6
Lochner, George Henry 87
Lodge, Joseph 12
Lofflerin, Magdalena 105
Lohrer, Conrad 97
Longstreth, Samuel 10
Looser, Conrad 90
Lorcher, Rosina 100
Loreher, Mathias Friderich 95
Loreherin, Christina 95
Lotz, John Philip 114
Lotze, Joseph 124
Lotze, Margareth 124
Lownes, Joseph 34
Lowry, Lewis 30
Luders, Thomas C. 49, 50
Ludy, Christian Junior 39
Ludy, Christian Senior 38
Ludy, Fredericka 33
Ludy, John Jacob 33
Ludy, Margaretta 38
Ludy, Maria 34
Ludy, Maria Elizabeth 34
Lum, Jacob 58
Lust, Catharina Dorathea 56
Lust, David 108
Lutz, Jacob 24
Lutz, Johan George 100

M

Machee, John 71
Machtle, Jacob Friderich 118
Macke, John 86
Maderin, Julianna 58
Madia, Joseph 101
Madison, James 9
Maier, Johan Georg 105
Maisch, Johan Ulrich 122
Mandel, Conrad 56
Mandry, William 94

Manner, Johan 113
Mantoft, Elisabeth 101
Marbacher, John 91
Marckle, Jacob 99
Mardini, Johan Samuel 70
Maris, Jesse J. 122
Mark, Jacob 120, 121
Marsch, Johan Ulrich 100
Marshall, Joseph 108
Marshall, Margaret 102
Martin, Emalls Junior 80
Mast, Christian 48
Maszne, Michael 110
Mattmuller, Johan Georg 73
Mattmuller, Johan George 74
Mattmuller, John George Junior 74
Mattmuller, Maria 73, 74
Mattmuller, Maria Barbara 74
Mattmuller, Maria Junior 73, 74
Maule, Jonathan 57
Maull, John 129
Maur, Salome 51, 52
Mayer, Anna Maria 71
Mayer, Eva Rosina 71
Mayer, Gottlieb 71
Mayer, Jacob 67
Mayer, Jacob Friderich 112
Mayer, Johannes 71
Mayer, John 63
Mayer, John Frederick 63
Mayer, John Jacob 56, 67
Mayer, Wilhelm 71
Mayerin, Barbara 120
Maysenhoelder, Charles 61, 122
McClellan, William 73, 74
McClellan, William Junior 73
McCormick, John 83
McCutchen, Ebenezer 56, 94
McDonald, L. 107
McIlhany, Louisa 69, 72
McIlhenney, Louisa 60
McIlvain, James 121, 122
McKenzie, Alexander 103
McKinley, Alexander 50
McKnight, William 45, 54
Means, William 81
Meier, Johan Georg 77
Meier, Margareta 77
Melbeck, John 37
Mentz, G. W. 52
Mentz, George W. 124
Mentzenheimer, Lazerus 124
Mercier, Charles 42, 65
Mertz, Christina Dorothea 62
Mertz, John David 62
Mesch, Lucas 39
Mesmer, Wernhard 16
Mesner, Simon 117
Messerschmidt, Elizabeth 33
Meyer, Abraham 39
Meyer, Christina 46
Meyer, Christoph 2
Meyer, George 46
Meyer, Joseph 48, 52
Meyer, Maria 48
Meyer, Mary 126

Meyers, Henry 60
Michlen, Anna Maria 119
Midlin, Walter 9
Miller, Caroline 128
Miller, Daniel H. 59, 83
Miller, Georg William 120
Miller, Johannes 70
Miller, John 41, 128
Miller, Jonas 86
Miller, Leonard 40
Milnor, William Junior 77
Mingle, John 76, 90
Mingle, John Junior 125
Miquet, Francis 3
Mohl, Elisabeth 102
Mohl, Hadwig Sophia 100
Mohl, Justus 99
Mohl, Maria Catharina 100
Mohl, Wilhelmina 102
Mohler, Daniel 44
Mollenkopff, John Jacob 5, 34
Montgomery, William Junior 56, 103, 123
Moore, Jacob Frederick 47, 49
Moore, James 104
Mootzar, Daniel 49
Mootzar, John 49
Morad, Fanchette 48
Morad, John 39
Morad, Joseph 43
Morad, Mariana 43
Morad, Marietta 50
Morgan, George W. 101
Morris, James P. 57
Most, Henry 14
Motz, Barbara 6
Motz, Christina Johanna 5
Motz, Jacob 5
Motz, John 6
Motz, John Michael 5
Motz, Rosina Catharina 56, 94
Mower, George 18
Moyer, Daniel 67
Muazungerin, Regina Catharina 126
Muhle, George 24
Muhlhauser, Christianus 85
Muhlhauser, Christina Margaretha 82
Muhlhauser, Elena 85
Muhlhauser, Johannes 81
Muhlhauser, Rosina Regina 85
Muller, Dominicus 12
Muller, Maria 12
Muller, Moritz 4
Muller, Philip 70
Munzunger, Regina Catharina 103
Murdoch, Samuel 109
Murdock, William 38
Musser, George 36, 100
Musser, Jacob 77
Musser, John 48
Musser, Sarah 102
Musser, William 35, 36, 38
Mutter, John 39
Myer, John 106
Myers, John Meyer 34

N

Nagel, Jacob 61
Nagele, Andreas 28
Nagele, Margareta 102
Nagele, Walburga 28
Nagle, George 77
Naglee, John 37
Neff, David 63
Neff, Doris 126
Neithhammer, Gottlieb 120
Neubold, John Gottlieb 69
Newbold, Michael 34
Newbold, Samuel 37, 106
Newbold, Thomas 34
Newbold, William 113
Nill, Christian Daniel 69
Nithhammer, Friderich 114
Nithhammer, Gottfried Friderich 114
Nitzel, Jacob 125
Nitzell, Jacob 92, 94
Noll, Anna Maria 49
Noll, George 37
Noll, Nicholas 37
Noll, Susana Catharina 48
Noll, Susanna Catharina 85
Nollin, Margaretta 37
Nollin, Salome 43
Norris, Isaac 51
Notton, John 114
Nutz, Leonard Junior 95

O

Oberholtz, Henry D. 40
Oberholtz, Isaac 42
Obrist, Abrahm 28
Obrist, Anna 28
Odlin, Woodbridge 14, 15, 17, 18, 19, 20, 21, 26, 27, 28, 29, 30, 31, 32, 33, 34, 35, 44, 51, 52
Oestereicher, Christian Frederick 42
Ogle, Thomas 88
Ollie, Carl 93
Osman, William B. 72
Osterheldt, Frederick 103
Osterman, Jacob 92
Ott, Anna Maria 76, 86, 120
Ott, Christian 74, 103, 120
Ott, Johan Georg 81
Ott, Johan George 87
Otto, Jacob S. 73

P

Packard, H. R. 128
Palmer, Christianna Catharina 78
Palmer, Jacob Wilhelm 78
Palmer, John 40
Paul, Joseph 65
Paulsen, Peter Mathias 124
Pearpoint, Robert 121
Peiffer, Jacob 108
Peisch, Johan Frederick 70
Pepper, George 88
Peter, Daniel 30

Peterman, George 61, 86
Peterman, Jacob 61, 86
Peters, Richard 121
Peterson, Jacob 86
Petter, Anton 116
Petz, Jacob 60
Pfeiffer, Catharina 21, 35
Pfeiffer, Michael 21, 35
Pfeiffer, Michael Junior 21, 29
Pfister, Amand 94, 95
Pfluger, Eva Catharina 101
Pflugfelder, Peter 117
Philler, Elizabeth 125
Phillips, Valintine 63
Phillipson, Simon 87
Picquet, Benjamin 58
Pierce, John 31
Pike, Marinus W. 29
Pissant, John 92, 93
Pitz, Henry 63
Planck, John 47, 49, 76, 87
Plank, John 114
Pleyfus, Christina 101
Pong, Diena Du 41
Poppel, George 75
Pott, Francis 88
Potter, James 35
Potts, William L. 42
Pradel, John 63
Pratt, Henry 118, 119
Preser, Jacob 61
Price, Chandler 101
Pries, Manuel 88
Priess, Manuel 125
Pulvermuller, Conrad 9
Pyle, Joseph 77, 121

Q

Quig, John 85
Quig, Margaret 85

R

Raab, Jacob 13
Raiguel, Abraham 98
Rapin, Joseph 60
Rapp, Frederick 70
Rasig, Diederich 17, 32
Rasig, Eva 17, 32
Rasig, Eva Margaretta 6
Rasig, Jacob 17, 32
Rasig, Magdalena 17, 32
Rass, Clement 30
Raster, William 63
Ratshiller, Anthony 122
Rau, Gottfried 25
Rauber, Jacob 110
Rauch, Peter 3
Rauleig, Greensburg L. 95
Rausch, Johan Jacob 70
Ravann, John Peter 54
Ray, Anna Elizabeth 87
Raybold, Philip 22
Rayhle, Carl 36
Rayhle, Catharina 37

Rea, John 88
Rebman, John Friderick 90
Reece, Enos 99
Rees, Charles B. 96
Rees, John 90, 91
Reeves, Benjamin 123
Rehfus, Gottlieb Frederick 57, 58
Rehm, John Jacob 34
Reichardin, Sarah 103, 123
Reichert, John Gottlieb 35
Reichmann, Jacob Frederick 130
Reigart, Daniel 7
Reindollar, Jacob 122
Reiner, Johan Georg 119
Reinhard, Peter 4
Reiniger, Barbara 15
Reiniger, Barbara Junior 15
Reiniger, Christian 15
Reiniger, Daniel 15
Reinwald, John 59
Reisz, Barbara 116
Reisz, Christian 116
Reiszner, Conrad 30
Reizner, Conrad 17
Remele, John 63
Renninger, John 59
Renz, Frederich 128
Resh, Henry 34
Resimont, E. F. F. Joseph De 6
Rex, George 99
Reyher, Johan Gotthard 99
Richard, Mark 67
Richards, Benjamin W. 94
Richards, George 7, 9
Richards, William 94
Richner, George 48
Rickebach, David 9
Ricker, George 2
Rickle, William 127
Ridder, Joseph 116
Riehle, William 75
Riesh, Henry 118
Rieth, Jacob 90
Riggebacher, Henry 42
Riley, Jacob F. 80
Riley, Tobias 80
Rilliger, Catharina 126
Rillinger, Catharina 114
Rinderknecht, Elizabeth 29, 35
Rinderknecht, Henry 28, 35
Rink, John 83
Ripberger, Francis 113
Ripperger, Conrad 94
Rising, E. 5, 6, 7, 10, 16, 35, 36, 37, 41,
    43, 46, 47, 50
Ristine, Jacob 63
Rittberger, Christiana 31
Rittberger, George 30
Rittberger, Gottlieb 31
Ritter, Johannes 69
Robbins, Samuel J. 5, 6
Rodgers, Denny 57
Roger, John Christian 61, 122
Roland, John 87
Roop, Christian 12
Rose, Robert H. 36

Ross, Clementina 61
Ross, Clementine 83
Ross, John 61, 92
Rost, Jacobina 87
Rotshiller, Antoni 58
Roy, Anna Elizabeth 71
Rubican, Daniel 64
Rudolph, Gottlob 14, 53
Rudolph, Johanna 14, 53
Rudolph, Johanna Junior 14
Rudy, John 84
Ruff, ? 77, 121
Ruff, John 44
Rummel, Johannes 109
Ruppert, John 55
Rush, Henry 117, 119
Russel, Edward 126
Russell, Edward 103
Ruth, Daniel 41

S

Sager, Michael 57
Sagesser, Jacob 55
Sagesser, John 55
Sailer, Frederick 52
Sailerin, Barbara 64
Samuel, James 9
Saner, Gottlieb 45
Sarmiento, Francis Cavellero 52
Sauder, John Amandus 24
Sauter, Ferdinand Carl August 116
Schacherlin, Margaretha Barbara 105
Schachterlin, Agatha 116
Schaeffer, Anna Maria 57
Schaeffer, Jacob 129, 130
Schaeffer, John 57
Schaefner, David 25
Schaffelin, Barbara 60
Schaffer, Adam 14
Schaffer, Catharina 99
Schaffer, Christiana 16
Schaffer, Jacob 14, 32
Schaffer, John 21
Schaffer, Michael 16
Schaffer, Solomea 14, 32
Schaffer, Solomea [Junior] 14
Schafflin, Catharina 64
Schaffner, Catharina 13
Schaffner, John 7, 13
Schalin, Sabina 9
Schanbacher, Anna Maria 77
Schanbacher, Catharina 78, 87
Scharr, Johan Georg 106
Schaubel, Johan Jacob 69
Schaufele, Johannes 111
Schaufelin, Catharina 71, 72
Schauffele, George Philip 91
Schauffler, Valentin 48
Schedlice, John L. 84
Scheel, Andreas 107
Scheerer, Jacob D. 130
Scheffel, John Jacob 58
Scheide, Christian 66
Schelling, Rosina 101
Schenck, Carl Ludwig 117

Schenck, Christian 127
Schenck, John 66
Schenck, Maria Margaretha 118
Schenck, Michael 49
Schenzin, Anna Dorothea 64, 65
Scherner, Johan Gottfried 115
Scherrer, Christian 79
Scherzinger, John M. 54
Schettler, Conrad 23
Schettler, Juliana 23
Schib, Maria 37
Schickin, Rosanna 76
Schifferin, Elizabeth 128
Schiffin, Elisabeth 105
Schiller, Christina 84
Schiller, Gottlieb 84, 102
Schiller, Johannes 83
Schilling, David 94
Schimelin, Elisabeth 123
Schimmern, Elisabeth 123
Schlegel, Anna 34
Schlichter, Daniel 40
Schliphach, Conrad 110
Schliphack, Christian 110
Schmidgall, Jacob 29
Schmidt, Andreas 111
Schmidt, Barbara 109
Schmidt, Casper 69
Schmidt, Christian G. 41, 56
Schmidt, Friderich 98
Schmidt, Georg Michael 109
Schmidt, Henrich 70
Schmidt, Jacob 26, 69
Schmidt, Ludwig 22
Schmidt, Maria Elisabetha 69
Schmidt, Maria Rosina 56
Schmolin, Friderich 112
Schnatz, Sebastian 91
Schneide, Catharina 98
Schneider, Elisabeth 75
Schneider, Fransiscus 98
Schneider, John Andrew 41
Schneider, Magdalena 98
Schneider, Maria Anna 98
Schneider, Rosalia 97
Schneider, Xaverius 98
Schninger, Jacob 82
Scholer, Frederick 54
Scholtheis, Nicholas 58
Schott, Anna Maria 109
Schott, Elisabeth 109, 115
Schott, George 117
Schott, Johan Georg 115
Schott, Joseph 115
Schott, Osgood 115
Schrack, Abraham 116
Schreiner, Henry 36
Schroeder, Maria 99
Schuhurt, Johan Friderick 92
Schultheis, Nicholas 63, 118
Schultz, Barbara 51
Schultz, John 24
Schultz, Joseph 51
Schultz, Magdalena 41
Schulz, Sophia 90, 121
Schumacher, Johannes 70

Schuster, Anton 69
Schuster, Catharina 69
Schuster, Christina 69
Schwager, Elisabeth 111
Schwager, Johannes 111
Schwar, John 8
Schwartz, Barbara 91
Schwartz, John 1
Schweitzer, William Godlob 6
Schwikkard, Frederick 59
Scott, Alexander 53
Seefried, Catharina 14
Seeger, David 63
Seggeser, Jacob 1
Seggeser, John 1
Seggeser, Verona 1
Seibert, Jacob 7
Seiffer, Elizabeth 2
Seiler, Anton 1
Seiser, John 130
Seitz, Christina Catharina 49
Seiz, Johan 113
Seuterin, Catharina 113
Sexton, Thomas 87
Sharp, Eli 61
Sheerer, Gottlieb 127
Sheerer, Jacob 129, 130
Shell, Henry 90
Shelly, Daniel 44
Shiller, Michael 49
Shoemaker, David 52
Shoemaker, Jane 98
Shoemaker, Samuel 56
Shott, John P. 114
Siddons, Joseph 118
Sieger, Maria Magdalena 56
Sigrist, Jacob 4
Simon, Gottfried 104
Simpson, Michael T. 13
Singer, John 89, 128
Singer, Simon 8
Smith, Benjamin 50
Smith, Charles L. 73
Smith, Christian G. 64
Smith, Daniel Junior 100
Smith, Eva 129
Smith, Jacob 129
Smith, James 92
Smith, John 54
Smith, John R. C. 53
Smith, Silas H. 46, 47
Smyser, Mathias Junior 11
Snare, William 54
Snyder, Erhart 127
Snyder, Frederick 130
Snyder, Henry 127
Sommer, Jacob 52, 103
Space, William 91
Spadin, Rosina Catharina 103
Spat, Joest 30
Spat, Maria Ursula 126
Sperry, Jacob 90, 94
Spietzl, Fransz 70
Spittelmeisler, Mathias 93
Sporr, Jacob Frederick 65
Staengel, Andreas 11

Stahl, Catharina 56, 68
Stahl, Christian 7
Stahl, Frederick 68
Stahl, Gottlebin 68
Stahl, John Gottlieb 68
Stahl, John Martin 68
Stahl, Martin 68
Stahl, Susanna Catharina 68
Staiber, John 45
Staiger, John Michael 53
Stall, Catharina 96
Stall, F. 96
Stall, Frederick 31
Stampfle, David 110
Starck, Johan Jacob 120
Starrett, David 72
Statz, John Nicholas 55
Staub, Catharina 95
Staub, Gottlieb Frederick 62
Staub, John Jacob 62
Staub, Maria Barbara 62
Stauffer, John 7, 8
Steel, John 59, 60
Steel, William 89
Stein, Abraham 59, 73, 124
Steinbran, Johan Georg 99
Steiner, George 36, 81
Steininger, Philip 22
Steinman, Georg 108
Steinman, Johan 108
Steinman, John F. Junior 108
Steinmetz, Christopher 91
Steinmetz, Jacob 64
Steinmetz, Rachel 81
Steman, Jacob 10
Sterki, Catherina 2
Stern, Ceron 113
Stern, Jacob 96
Sterrett, Sarah 95
Sterrett, Thomas 95
Stevenson, John 109
Stewart, Thomas 92
Stieg, John 8
Stierlen, Johannes 99
Stock, John 87, 124
Stocker, John 41
Stoll, Jacob 40
Stoltz, John 40
Stoltz, Michael 122
Stoltzfuss, Abraham 12
Storr, Friderich 101
Stouffer, Abraham 40
Stouse, Joseph 94
Straatman, Anna Elisabeth 98
Stracker, Albert 107
Straub, Gottfried 93
Straub, Jacob 69
Straub, Johan George 67
Streeper, Daniel 85
Streeper, Richard 60
Stregel, Anna Maria 5, 41
Stregel, Landolin 5, 41
Strohm, John 30
Studer, Anna Maria 49
Studer, Jacob 49
Studer, Joseph 49

Stum, Andrew 33
Stum, Elizabeth Catharina 33
Stump, John 40
Stumpf, Nicholas 24
Stup, Leonard 46
Sturgis, ? 113
Sturm, Christian 105
Sulger, Jacob Junior 73
Sulzer, Johannes 96, 97
Supfle, Gottlieb 113
Supflein, Christina Dorothea 63
Sutter, Fransiska 85
Sutter, Joseph 85, 123
Sutter, Marianna 75, 123
Sutton, William 16
Swertswelder, Jacob 50
Swertzer, Henry 120

T

Tantzer, Barbara 51
Tantzer, Elizabeth 50
Tantzer, John George 50
Tantzer, Theresa 51
Taschner, Carl 99
Tatham, James 51, 71
Taubenhein, Friderich 105
Tay, Anthony 108
Taylor, Anthony 93
Taylor, John M. 57
Taylor, Joseph 23, 73, 97, 123
Taylor, Levy 124
Taylor, Michael 83
Taylor, William Junior 8, 51
Teisseire, Anthony 41
Teisseire, James 101
Thal, Joseph Anthonia 16
Thall, Tyonius 16
Thommisont, August Gabrael 122
Thompson, Thomas 117
Thornton, Joseph 74
Thron, Peter 40
Tiedemann, Christina Wilhelmina 123
Tiessiere, James 121
Tietjens, John Nicholas 129
Toppal, George 36
Trago, Joseph 1
Trautwein, Christopher 25
Trautwein, Johannes 68
Treffinger, Philip Bernhard 91
Trefts, George A. 106
Treftz, Wilhelm 66
Treisendanz, John Michael 59
Troscher, Frederick 16
Troscher, John Ludwig 16
Troscher, Louisa 16
Trotter, Nathan 37
Troxler, A. M. C. Rosina 122

U

Ulman, Lazerus 124
Ulrich, Dorothea 63
Ulrich, Michael 3
Urban, Carlina 114
Urban, Catharina 71

Urban, Clemenz 44
Urban, Francis Joseph 45
Urban, Francis Joseph Junior 45
Urban, Johan Casper 71
Urban, Sophia 108, 109
Urban, Wilhelm 114
Urffer, David 43
Urspruch, Henry 128
Urspruch, Henry Junior 128

V

Van Uxem, James Junior 2
Vanarsdalen, Christopher 117
Vernon, John 91
Vogt, Anton 31
Vogt, Christina 83
Vogt, Johan George 86
Vogt, John George 31
Vogt, Margareta 84
Vogt, Maria Agatha 31
Vogt, Norbert 31
Vogt, Philip Jacob Junior 53
Volkner, Henry 78
Volmicker, Elizabeth 45
Volmicker, Jacob 45
Volmiker, Catharina 42
Volmiker, Jost 41, 42
Volz, John Jacob 6
Vonbun, Anton 96
Vonbun, Xavier 96
Voule, L. H. 71

W

Wagner, Christian Friderick 90
Wagner, Christopher 8
Wagner, Elisabeth 125
Wagner, Eva 124
Wagner, Jacob 107
Wagnerin, Dothothea 77
Wagnerin, Magdalena 72
Wahl, Christian 86
Wahl, Magdalena 86
Wahly, Johannes 101
Waiblin, Catharina 81
Walbold, Jacob Friderich 114
Walch, Eberhart 108
Walke, John 65
Walker, John 42
Wallace, James 49
Wallace, William 81
Walsser, Doris 53
Walsser, Maria Anna 53
Walter, Casper 93
Walter, Jacob 96
Walter, Simon 91
Walter, Urich 110
Waltman, Catharina 96
Wampole, Isaac 72, 73
Wandel, Augustin 92
Ward, William 4
Warden, Jeremiah 64
Warden, Jeremiah Junior 64
Warner, John 114, 120, 126
Warrance, William 120

Warren, William 86
Wasman, Friderich 70
Watson, James T. 61, 62, 63
Way, James 96, 103
Weaver, Henry 56, 82
Weber, Fransz Joseph 77
Weber, Gottfried 84
Weber, Johan Georg 119
Weber, Philip 14, 32
Weberin, Susanna 99
Weder, Kraft 115
Weder, Maria 115
Wegman, H. R. 123
Weidlein, Anna Sabina 119
Weidleinin, Maria Catharina 120
Weidlin, Catharina 118
Weidman, John 29
Weimer, Daniel 56, 82
Weimer, George 56
Weimer, John Jacob 65
Weimer, Maria Magdalena 60
Weinman, Christina Sophia 64
Weinman, Jacob 64
Weinmanin, Friderica 103
Weisenberger, Genevesa 72, 87
Weisenberger, Geneveva 124
Weisenberger, Julianna 72
Weisenberger, Therese 72
Weiss, Bastian 121
Weiss, Frederick 36, 81
Weiss, John 121
Weld, Christian 72
Weller, Anna Margaret 106, 124
Weller, Elisabeth Margaretha 106
Weller, Johan Georg 97
Wenner, George Junior 32
Wentz, Samuel 72, 74, 124
Wentzel, Christian 104, 106
Wentzel, Elisabeth 106
Wentzel, Peter 106
Werner, Dorethea 55
Werohe, Friderich 113
Werthele, Agnus Magdalena 61
Werthele, Christianna Walburg 62
Werthele, Elizabeth Rosina 59, 61
Werthele, Johanna Dorothea 62
Werthele, Philip Jacob 61
Werthele, Rosina Fredericca 61
Wethele, Daniel 61
Wethele, Walburg 61
Wetheral, Samuel W. 54
Wetterin, Catharina 59
Weyhemerger, Charles William 70
Weyhenmeyer, Charles Wilhelm 92
Weymer, Catharina Elizabeth 59
Whiteall, John L. 109
Widmeyer, Christian 60
Widmeyer, Dorothea 59
Wiedmanin, Elizabeth 60
Wieland, Adam 116
Wilbank, John 101
Wilbur, Backus 43
Wilde, Elizabeth 26
Wilde, Hartman 26
Wildemuth, Johan 117
Wile, G. 108, 110, 112, 113, 114, 115

Wilhelm, Gottlieb 96
Williams, James 54, 84
Willig, George 81, 87, 101
Willig, George Senior 77
Wilson, John 58
Wilson, Robert 34
Wilson, Thomas 86
Wilson, William J. 67
Wilt, George 44
Winter, Lorenz 37
Witman, Margaret 65
Witmanin, Maria 96, 99
Witmire, Barbara 130
Witmire, Fredericka 130
Wittel, David Melchier 66
Wizeman, Jacob 122
Wizeman, Johannes 120, 122
Woelpper, David 59, 61, 64
Wohrer, Charles Frederick 129
Wohrer, Christian Frederick 129
Wohrle, Johan David 97
Wolf, Catharina 118
Wolf, Dorothea Maria 60
Wolf, Fredericca 61
Wolf, Henry Junior 61
Wolf, Jacob 64
Wolf, Johan Adam 70
Wolf, John George 64
Wolf, John Gotlieb 55
Wolf, Philip 37
Wolf, William F. 72
Wolff, Daniel 127, 128
Wood, James 39
Woods, Nathan 16
Woolston, Benjamin 57
Woolston, Jeremiah 102
Worth, James 107
Wray, William 64
Wunderlin, Francisca 39
Wunderlin, Theresia 48
Wurster, Johan Jacob 108
Wursthorn, Magdalena 51
Wurtembergerin, Regina 90
Wurtzburger, Johan 79
Wurtzburger, Maria 79
Wuterich, Catharina 6

Y

Yohe, George 8, 53
Young, Daniel 45
Young, George 45, 49
Yourhaus, Henry 103

Z

Zahnin, Regina 89
Zechele, Frederick 129
Zeile, George 40
Zell, Jacob 103
Ziegle, Conrad 115
Ziegler, Christina 103, 126
Ziegler, Eva Margaretha 101
Ziegler, George 128
Ziegler, Mr. 33
Zimmerman, Carl 78

Zimmerman, Catharina 40
Zimmerman, John 125
Zimmerman, John Christian 37
Zimmerman, Martin 40, 41
Zoller, Friderich 111
Zuber, Maria Anna 2
Zug, Christian 57
Zwisele, Pius 77, 121